RSAC

D11199533

Rape Crisis
Responding to Sexual Violence

SEP 2008

MANCHESTER RAPE CRISIS
UNDER THREAT!
Council plan to "Review"
our funding!

We provide free, confidential
counselling to women & girls who
have been raped & sexually abused:

- by telephone
- face to face
- in survivors groups.

We are the ONLY organisation funded
by MCC who provide this service.

Without Council

we cannot sur

PLEASE HELP.....

PLEASE write IN PROTEST t
of the Social Services Co
the Town Hall.

PLEASE contact your own C

IMPORTANT!!
If MRCL has helped YOU -
in your letter, which CAN

WOMEN'S CANDLEL

7.00pm in Alber
MONDAY 18TH MARCH

FOR MORE DETAILS : PO BOX 336, MCR.
TEL. 061 228 3602

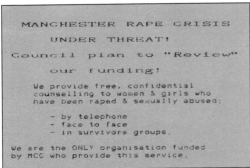

Campaign to End Rape

Campaigning Priorities:

Increasing the conviction rate

Better treatment and
representation of raped
women & children in court

Changing the law on consent

A National Conference

Rape & the Criminal Justice System

Saturday 14 June 1997

Institute of Education
Bedford Way
London
WC1H 0AL

Speakers
Olive Braiden, Ruth Chigwada-Baily,
Helen Grindrod QC, Liz Kelly, Sarah Maguire,
Det. Supt. Stephanie Yearnshire

& from the USA
Alice Vachss, prosecutor known for winning
'unprosecutable' sex crime cases

Chair for the day: Helena Kennedy QC

This event is sponsored by:
The Justice for Women Organisation, Rape Crisis Federation, England

Some campaign materials from the 1990s, picture of Manchester Vigil by fletcherfernie.co.uk

Rape Crisis

Responding to Sexual Violence

Helen Jones and Kate Cook

Russell House Publishing

First published in 2008 by:
Russell House Publishing Ltd.
4 St. George's House
Uplyme Road
Lyme Regis
Dorset DT7 3LS

Tel: 01297-443948
Fax: 01297-442722
e-mail: help@russellhouse.co.uk
www.russellhouse.co.uk

© Helen Jones and Kate Cook

The moral right of Helen Jones and Kate Cook to be identified as the authors of this work has been asserted by them in accordance with The Copyright, Designs and Patents Act 1988.

All rights reserved. No part of this publication may be reproduced, stored in a retrieval system or transmitted in any form, or by any means, electronic, mechanical, photocopying, recording or otherwise, without the prior permission of the copyright holder and the publisher.

British Library Cataloguing-in-publication Data:
A catalogue record for this book is available from the British Library.

ISBN: 978-1-905541-27-0

Typeset by TW Typesetting, Plymouth, Devon

Printed by Alden, Oxford

Russell House Publishing

Russell House Publishing aims to publish innovative and valuable materials to help managers, practitioners, trainers, educators and students.

Our full catalogue covers: social policy, working with young people, helping children and families, care of older people, social care, combating social exclusion, revitalising communities and working with offenders.

Full details can be found at www.russellhouse.co.uk and we are pleased to send out information to you by post. Our contact details are on this page.

We are always keen to receive feedback on publications and new ideas for future projects.

362.883 J717r 2008
Jones, Helen (Helen D.)
Rape crisis : responding to
sexual violence

Contents

List of Tables and Figures

Tables

Table 1.1 Opening dates of Rape Crisis services

Table 3.1 Services provided by Rape Crisis centres

Table 4.1 Arguments for and against a network

Table 5.1 Expenditure of charities – groups with limited or no financial history

Table 5.2 Expenditure of charities – groups with less than £15,000 per annum expenditure

Table 5.3 Expenditure of charities – groups with more than £100,000 per annum expenditure

Figures

Figure 2.1 Range of 'violences' and 'causes' identified by Rape Crisis volunteers at a training session

Figure 2.2 From Manchester Rape Crisis – Policy Document, circa 1990

Figure 2.3 Notes from Manchester Rape Crisis Training

Figure 5.1 Rapes reported in Ireland in 1996

Figure 5.2 Rapes reported to the police in Scotland in 2000

Figure 5.3 Support received from SARCs, friends and relatives

Figure 5.4 Expenditure of Rape Crisis centres 2004

Dedication

This book is dedicated to the memory of Richard Edward Cook.

Acknowledgements

This book was in our hearts and in our heads long before it made it onto paper. We have many people to thank but we would like to start with the publishers whose patience has been generous, throughout.

The book would still be an idea without the women who have contributed by: completing questionnaires; giving interviews; making comments; reading drafts; contributing diagrams and illustrations and entries for the glossary. We especially want to thank: Sheila and Lee, Maggie, Jenny, Cath L., Sheila B., Sandra Mc., Jude, Nicole, Shahidah, Sue, Kay B., Julie B. and everyone who completed the questionnaire and who took part in impromptu interviews.

We try to acknowledge the passion of the women who started this movement and who have nurtured it, throughout this volume. We also need to acknowledge our own personal debt to those women here. Many women have enriched our lives and the lives of the thousands of women who have used the services of Rape Crisis throughout its more than thirty year existence. We could not have written this book without any of them because **they are** Rape Crisis. They have listened to us while we were on our soapboxes and challenged us when they felt we were wrong. The sisterhood we have received has been beyond measure.

We have friends within the movement, and in other parts of our lives, who have provided support and strength, even if they weren't aware of it at the time. For wisdom and downright feminist awareness (that sometimes leaves her staggered) Helen wants to thank Julie Mc.; for showing me the way but not always agreeing, Kay; a loyal friend and mentor, Eileen; my rocks, Maggie and Paula; always there for a coffee and a sounding board, Maria; my amigos, Gill and Sarah; someone who taught me that you don't let anyone or anything get you down, Marcia; and Julie and Kathy whose transatlantic friendship has often been a lifeline. Helen also wants to say thank you to her husband David who frequently put a cup of coffee in front of her at the computer while she refused to speak because of the 'very important sentence rattling around in my head'; her children Barry and Sally have been very supportive of mum's strange research area and are very loved; her ma-in-law; Doreen and her mum and dad are unlikely to ever read this book (but they might read this part if told they get a mention); so thanks go to Val and Stan and also her two brothers Ricky and Stephen.

Kate wants to thank all of her friends who have ever shown an interest in 'the book' but in particular to acknowledge the endless support from Annie Muse, Margaret Cook and Stevie. Thank you all, so much.

About the Authors

Dr Helen Jones hates to be put in a box but will describe herself as a feminist, teacher, researcher, writer, website monkey and activist. She has taught in universities in the UK and the US and is currently employed at Manchester Metropolitan University, where she works with some of the brightest students in the country. There she teaches on a range of criminology and criminal justice topics and enjoys introducing her students to issues that really matter in the world. This, combined with feminist activism, has seen her involved in the Home Office Sex Offences Review, the Victims of Violence and Abuse Prevention Programme (VVAPP) and the Inter-Ministerial Advisory Panel on Sexual Violence. Over the years she has been a collective member and unpaid consultant to the Rape and Sexual Abuse Centre in Merseyside and often speaks about the Rape Crisis movement at conferences, on the radio and in the press but doesn't like being on television.

Dr Kate Cook is a radical feminist activist, who is also a lesbian, a teacher and a writer. She began working in Rape Crisis as a volunteer in 1990, after a summer school for the legendary OU women's studies course *The Changing Experience of Women*. Her experience duly changed at that point and she became a busy member of the Manchester Rape Crisis collective, acting as a support worker as well as becoming involved in all of the aspects of running the centre, from painting and maintenance through to training volunteers and outside speaking. Through this work she has met a number of wonderful women (including Helen) many of whom have contributed to this volume. She has also developed some skills which she tries to give back to the movement through continued links with Rape Crisis, through campaigning work with CER; TAR and JFW (see Glossary of Abbreviations) and through her teaching. At various times Kate has also been a member of the *Manchester Women's Liberation Newsletter* and *Eve's Back*.

Preface

Thank goodness this book has been written! This might be a strange phrase to begin a book with, but it is the honest reaction that will ripple through the Rape Crisis movement as they read this book. Across the world, Rape Crisis work has gone on relatively quietly, unassumingly, for the last three decades. The focus of individual Rape Crisis centres has been to provide high quality, woman-centred support to as many survivors as they are able to, although demand for support is high and funding low. On the ground this often feels like a continuous uphill struggle. At the national level, the Rape Crisis Federation (1996–2003) and now Rape Crisis England and Wales (2003–) has been focused on supporting the work of the network of individual centres, and on fundraising and campaigning for change at a national level (alongside its sister organisations in Scotland and Ireland). Admittedly, this 'head down and get on with things' approach has led to ours unintentionally being a fairly insular movement. This is why this book will be so highly valued by members of the Rape Crisis movement – at last there is an opportunity for those outside the movement to learn about some of our work, and hopefully understand our motivations.

Rape Crisis: Responding to Sexual Violence represents a tentative opening of a door that has been largely shut for three decades. It documents the Rape Crisis movement's simultaneously depressing and inspiring journey. Depressing because it highlights the myriad of problems faced by even the strongest of centres. Depressing because it emphasises the ubiquitous nature of rape. Depressing because it represents reality – we simply do not have enough Rape Crisis centres left to provide the support that every survivor needs and deserves. On one level the book charts the gradual decline of the Rape Crisis movement. However, on another level, it stands as a testament to the strength of so many women. Brave women who ring our helplines and visit our centres, using words they never thought they could. Inspiring women who have dedicated their lives to supporting survivors. Dedicated women who refuse to rest until things change. Focused women who have a vision of a world free from rape. Passionate women for whom the term 'good enough' does not feature within their vocabulary.

This book will come as a welcome read for anyone who despairs that sisterhood is over. It will comfort those who think sisterhood is meant to be easy! It may surprise those who question the need for feminist politics in contemporary society. *Rape Crisis: Responding to Sexual Violence* reminds us why the personal is still the political. It reminds us why we must never give up.

Dr Nicole Westmarland, Chair of Rape Crisis (England and Wales)

Introduction

It is estimated that in 2003 about 80,000 women experienced rape and attempted rape (Walby and Allen, 2004) in England and Wales but that only 629 cases resulted in successful prosecutions. If you reported a rape to the police in 2003 you had a mere 5.6 per cent chance of getting the rapist convicted. All of this is well-publicised now: there is a crisis in the Criminal Justice System's response to rape. However, this book focuses on a parallel concern. At the same time as Britain is failing survivors of rape in the courts there is an erosion of the most effective method of supporting survivors of rape – the Rape Crisis movement.

The need for support

Any woman might ask herself what she would do if she was raped – and some of us know the answer to this question, as we have lived through rape. For many, we are not sure about going to the police, or going to court and with the conviction rate at an all-time low that is not surprising. However, many of us do know that we want or we would want some support, from someone who understands what rape is about and how hard it is to live with. For around 30 years now that support has most often come from a Rape Crisis centre. However, most of the public know little about these centres or how they are run. This book documents the story of Rape Crisis in the UK, from its small beginnings, to a peak in the 1990s and through to a decline, at the beginning of this new century. However, this is not a history book. It does not attempt to document the often turbulent stories of the individual centres. Instead it tries to create a permanent record of the philosophies and ideas that underpinned the original Rape Crisis centres and to show how these centres have changed and evolved, during their 30 year history. The book provides the reader, whether an interested individual, a student or academic, a professional or voluntary worker, with something of the flavour of the original Rape Crisis work, whilst evaluating the place of that work in British society of the twenty-first century.

The emergence and development of the Rape Crisis movement

Both of the authors of this book have worked with the Rape Crisis movement in the UK, been part of the movement and taught about the movement. So often we would sit down, drink coffee (or beer, on a good day) and bemoan the fact that no single book existed to tell the story of how Rape Crisis emerged, to give voice to the women who work within the movement and to document the services, struggles and successes that make up one of the most enduring features on the feminist landscape. So we decided that it was about time that we did it ourselves. We regard this book as a step in the process of documenting Rape Crisis in the UK. We hope that it can act as a catalyst to encourage others to do further research, and write about the centres and the aspects of the work that we have (inevitably) not done justice to. With this in mind we have tried to document our sources well, to help any future researchers. Additionally, and as our biographies make clear, we are both feminists who have worked within the groups we are writing about, and we are clearly aware that this impacts upon the way we write, the questions we ask and the subjects we choose to explore. However we make no apology for our *a priori* interest since the radical feminism which is the heart of the anti-rape movement argues that the standpoint of belonging gives a clear and important place from which to critique, to document and to develop. We do not claim the traditional objectivity of the academic author because we do not strive for that position. Instead we merely draw your attention to our experience and our leanings and leave you to decide whether these fit us to write about the movement we love so fiercely.

We have no wish to dismiss the range of feminist writings that have discussed theories of rape, the impact of victimisation and the relevance of statistical data on sexual violence; indeed we draw on some of this work within our volume. However, what this book does is something different. It aims to provide the reader with a clear understanding of the context in which the Rape Crisis movement emerged in the UK. It tells something of the beginnings of the Second Wave of Feminism (see Glossary) and of the power of the tool of consciousness-raising (or CR) (see Glossary). It moves on to examine the structures and policies of Rape Crisis, its poverty and weaknesses as well as its astounding strengths and successes. This volume enables any reader to understand what the Rape Crisis movement is, whether their interest is personal or professional. We end this book with a Glossary of terms and groups, to try to help fill in any missing 'herstory' where we may take ideas and terms from feminism for granted, but which readers might be less familiar with.

We chart the political context of the Second Wave of Feminism and the theoretical developments that ran alongside the emergence of the anti-rape movement which had its roots in the CR groups of the Women's Liberation Movement in the United States (Brownmiller, 1999). The book explains how feminist groups spearheaded the early development of Rape Crisis centres in the UK, examines the state of the Rape Crisis movement in the first decade of a new century and finds that storm clouds may be looming. In the US, it has been suggested that the future of independent Rape Crisis groups is uncertain (O'Sullivan and Carlton, 2001). This declaration could just as easily be made in the UK. As in the US, new legislation has been heralded as women's salvation, Sexual Assault Referral Centres (SARCs) have been formed providing a one-stop shop for reporting rape and receiving health treatment, and local Victim Support groups support survivors of sexual violence, as do some hospitals. Additionally, GP surgeries, social services and criminal justice agencies are now signposting services to primary and secondary care counselling or clinical psychiatry services. To an extent these changes have come in response to feminist challenges. However, they have also been influenced by other non-feminist shifts towards professional counselling, also emanating from the United States.

Rape Crisis – now and in the future

In light of these changes, perhaps then the need for Rape Crisis groups is no longer real? Those working at the front line will tell you otherwise. Speak to Rape Crisis workers and they will be happy to tell you about the range of services they provide which are both unique and necessary. Happy, that is, if they are not too busy trying to provide frontline services, whilst constructing funding bids for grants to keep the centre running, holding recruitment and training sessions to maintain the number of volunteers required and attending inter-agency partnership meetings to try to influence practice and policy in local statutory agencies. The Rape Crisis movement in the UK may have a similar future to that of its sister movement in the USA: indeed this would not be surprising as each movement has shared much in terms of political and practical development. To know whether this is really likely, however, we need evidence of the development of the Rape Crisis movement, here in the UK. To date, there is surprisingly little to go on. Whilst a constant stream of literature on the nature and extent of rape has been produced in the past 20 years, there is a space in the body of knowledge. This book aims to fill that gap, specifically outlining the work of Rape Crisis centres in England and Wales and also drawing comparisons with similar centres and networks in Scotland and Ireland.

In order to document the movement we have collected data from many sources, including annual reports and other documentation kindly supplied to us by Rape Crisis centres. We also draw upon an archive of the papers of the (now defunct) Rape Crisis Federation of Wales and England and upon a number of published sources. However, we felt the need to try to paint an up-to-date picture of the movement and so we have also asked groups about structures via a questionnaire, seeking some outline data on their organisation and its history. Representatives from a smaller number of groups have then participated in detailed interviews which create core material for the case studies used in this work.

In the early days, Rape Crisis centres struggled to provide telephone support to women who had been raped, but centres have developed since then to provide ever more services to wider groups of women and girls. This volume therefore examines these changes and considers some of the critical issues facing the work of Rape Crisis today. This began as a movement of women joined together in small and somewhat isolated groups which generally operated on a 'collectivist' structure (see Glossary). Today those collectives have largely disappeared. It has been argued that as Rape Crisis centres changed in their structures, so their philosophies changed (Campbell, Baker and Mazurek, 1998; Bevacqua, 2001) and, to some extent, the move towards 'professionalism' (see Glossary) has impacted on their political stance (Collins and Whalen, 1989). We try to unpick these trends in our discussions.

About this book

Chapter 1 begins by outlining the background, explaining the birth of the Rape Crisis movement in 1972, emerging from the fresh ideas of American second-wave feminism. The aim of this chapter is to allow an insight into the formation of the British Rape Crisis centres, which came later and so, we need to start out with the pioneers who inspired our own Rape Crisis founders. The chapter looks at the radical feminist ideals behind Rape Crisis and sketches the events that led to the formation of the very first centres. The American groups have tended to move towards professionalism and away from their radical grounding, in the years since (Matthews, 1994) and the chapter provides a little discussion of that shift. However, the reasons for change are not necessarily the same in the US as in Britain and the main focus of this volume remains the British Rape Crisis groups. The second half of the chapter therefore moves on to examine the foundation of Rape Crisis here in Britain, beginning in London, in 1976 but also gives some idea of the spread of the idea of Rape Crisis across the UK and Ireland. The chapter goes on to outline some of the core values that have defined the (British) Rape Crisis movement, in its approach to work and to the outside world, looking in particular at links between this fledgling movement and other feminist groups existing at that time.

This allows **Chapter 2** to begin to look at the development of the movement, since those early days. This chapter discusses some key changes and challenges that the early groups went on to face and critically evaluates whether the politics of the movement have changed with these shifts. The chapter also draws on interviews with three of the existing groups, to provide some outline of the development of these groups from their early beginnings. In turn, all of this sets the scene for Chapter 3 to develop a closer examination of the range of services offered by the groups today, drawing on interview and questionnaire results. This includes some analysis of internal stresses, which influence the lived reality or 'living dynamic' of Rape Crisis work. The concept of the 'living dynamic' is introduced in Chapter 2 but can be used to unpick a number of the aspects of this form of feminist engagement. We have already made it apparent that we know we have both gained much from our involvement in this movement. However, it is fair to say that other women who have become part of Rape Crisis have sometimes found this a terribly uncomfortable and stressful experience. **Chapter 3** tries to examine why this is so, moving on to look at the women who take part in Rape Crisis work and to draw out the pressures that the work creates for individuals. This chapter also examines a modern trend in service provision, which is involvement in the wider sphere of local services, through inter-agency partnership work.

Although the Rape Crisis movement was formed in the 1970s, early groups had no nationally organised body. Later however this began to shift, with meetings between groups and, eventually the formation of the Rape Crisis Federation (RCF) in the mid-1990s. **Chapter 4** documents this development, examining the pros and cons of forming a national network and showing that while there were difficulties involved in bringing together a movement 'often divided on fiercely held ideological beliefs' (Grant, 2001) the move to organise was successfully accomplished, if short-lived. The RCF closed in 2003, but, like a phoenix from the ashes of that group another co-ordinating group emerged to continue to provide a national voice for the movement and rebuild a network of the remaining Rape Crisis centres. Chapter 4 ends with a look at this new group and at the lessons which can be learnt from the troubled story of the RCF.

Chapter 5 rounds up our look at the support work of the centres by providing a snapshot of the Rape Crisis movement at the time of writing. This chapter draws on data from the Scottish and Irish Rape Crisis networks and from other sources. The chapter also evaluates the relationship between the Rape Crisis movement and statutory services for women experiencing sexual violence.

As Susan Brownmiller's history of the American Women's Liberation Movement shows, the beginning of the anti-rape movement saw the issues of supporting survivors and campaigning for change as entirely intertwined (Brownmiller, 1999). Today this is no longer the case: although many groups would wish to be involved in campaign work they find it hard to devote any time or energy to that side of the 'crisis'. **Chapter 6** looks at this trend and at the current campaigns which are often peopled by women who have worked within Rape Crisis or other support services (such as Women's Aid). The book concludes, as it began, by looking at the links between theory and practice, and by drawing the various strands of this work together; by offering some ways forward, in terms of practical tools for survival which might help to ensure that there are Rape Crisis centres for as long as there are women who need the support these specialists can offer.

CHAPTER 1

A Movement is Born: (E)Merging Theory and Practice

Introduction

Today, feminism is often seen as an idea which has had its day, an old-fashioned and 'un-cool' movement supported by hairy-legged and dungaree-wearing women in the 1970s. The reality is that feminism is almost never fashionable, as it is too revolutionary for comfortable consumption and it does not render itself easily into media sound-bites. Even the idea that 'feminists' are dull is not new:

> *To be called a feminist has become an insult. Even many contemporary women radicals go to great lengths to deny connection with the old feminism.*
> (Firestone, 1968, quoted in Firestone, 1970: 2)

Shulamith Firestone, one of the founding voices of the anti-rape movement, is talking here of the view of feminism in the early 1970s, at the beginning of the Second Wave of Feminism. The 'old' feminists she speaks of are those who struggled for the vote. Interestingly, to us, at the beginning of the twenty-first century those suffragettes now appear as heroines, whilst Shulamith, the Susans (Griffin and Brownmiller) Robin, Kate, Simone, Betty and all the others we are going to discuss here are now viewed as passé and dull. This is so far from the truth as to be a tragedy. Each of these women contributed to an amazing movement whose forces are still being felt today. This chapter begins to tell the tale of just one of the institutions that grew from that movement, Rape Crisis.

A good place to start is with a brief outline of the beginnings of Second Wave Feminism in the United States. We need to start over there, to document the origins of the Rape Crisis movement, since the US was the birthplace of anti-rape feminism, and the Rape Crisis idea developed from what Catharine MacKinnon has termed the 'method' of the Women's Liberation Movement, the practice of consciousness-raising (see Glossary) (CR). From this sharing of the reality of womanhood came the notion of speaking out about the damage that the patriarchy had brought upon female bodies. In turn, the public version of personal testimony, the

speak-out, created the realisation that contrary to common belief, rape was far from rare. This led to the idea that women who experience rape need support, from other women. Here then were the seeds of anti-rape feminist theory and its practical sister, the Rape Crisis movement.

The radical feminism (see Glossary) which created this movement was born straight from activism, with little pause for the development of theory. The formal theory was often written down later, as the movement grew and women found the time and confidence to occupy space in the academy. Sadly the academic feminist has not always served her activist sister well, particularly when, as time passed, the position of radicalism within feminist theory became devalued and marginalised (see Crow, 2000: xi). This chapter tries to help recreate the sense of purpose of radicalism by drawing on some of the first person accounts of the early days of anti-rape activism, to sketch out the stories of those beginnings. It begins to outline the development of the Rape Crisis movement on both sides of the Atlantic, in preparation for later chapters which focus more closely on groups in Britain. We also begin to unpick the origins and purpose of the collective structure which the early Rape Crisis centres tried hard to create.

No more handmaidens: birth of the Women's Liberation Movement

For many Americans, the woman who kick-started the second wave of feminism was Betty Friedan. She was born in 1921 and was a married woman with children who wrote about the concerns she had over the structure of women's lives. Her groundbreaking book, *The Feminine Mystique* (1963) led her to prominence and Friedan went on to found the National Organisation of Women (NOW) in 1966 which still has over half a million members (male and female) today (http://www.now.org). NOW concentrates on liberal feminism which is interested in obtaining equal entry into the professions for women and is not the version of feminism we are centrally interested in here. A visit to the NOW website will reveal tht they do campaign on rape issues these days; however this was not where they began (original concerns were about equality of opportunity in employment and education: see Ware, 1970: 21–3) and it was not these women who started the Rape Crisis movement.

There were (and still are) a number of different 'feminisms' and Cellestine Ware's early work (1970) documents some of the first shifts and re-formations of groups and ideas. The mass media on both sides of the Atlantic has rarely grasped this complexity however, so that the mainstream image of feminism is often too bleached-out to be recognisable. In reality, splits, shifts and schisms make it difficult to chart the exact development of the theories we take for granted today but there appears to be some consensus as to the way in which the (American) anti-rape movement began.

The Women's Liberation Movement (as opposed to Friedan's liberal feminism) grew out of student activism. In the mid-1960s there were a number of lobbies for change in the US, the most prominent being the Civil Rights movement and the hippies. It is probably reasonable to characterise these as two very different groups, as the Civil Rights movement was largely made up of Black working people, and the hippies consisted of disenchanted middle-class youngsters. However there were groups which crossed boundaries and one of these was the student organisation, Students for a Democratic Society (SDS). This was a body which was founded at the end of the 1950s and which, in the 1960s, became involved in supporting the struggle for Black rights. It was out of exasperation with being forced to 'play peahen to the peacocks, administresses to the agonists, handmaidens to the lords' (Ware, 1970: 17) that women within this student movement began to act on their own behalf.

Some of the women wanted to work on the question of Women's Liberation alongside Civil Rights and the first attempt to formalise this desire was by the women's caucus at a national SDS conference in 1967. This was the presentation to conference of a 'Women's Manifesto' which was formally accepted by the conference but not acted upon. As a consequence, the women involved began to realise that they needed to act independently of men if they wanted to change their own situation. (Brownmiller, 1999: 12–15,

gives a fuller version of this story. For more on the background and the women involved, see Chapter One of Alice Echol's account (1989: 23–50). The 1990s documentary film *Berkeley in the Sixties* from Kitchell Films also tells of this rise in student activism).

The popular media often aligns this women's movement with the introduction of the contraceptive pill. What they tend not to appreciate though is that it was actually the failure of the pill to solve women's problems (profligate, unkind or uninterested lovers, for example) which enabled this generation of women to voice their dissatisfaction with women's lot. Finally, at the end of the 1960s, American women began to speak out about male dominance and to explore what effects that had on their lives. From small actions, such as the 'Women's Manifesto', women began to get together to discuss their situation in what were to become consciousness-raising groups. These were meetings of women who would 'rap' about things that were concerning them, in their lives. They might discuss: their friendships or relationships; housework; childbirth or child rearing; menstruation; or any one of a thousand other topics. The groups differed in levels of formality, but all had an egalitarian structure and tried hard to ensure that each woman present had space to talk about her own understanding of her world. Thus, the aim was for each woman to be able to 'grow' in terms of freeing her consciousness from the effects of a lifetime of oppression (there are many sources on the detail of consciousness-raising, some useful extracts can be found within Barbara Crow's collection, 2000: 271–300). This approach to organising has been important within the Rape Crisis movement as well as within the formation of feminist theory, and so we return to both collective working and consciousness-raising, later in this chapter.

Whilst influenced by Betty Friedan's work, the women within this new movement drew more directly on the writings of the French writer, Simone De Beauvoir. Anti-rape pioneer Shulamith Firestone dedicates her *The Dialectic of Sex* to De Beauvoir 'who endured' (Firestone, 1970: Dedication). Similarly, the early and influential radical feminist group the Redstockings describe De Beauvoir as having 'exposed male supremacy' and say that she 'gave us our feminism' (1979: Dedication).

De Beauvoir was interested in the oppression of women, whilst Friedan was concerned with moving them out of the home. One approach considered female oppression to be at the heart of the current model of society, whilst the other wanted to make some reform, in order to loosen the girdle that women were wearing (almost from choice). Radical feminism does not wish to turn women into men, but wants to create a world where all can live freely, without the chains of 'masculinity' and 'femininity' to bind us. In acknowledging their debt to the work of De Beauvoir both Firestone and the Redstockings are aligning themselves with a more radical form of feminist theory.

Radical feminism: the birth of the anti-rape movement

Shulamith Firestone was a New York based activist who was a member of the New York Radical Women (NYRW), one of the earliest groups of radical activists within the movement. Others in the group included Kathie Sarachild (still active in Redstockings and who gives us an early example of women renaming themselves by creating a matrilineal last name) and Robin Morgan. In 1968, the group mounted a protest in Atlantic City, against the Miss America pageant. There were many public protests at that time in the US against the war in Vietnam and these often featured the burning of draft cards. The Miss America protestors came up with the notion of a 'Freedom Bonfire' in which various symbols of oppressed femininity could be burnt. Robin Morgan then gave a newspaper interview and the journalist chose to highlight bra burning, (even though in reality, no bras were burned) creating a stereotype of feminist activism, which has yet to be lived down (Brownmiller, 1999: 35–41. Carol Hanisch gives her own account in DuPlessis and Snitow, 1998: 197–202).

NYRW remain important to us today, as they documented much of their early work (in *Notes from the First Year*, 1968 and other publications. Duke University Special Collections, has transcriptions: http://scriptorium.lib.duke.edu/wlm/notes, last accessed 20.07.07). The group's development also demonstrates how the idea of liberation took hold. NYRW grew quickly and had 150 women attending meetings, which naturally became impractical and at the end of 1968 they split into three (Ware, 1970: 33–5). One of these emergent parts went on to become the Redstockings, a group which, quite remarkably,

is still working for feminism to this day (see their website http://www.afn.org/redstock/ last accessed 20.07.07).

This short précis gives a glimpse of how things moved on, at great pace, from the beginnings in 1967. Within a few short years, New York, Chicago, Boston and many other US cities had Women's Liberation groups formed and reformed. Newspapers were being produced documenting the ideas and actions being generated and, by 1970, books and collections also began to appear. What these women had in common was an opposition to 'dominance in human relationships' as this was understood as the 'basic evil' within a society (Ware, 1970: 16). Here then is one early interpretation of the meaning of the idea of 'radical' feminism. It is radical in the sense that it is willing to reconsider life from the ground up. Radical feminism sees the problems of oppression as complex and multi-layered, meaning that solutions are not to be found in easy applications of new law, or new policy. To remove dominance from human relationships in a (first) world which founded its basic human units on the institution of marriage, whereby one partner was to 'honour and obey' the other, was always a tall order. Not surprisingly then, Women's Liberation was both exciting and frightening for the women involved and for those around them. The process of creating the movement clearly cost many individuals dearly (and Brownmiller and Ware's works are testimony to this point, as is the short life of the activist Valerie Solanas, the authoress of the *SCUM Manifesto*; see Brownmiller, 1999: 27–30). The movement that emerged has been variously criticised for being too middle-class, too white and too heterosexual. It is clear, however, looking back that if those trends emerged they were not intended. The women who started this movement were concerned with any form of dominance within human relationships, not only those founded on sex. They also wanted to take all women with them, even though they may have lacked the tools to create that utopia.

Writing much later, Barbara Crow has summarised the distinct elements of radical feminism (from the era 1967–1975) to be: that the women saw 'women's oppression as the first, the oldest and the primary form of oppression . . . to which all other forms . . . are related and connected' and that the women drew their knowledge from the practice of consciousness-raising (Crow, 2000: 2). The earliest usage of the term 'radical feminism' dates back to the Redstockings, *Notes for the Second Year* (1970, ibid.: 8). However, in those early days, radical feminism was often simply termed 'feminism'. The need to draw distinctions only came later. As Redstockings stated in 1969, 'we do not ask what is "radical", "revolutionary", "reformist", or "moral" – we ask: is it good or bad for women?' (Redstockings, reprinted in: 1979: 11).

Meanwhile, within their CR groups around the country, women began to speak about the uncomfortable sensation of being ogled by men, of being hassled in the streets and elsewhere and, eventually, of being raped. Susan Brownmiller describes the beginning of this process in her own group, in late 1970 and of how this led to a public meeting where women came and spoke of their personal experiences of rape (Brownmiller, 1999: 194–201). This 'speak-out' strategy had been used in 1969, by the Redstockings, in relation to abortion issues (ibid. and see papers on the Redstockings website). As one founder said:

> *It showed the power of consciousness-raising, how theory comes from deep inside a person's life, and how it leads directly to action.*
> (The late Irene Peliskis, quoted in Brownmiller, 1999: 108)

And so it was for rape. The first speak-out was held in January 1971 with free entry for women and an entrance fee for men (who could only attend if accompanied). Over 300 women attended and at least 30 testified to their different and compelling experiences of forced sex (ibid.: 199–200; also Matthews, 1994: 9). To a generation raised on *Oprah* and the many other versions of the televised 'speak-out', it is hard to imagine the power and significance of this meeting. Here was the truth of the slogan 'the personal is political'. Women's stories (of their own violations) came together to create a powerful force for change. The day produced knowledge and impetus which Brownmiller says left the participants reeling. A future conference on rape was quickly in the pipeline. Brownmiller herself went on to produce *Against Our Will: Men, Women and Rape* (1976), still the starting point for feminist consideration of rape, some 30 years after its publication.

Anti-rape work began to spread out from this beginning. In 1971, in various cities in the US, Women Against Rape (WAR) groups were founded. In Los Angeles for example, Bay Area Women Against Rape (BAWAR) was set up in 1972 and created information packets for women who had been raped (Matthews, 1994: 9). Working in Berkeley, California, the poet and author Susan Griffin published an article entitled *Rape: The All-American Crime* (Brownmiller, 1999: 205). In San Francisco, Diana Russell began a lifetime of work on violence against women with a pioneering study on the prevalence of rape (Russell, 1982). Groups working on this new topic carried on using the egalitarian model they had brought with them from their other activism. Ware describes the methods of organising within the early group *The FEMINISTS* (1970: 26):

> *The work of the group is divided into two categories: routine and creative. Routine is typing, answering the telephone and envelope stuffing. Giving lectures, press conferences, writing position papers and giving radio and television interviews is creative work. Chairwomanship of the meetings is lot-determined and changes with every meeting. A secretary and treasurer, also chosen by lot, hold these offices for one month. No person takes a second turn at any task or office until everyone has had a turn at that work.*

This way of working clearly required considerable commitment from all concerned and was always quite time-consuming in sharing knowledge and skills. Yet this type of model was widely used (though not always with this level of formality) as the women considered it tremendously important to enable all involved to share in the power of the process. As Redstockings put it; 'we see the key to our liberation in our collective wisdom and our collective strength' (quoted in Ware, 1970: 39). In order to struggle against dominance within relationships of any kind, the women wanted to create truly non-hierarchical organisations where everyone shared knowledge and skills.

This then is the background to the beginning of 'Rape Crisis'. Women were organising and writing about rape, and developing the methods of working that would create the new anti-rape support network. However, before looking at the formation of those first American groups it is perhaps worth considering the work these activists were engaged in, a little more broadly.

Understanding rape

It could be argued that the work on rape is the most courageous effort of Second Wave Feminism, given that it was difficult to find very much serious consideration of the topic within mainstream writings. Brownmiller's magnum opus is testimony to the lack of understanding or knowledge of rape, in what went before (1975: 11–15). Rape was considered to be extremely rare, and graphically violent. Rape was believed to be committed only by crazed strangers, in circumstances forced by their own pathological illnesses. Second Wave Feminists have had the courage to examine rape and to find that it is the same crime, whether it is committed in this stereotypical way, or in some more mundane fashion. When a work colleague rapes, the pain is the same; when the rapist is a landlord, who is smoothly dressed and freshly perfumed, the hurt is equally dramatic. More contentiously, when a father rapes or when a husband rapes then the event is the same, but there is an additional burden in terms of the destruction of existing relationships. We take this knowledge for granted today, even if our law has trouble in applying it with honesty. None of this was known, however, back in 1970.

It is also due to these pioneers that we now understand that rape is, sadly, terribly common. Russell (1982) was the first to find that around one in four women experiences rape or attempted rape during our lifetimes and that the most common assailant is a partner or former partner. Her work has now been backed up by other studies, in several countries (Hall, 1985; Painter, 1991; Statistics Canada, 1993; Kelly and Regan, 2001) so that, again, we can all now produce these statistics with confidence and understanding. However, there is real danger in that confidence.

Firstly, there is the risk that we lose sight of the enormity of what the anti-rape feminists took on. To move public understanding from a place where rape was considered very rare, to a place where it is widely accepted today as actually common, was a huge undertaking. Secondly, we need to remember that this is an extremely uncomfortable truth. When rape is rare it can be held at a distance. Once rape is acknowledged as common, then this becomes harder to achieve. All too often, it appears to us that responses to women who have been raped, responses to Rape Crisis and to anti-rape feminism are filtered through this discomfort. For many people, the truths that anti-rape feminism speaks are much better left silent. Hostile responses may come from men, who fear that their own behaviours will be examined. They may come from organisations who do not want to be associated too closely with a dirty word like 'rape'. They may also come from individual women or girls, who are trying to get on with their lives and

minimise the impact of rape in these lives and within the wider society. All of this makes anti-rape feminism important and difficult.

Brownmiller and the others (Susan Griffin, Kate Millet and more) were creating a new theory of rape, which rejected the psychological ideas of the past. They saw that rape was common and knew from this that there was either a large number of men with pathological illnesses, or that to rape was a more normal part of masculinity. They argued that rape was not an aberration, but acted as a useful tool which could be used to keep women under control. Brownmiller contended that 'the discovery that his genitalia could serve as a weapon to generate fear must rank as one of the most important discoveries of prehistoric times' (1975: 14–15). Anti-rape feminism was uncovering ancient truths about male behaviour, which had always been present (according to Brownmiller) but which had not been noticed before. Rape was analysed as a 'conscious process of intimidation by which *all men* keep *all women* in a state of fear' (ibid., emphasis in original). Rape was not an accident of illness, but a process for subjugation. This insistence on rape as a *conscious* process was important, but also uncomfortable, for those outside of feminist consciousness.

A common accusation is that radical feminist anti-rape theory is essentialist. To put it another way, the charge laid against anti-rape activists can be that we think 'all men rape' and therefore hate men, dismiss men, marginalise men or are simply unrealistic. This is, in part, a misreading of Brownmiller's original analysis. What Brownmiller speaks of is the force of rape, the power of rape or the fear of rape. She argues that the effect that the danger of rape has on women is to limit our freedom. This can be shown simplistically in research about women's fear of violence and the effects it has on our lives (not going out alone after dark, not feeling safe alone, etc.). Brownmiller and the other pioneers saw that all men benefited from this, in terms of their own freedom and their ability to 'look after' women, which enhances their power and permission to act. Clearly then, this is a long way from saying that all men rape. There is no need for all white people to practise racist violence to benefit from racial power. Similarly, men do not have to be actively violent to benefit from patriarchal power.

In reality, the radical feminist anti-rape movement has always maintained that rape is the product of a particular socially-constructed version of maleness, as machismo. This version of masculinity is so all-powerful within society that it can be argued that it renders any man a *potential* rapist, but this is not a biological argument. Feminist theory assumes that masculinity can be defined differently and that the challenge of changing the dominant version is one of the tasks of feminism. Ultimately the aim is to create a world where it is no longer true that 'like indiscriminate terrorism, rape can happen to any woman, and few women are ever without this knowledge' (Griffin, 1979: 13). Nonetheless, many people, men and women, still find these arguments difficult to take on board:

> *Sex class is so deep as to be invisible. Or it may appear as a superficial inequality, one that can be solved by merely a few reforms, or perhaps by the full integration of women into the labour force. But the reaction of the common man, woman, and child – 'That? Why you can't change that! You must be out of your mind!' – is closest to the truth ... This gut reaction – the assumption that, even when they don't know it, feminists are talking about changing a fundamental biological condition – is an honest one.*
> (Firestone, 1970: 11 emphasis in original)

In this radical feminist analysis then, rape is understood as an exercise in violence which helps to maintain the patriarchal status quo. Kate Millett's *Sexual Politics* (1970) clarifies this relationship arguing that patriarchy relies upon the sexual violence epitomised by rape, to help maintain its force. Barbara Burris, also considers rape briefly, in her *Fourth World Manifesto* originally written around 1971 (reprinted in Crow, 2000: 238–64). 'Rape is an individual male imperialist act against an individual woman' (ibid.: 247. The territory of this form of imperialist invasion is a woman's body and that body may come in many different forms. It may be Black or white, young or old, beautiful or exhausted. It may be saucy or virginal. Rape is rape, no matter who does the invading act and upon whom it is practised.

This knowledge, coupled with the original insight that even radical males were not interested in the women's struggle, meant that the question of women-only space was resolved. To work around rape, it was clear from the outset that women would need their own room. Ware quotes incidents from the early days of the movement when women speaking publicly for liberation were heckled ('take her off the stage

and fuck her!') and even urinated on (at the University of North Carolina) by men who were supposed to be political radicals themselves (Ware, 1970: 36). This is the background to the clear knowledge of a need for women-only space, to advance the struggle for female liberation within the anti-rape movement.

Starting small: Rape Crisis in the US

The original Rape Crisis centres were set up in the US by women from within the anti-rape movement. These centres aimed to 'provide services to victims in crisis, to educate communities on violence against women, and to mobilise efforts for social change' (Campbell and Martin, in Renzetti et al., 2001: 228). Women came together to create these centres within their own homes, with no funding or prior expertise in the field. This was passion put into action, with a view to responding to the need that consciousness-raising (and the speak-outs) had revealed. From the documented histories, it seems likely that the very first Rape Crisis centre was the one in Washington DC (Brownmiller, 1999: 206).

After attending a conference on rape in April 1972, a group of eight women in Washington met to set up a new service for women who had been raped. These women were linked through Women's Liberation in Washington and they wanted to provide emergency information and advice via a telephone helpline. They started up that summer, with a 24-hour telephone line, run out of a shared house where one of the women lived (ibid.; see also Matthews, 1994: 10). 'We put an extra bed in the hall in case a raped women didn't want to go back to her house and needed a place to stay' (Karen Kollias, quoted in Brownmiller, 1999: 206). The work of the organisation grew, and they were quickly getting 200 or so calls per month (Brownmiller, 1999: 207; see also Matthews, 1994: 10: who quotes 20 calls per day). Yet the aims were not only to provide support: 'From the beginning we saw our mission as political education *plus* practical service' (Karen Kollias, quoted in Brownmiller, 1999: 208: emphasis in original). This was a long way from a mainstream social services model. The group was personally involved with the women they supported, even offering shelter if needed. The way of working clearly grew out of the women's concern for individuals as well as from their wish to change the world.

At about the same time, another service was being developed by the Bay Area Women Against Rape (BAWAR) women in San Francisco. In March of 1973 Matthews reports that the group applied for $25,000 of city money to set up a funded Rape Crisis centre having previously provided some facilities on a voluntary basis (Matthews, 1994: 10). There is some difference of account here as, according to Brownmiller, the second centre was opened at Ann Arbor in Michigan and the third in Philadelphia (1999: 208). Susan Griffin has a section in her book entitled *Rape: The Power of Consciousness* (1979: 69–102) where she notes dates for the founding of various centres and the first service she names is 'Women Organised Against Rape (24-hour crisis centre) Philadelphia' in 1971. However, what is clear is that the idea of Rape Crisis spread quickly. In early 1973 the Washington group was producing a newsletter which shows that there were at least 15 other groups by February of that year (Matthews, 1994: 10).

Each of these individual groups grew, and more groups developed elsewhere. Washington created a booklet on how to set up a centre (Brownmiller, 1999: 208) which appears to have been widely distributed. The early groups provided broadly similar services (perhaps due to the guidance in the pamphlet from Washington): 'Most had 24-hour crisis hot lines to provide information, referrals, and crisis counselling' (Campbell and Martin, in Renzetti et al., 2001: 229). Centres also had volunteers who were able to act as legal and medical advocates, to go to the police station or hospital along with women. They were also involved in organising public actions, demonstrations, protests and in lobbying the State for legal changes (ibid.). In the end, the groups aimed to change the world:

> *[Rape is] a political issue, where men violently exercise their power over women. It logically follows that rape will not end until men do not have power over women.*
> (*Washington Rape Crisis Newsletter*, 1973, quoted in Matthews, 1994: 13)

The old views (that rape is rare; or that Black women are more provocative and so 'rape-able'; or that rape of a virgin is more serious; and so on) were now characterised as 'myths and misconceptions' about rape (Brownmiller, 1976) and were to be challenged whenever they were met.

It must have become clear very quickly to the women involved that the need for their service was huge. At the same time, however, they were trying to provide education and become a force for change and do all of this in circumstances where 'nobody got paid' (Karen Kollias, quoted in Brownmiller, 1999: 208). These were often truly voluntary organisations, run on a collective basis, with time-consuming group decision-making to undertake as well as this burgeoning work. Not surprisingly then, others apart from BAWAR also began to look for funding from local government and other organisations (Matthews, 1994: discussed in Chapter 4). As these attempts succeeded they heralded the beginning of the end for collectivism (see Glossary), as this extract from the centre history given on the Washington DC website reveals:

> *In the beginning, the Center was organised as a collective with decision-making based on group consensus in weekly meetings. As more women became involved, decision-making and tasks were organised into ongoing committees. The weekly meetings then served as a place for committees to report on their work and to receive feedback from the collective.*
>
> *When the first DC government funding contract was received in 1975, the members of the Center saw a need to formalise their organisational structure to adhere to re-quirements of the Internal Revenue Service, the city government, and foundations. The Center adopted by-laws which set forth agency objectives and definitions of various decision-making groups within the organisation such as the Board of Directors, the Steering Committee and the Board of Trustees.*
>
> (http://www.dcrcc.org/history.htm, last accessed 20.07.07)

Chapter 2 shows that these same reasons were given later, when British Rape Crisis centres began to abandon their collective structures. Yet in reality, it would have been possible to find ways to satisfy the funders and regulatory bodies without actually ceding this form of idealism.

Increasingly attracting mainstream funding, the numbers of groups across America continued to grow. By the end of the 1970s it is reported that there were 600 centres (Tuttle, 1986: 271) though there was apparently a downturn, following cuts in government funding at the beginning of the 1980s (ibid.). To come up to date, according to Campbell and Martin there were around 1,200 RCCs in the US as at 2001 (in Renzetti et al., 2001: 227–41). However, with all of this growth, the original political imperative towards change was lost. Initially built as institutions organised in such a way as to 'prefigure the society we wanted' (Hartsock, 1998: 10) the early Rape Crisis groups paid as much attention to *how* they worked as they did to the work itself. Collective working and a partnership between support and activism were seen as a step towards a post-patriarchal existence. Sadly, few such groups remain, as the American Rape Crisis movement has been gradually co-opted into the mainstream of social agencies. According to Helen Benedict (1992), the profile of rape as a social issue, in the United States, tended to decline during the 1980s and 1990s. Many Rape Crisis centres have closed, and others struggle to stay afloat. The National Center for the Prevention and Control of Rape, an influential funder of research projects, has been downsized and absorbed into its parent organisation and 'along with this loss of interest has come a loss of understanding' (Benedict, 1992: 251).

Anti-rape feminism and the Rape Crisis movement grew from the same core of knowledge, that patriarchal power had led to dominance in human relationships and that this needed to be changed. The original movement was to be a part of that process of change. In the US it appears to have become something more closely resembling a liberal feminist blanket. The dominant model for Rape Crisis US-style now appears to provide a safe place for women to speak of their rape but not a venue for changing the social conditions that sustain rapists. Women may be held safely in the warmth of the blanket, but they are no longer invited to become a part of a movement to free their daughters from violence against women. Charlotte Bunch says that, within feminism, it is important that 'alternative institutions should not be havens of retreat, but challenges that weaken male power over our lives' (1987: 114). Whilst Rape Crisis centres certainly began as this form of challenge, it appears that in America they might now benefit from a renewed involvement in a movement for change. In the UK meanwhile, it took a little longer for the Rape Crisis movement to begin and it is also taking longer for the vestiges of feminist activism to leave the groups.

Into a hostile silence: Rape Crisis in the UK and Ireland

As in America, the Rape Crisis movement here grew straight out of consciousness-raising and other discussions about the reality of rape. The women who started the first Rape Crisis groups were clearly identified as feminists. Here too, they provided a women-only service, although there have also always been differences between the American Rape Crisis model and the British imitator. Most obviously, few Rape Crisis centres here have ever contrived to keep a 24-hour telephone line open. London Rape Crisis managed this feat for a number of years, though this group has sadly now closed. Other clear distinctions between Rape Crisis centres in the UK and US are that the British groups remained independent from one another for a full 20-year period (whereas the American groups have formed different kinds of alliances and groupings: see Matthews, 1994 for discussion) and that, in many instances, the British groups still exist on shoestring funding (see Chapter 5). In Britain, few centres ever achieved the kinds of mainstream assistance that came, fairly swiftly, to American Rape Crisis and this may account for a greater level of radical politics within the British movement.

The London group was the first to open, in North London in March 1976, after a loose collection of women had been meeting since some time in 1972/3, discussing rape (London Rape Crisis Centre (LRCC), 1984: ix; Tuttle, 1986: 271; Bowen et al., 1987: 49).

> *It was a group of about 40 women who met because they wanted to do something about rape. Different women had different ideas about what it was they wanted to do ... One group became a support group, the others decided they wanted a campaign. It was out of this group that the idea for a Rape Crisis centre came – I think there was about ten of them to begin with.*
> (Bernadette Manning, quoted in Bowen et al., 1987: 49)

According to Tuttle, this Rape Crisis group originally set their line up in a house donated by the Department of the Environment, but without official funding (ibid.). Former members Bowen and Manning, interviewed in 1987 do not say this, but do comment on the lack of mainstream funding. According to them the start-up funding came from the Barrow and Geraldine Cadbury Trust (http://www.bctrust.org.uk, accessed 20.07.07) but there was also money from a number of other sources in the early years (Bowen et al., 1987; Green, 1976 comments on applications being made for 'Urban aid and other government grants', in *Spare Rib Reader*: 465). As in the US, the Rape Crisis movement in Britain also started with the feeling that they were working within an environment which had no understanding of rape:

> *It is difficult for women to speak about experiences of sexual violence. Society perpetrates a hostile silence which denies reality for women who have been raped. In the Women's Liberation Movement we have learnt that talking and working together to break this silence can be enormously strengthening.*
>
> (LRCC, 1984: ix)

The sense of working in an alien environment was heightened by harassment from men. In the early days of the London group, Romi Bowen reports that the door to their office was kicked down by a group of men (Bowen et al., 1987: 50) and there were always abusive and threatening phone calls too (ibid. 51). Green tells of 'men ringing with obscene threats' when the phone number was first announced and of a bomb attack on a sister centre, in Sydney, Australia (1976, in *Spare Rib Reader*: 467).

At the very beginning though, it was 'exciting for the phone to ring' (Bowen et al., 1987: 50) and many calls were, of course, genuine. The number of callers quickly grew and the LRCC worked out a system to enable them to keep the line open 24 hours a day (ibid.). Initially this meant women sleeping overnight in the office but eventually the phone was re-routed to women's own homes during the night hours. Other groups appeared around the country, and as with Washington in the US, the London group offered advice to women wanting to set up local services (ibid. 55).

Generally, other groups in the UK have not managed to offer a 24-hour service, but otherwise there was a pattern to the range of services generally undertaken by the early groups. All offered a telephone line for as many hours as they could manage. This might be staffed by paid employees for some of the time, where the group had paid workers, but often the bulk of this work (or all of it in less well funded groups) was done by volunteers. Groups also tended to provide practical information about the police and court systems (usually via leaflets as well as over the telephone). They helped with information about 'VD' testing (or sexually-transmitted infections in modern parlance) and pregnancy testing and abortion. Some also had information available about 'lists of non-sexist doctors or self-defence classes' (Tuttle, 1986: 271). From the early days, Rape Crisis groups also offered a face-to-face

service, visiting women in their own homes if needed (Bowen et al., 1987: 51). At some point the idea of the self-help group emerged and some centres ran groups for women who had been raped. However, LRCC opposed this therapeutic response, at least in the early days. Bernadette Manning says that their approach was to encourage women to join CR groups, rather than becoming isolated into specialist groups for raped-women only (ibid.: 52, we also return to this topic in Chapter 3). This approach from London also shows that, crucially, groups also worked to change public opinion:

> *The counselling work and the other work that creates change are not separate – they are brought together so that they can strengthen each other.*
>
> (Bowen, 1987: 50)

According to Bernadette Manning the work was on three levels. Firstly, there was the direct work with women; there was also the experience of working within a collective structure that had a political commitment to women-only work, and finally there was the public education element of the work. All of this came together to make being part of Rape Crisis a 'wonderful, wonderful experience' (Bowen et al., 1987: 50–1).

Once the London centre had opened, the number of groups then grew rapidly, just as it had done in America. Kent Rape Counselling and Research Project was formed in 1977, Tyneside Rape Crisis Centre was founded in 1978 and remains the longest established, continuous Rape Crisis service in the UK, and Birmingham Rape Crisis opened in 1979. The Canterbury based group is still active, now as East Kent Rape Crisis and the Tyneside centre is also thriving (http://www.tynesidercc.org.uk). There is still a group in Birmingham, but this has moved outside of the main Rape Crisis grouping and provides services to both men and women survivors (the Rape and Sexual Violence Project, Birmingham). Both the Sheffield and Manchester groups had formed some years before opening their helplines in 1979. The Sheffield group was originally the 'Sheffield Rape Counselling and Research Group' but later became Sheffield Rape Crisis. Both of these groups are still in existence and took part in the survey we sent out for this book, as did Tyneside.

In Scotland, Rape Crisis also got off the ground quickly with Glasgow opening their first centre, in 1976, and Edinburgh following shortly afterwards in 1978 (Rape Crisis Scotland website).

Glasgow changed their name to Strathclyde Rape Crisis, in 1982, following a change in funding (ibid.). To this day, Scottish groups aim for collective structure where possible. Their policy statement says:

> Collective working is about sharing the power and responsibility in the organisation and allowing women involved to determine the direction and priorities – collective working does not mean everyone has to be the same.
> (http://www.rapecrisisscotland.org.uk)

Into the 1980s Rape Crisis centres continued to spread and the LRCC book, published in 1984, included a list of groups dated May 1983. This showed a total of 26 groups, including that in London itself. However, there appear to be errors in this listing as there is no mention of the group in Canterbury. Both Bradford and Coventry (see Table 1.1 below) do appear. In writing this précis we are also aware of groups that slip between the lines of our summary and are in danger of disappearing. These include Cumbria Rape Crisis, based in Carlisle and included in the 1984 listing. This staunchly feminist group appears to have closed in the late 1990s and although there is now a successor group, West Cumbria Rape

Crisis, this is differently established, and works with men and women. The 1984 list does also include one group in Wales, South Wales Rape Crisis (this sadly closed in 2005, due to funding problems) and four in Scotland (Aberdeen, Edinburgh, Highlands and Strathclyde). Irish groups in Belfast, Cork and Dublin also appear (LRCC, 1984: 136–7). Clearly then, the idea of Rape Crisis had spread throughout the UK and Ireland during the seven years since London first opened their line. The Belfast group opened in March 1982 and remains the only centre in the north of Ireland (Rape Crisis and Sexual Abuse centre, Northern Ireland website, http://www.rapecrisisni.com, last accessed 20.07.07). By 1985 the six groups in Ireland (including Belfast) had formed a network (Rape Crisis Network Ireland website, http://www.rcni.ie, accessed 20.07.07). It took the English and Welsh groups more than another ten years to achieve the same step.

Finally, Table 1.1 below gives some more information about the spread of Rape Crisis groups within England and Wales, showing what we have been told about opening dates by groups not yet mentioned here, who completed the questionnaire.

Table 1.1   Opening dates of Rape Crisis services

Group name	Year of formation
Bradford Rape Crisis Group	1981
Coventry Rape Crisis	1981
Plymouth Rape and Sexual Abuse Line	1982
Peterborough Rape Crisis Counselling Group	1983
Grays Thurrock Rape Crisis Line (later adding North Kent)	1984
Bangor Rape Crisis Line	1984
Doncaster Rape and Sexual Abuse Counselling Centre	1984
Gloucester Rape Crisis Centre	1984
Southampton Rape Crisis Line	1985
Rape and Sexual Abuse Support Centre (Croydon)	1985
Rape and Sexual Abuse Counselling Agency (Wirral/Merseyside)	1986
Rape Crisis (North Staffs and South Cheshire)	1986
Herts Area Rape Crisis and Sexual Abuse Centre	1986
Hereford and Worcester Rape Crisis	1986
Barnsley Rape Crisis	1987
Watford and South West Herts Rape Crisis	1988
Colchester Rape Crisis Line	1989
Rape and Sexual Assault Centre (Guildford)	1992
Durham County Rape Crisis	1992
Women's Rape and Sexual Abuse Centre (Cornwall)	1994
Milton Keynes Rape Crisis (which has now closed) spawned two other groups in the early 1990s, both of which eventually became independent centres, Aylesbury Vale Rape Crisis (1995) and Wycombe Rape Crisis (1995)	1995

It is fair to acknowledge that this book will not do justice to individual memories of those who have worked within the movement, been supported by Rape Crisis or, perhaps, felt that they were let down by the movement. Our emphasis instead, has been to pull together some of the existing written sources, adding to these from our own experience and that of the women who have talked with us about other Rape Crisis centres. Our discussions above also make it clear that the Rape Crisis movement has diversified in styles over the years since London set up that first centre and we return to explore these shifts further, in following chapters. The next section shows how this knowledge is used to set down some of the key features of Rape Crisis work.

Core values

Right from the beginning there were a number of facets of Rape Crisis work which made it different from other forms of support that might be available to women. Being feminist and saying so, was always the most obvious of these and the use of a non-hierarchical organisational structure would be another, less visible, difference. However, there were other core values, coming out of feminist politics, which informed the groups' ethos. This section tries to set the scene of the early British Rape Crisis work by laying out some of these core values. This list may not be complete and does not try to provide an historical timeline, but aims to show how feminist collective working and consciousness-raising came together to create a vital and radical form of support work. The hope here is to allow readers to appreciate where Rape Crisis started and why it had specific values relating to:

- Believing women.
- What constituted 'rape'.
- Not naming callers and not 'counselling' them.
- Providing support which was not non-directional.
- And respecting women's confidentiality and autonomy.

These core values will be returned to and expanded upon as the book develops but it is important at this stage to define and explain them.

One of the core values is expressed in how Rape Crisis responds to callers. Rape Crisis

workers consider that a central issue for survivors of rape is belief. Before the advent of Rape Crisis, a woman or girl who experienced rape might have gone to the police with her complaint or might have confided in family and friends. In some cases she would seek medical help, for injury or possible sickness or pregnancy. In any of these circumstances women have tended to be met first with scepticism, and sympathy only where they passed the test of honesty. Women within consciousness-raising groups spoke of these experiences of scepticism and so, by the time Rape Crisis was created, a need to behave differently had already been identified.

When women are raped, doctors consider whether their injuries measure up to what is expected of rape, and a range of professionals evaluate the woman's mental health to establish whether she is prone to fantasy or truth-telling implying that the law can be understood as having a primary aim of rooting out false accusations, rather than punishing rapists. In other words, the attitude of these professions suggests an interest in maintaining the stability of a society that believes that rape is rare. Only rarely then, can such professionals offer support. As a part of a radical movement for change, Rape Crisis could afford to take a different position on this important issue, and did so. A key core value within Rape Crisis has always been to believe what women tell us. As the comments of London Rape Crisis have already shown, societal values are there to deny rape and it is therefore the task of the Rape Crisis support worker to begin to redress that imbalance. The theoretical insight to create this practical policy came out of women's lived experience, as reported in CR and so this is a good example of the way in which the stories from CR have informed radical feminist theory and practice.

Another lesson from CR was that women have different definitions of 'rape' than those of the law or other professions. And so, from early on, women campaigned to change the legal definition of the act of rape (for more on this see: Ginsberg and Lerner, 1989; Cook and Jones, 2007). This knowledge also impacted on the core values of Rape Crisis work in that it meant that collectives would always speak with women no matter how the law might describe what had happened to them. In some strict sense then the name 'rape' crisis was always a misnomer. Within feminism though, it acted as recognition that women describe their experiences as 'rape' far more willingly than the law, the police or other agencies might. Again, given that these organisations are vested with maintaining the social stability they perceive to exist, it is not surprising that they act to minimise women's hurt by re-naming it as 'assault' or 'indecency' or 'exposure' and so on. Again, given their radical roots, Rape Crisis could afford to stand outside of this safety net and name the violence as women do. This made Rape Crisis welcoming to women, but also helps to explain why the collectives had edgy relationships with police and other agencies, from the beginning (Lupton and Gillespie, 1994). Later on (as Chapter 2 shows) these differences eventually led to structural changes and name changes within a number of Rape Crisis centres, which may also have marked a watering-down of their political edge.

Yet another characteristic which has tended to distinguish Rape Crisis from other agencies is language. Rape Crisis workers tend to term the women they work with as 'women' not 'clients' or 'users' and as 'survivors', not 'victims' (see Chapter 3 for more on the issue of terminology). The impetus for this careful use of language also came straight from consciousness-raising. As women spoke out about their experiences of being women they began to realise how words were used to belittle and subject women further. So it was that feminists avoided using words such as 'bitch' or 'cow' to describe other women and this awareness over language was also transferred into the new work on rape. At the time of the first edition of the London Rape Crisis book, the term survivor had not yet emerged. The collective were, however, clear about the problems of the term 'victim':

> *The word 'victim' does not appear in this book. It does not adequately describe women who are part of and have contacted the London Rape Crisis Centre. Rape does affect women for some time after it happens, but it often unleashes anger that has never been able to find its target before, which is strengthening. There is not a separate category of women who are 'victims' just as there is no category of men who are 'rapists'. Using the word 'victim' to describe women takes away our power and contributes to the idea that it is right and natural for men to 'prey' on us.*
>
> (LRCC, 1984: x)

In addition, the term 'victim' raised other problems. The 'notion of women as victims separates women who have experienced sexual and physical violence from other women and therefore seeks to deny the commonality of women's shared experiences of violence and abuse' (Lupton and Gillespie, 1994: 6). By the time the third edition of the LRCC book appeared the Preface had been amended to indicate the use of the alternative term 'survivor' (LRCC, 1999: x) as an affirming alternative to 'victim'. Use of the term survivor is now widespread within many services, both voluntary and statutory. This debate on terminology even saw the government shift on its language use and many reports and publications now use the term 'survivor' or 'victim-survivor'.

However, there are also arguments against this term, as Romi Bowen demonstrated in 1987. She commented that both 'victim' and 'survivor' have the effect of defining women in terms of the violence we have experienced and that she did not find this helpful (Bowen et al., 1987: 52). Whilst 'survivor' is much more positive as an identity, it may not be a positive choice to identify oneself so absolutely in terms of a rape or rapes. Clearly then, the most broadly accepted label is 'woman'.

Similarly, groups often tried to avoid terming their work as 'counselling', to keep themselves distinct from the various schools of therapy that were also being imported from the United States at that time. Even in the 1990s, Manchester Rape Crisis and others continued in this trend. Indeed this developed to become part of a broader critique of the determinist approach of mental health professionals and doctors. Within this critical discourse, mental illness was understood as a social construction, rather than as a function of biology. In other words, there was a questioning of the willingness of the medical professions to assume that depression and other conditions were caused by chemical imbalances. For Rape Crisis then, this meant that the work with women would instead be referred to as 'support work' or simply 'work'. This helped to emphasise the practical nature of what went on (the work often included advice and information regarding medical, legal and other issues already mentioned briefly). It also made it clear that, within feminism, women who had been raped were not viewed as in need of 'therapy' or 'healing', since they were not ill. They had been violated and that had had untoward effects, they wanted support and they wanted information, but that was not the same as needing 'fixing up', in the way that therapy or counselling seemed to offer.

It would also be wrong to characterise the work of Rape Crisis as non-directive. Rape Crisis has always been clear about the need to challenge rape myths wherever they are encountered. This includes the myths which women repeat to us, over the phone. For example, if a woman tells a worker that the rape was her fault (because she was dressed in such-and-such a way; or she was out late; or she had been drinking; or whatever else) then the Rape Crisis worker will always challenge that view (Bowen et al., 1987; Lovenduski and Randall, 1993). Clearly, in this is the skill of Rape Crisis work, as to do so could be confrontational and ineffective. However, with practice and training workers become expert at saying: 'we all feel like that but you know, it wasn't your choice to be raped, it was his choice to do that to you' or something along those lines. This then is a part of the belief, which we have already discussed above. Inherent in the value of 'believing women' is the notion that Rape Crisis has faith in women's actions, even when those women may find that hard themselves. Rape Crisis has a politics and an ethical system to show to women, and that system says that women are not responsible for the violation which they have had visited upon their bodies by men. Nevertheless, where a woman says that she has aspects of what happened that she does not want to talk about or that she does want to talk about, then the Rape Crisis worker will always listen to her position. In this version of Rape Crisis work, some of the most obvious successes are the women who join a CR group or go on to become part of Rape Crisis themselves. For many others the experience is less directly life changing; and limits on service provision have also meant that being a caller to Rape Crisis can, at times, feel very frustrating indeed. Later chapters examine these threads in more detail and draw out the services provided by the centres over the years since their foundation. For now, we continue this examination of the values underpinning Rape Crisis work.

When a woman does say that she cannot discuss her sex life; or needs to talk about the way that she feels she led a man on; or some other specific aspect of what happened to her; or the effect she perceives it to have had, then the impetus of Rape Crisis is to do as the woman wishes. This is because of another core value, and perhaps the starting point for these values, which is to give back power. This chapter has already shown that feminist theory has understood rape as an exercise in violence which uses sex as its

mode of operation. For the individual woman who is raped, this acts as a profound theft of her bodily autonomy. For Rape Crisis then, the philosophy has always been that workers must try to act in such a way as to be deeply respectful of women's autonomy in order to try to rebuild that sense of having rights over one's own destiny. When *Spare Rib* wrote about the opening of the London centre, they were told:

> The primary purpose of the collective is to help raped women regain their strength as individuals.
> (Green, 1976, in *Spare Rib Reader*: 465)

Another linked issue is confidentiality, in the sense of not repeating women's stories to others outside of the Rape Crisis setting and not using those stories in the public aspects of Rape Crisis work. Rape Crisis workers began from the perspective that, whilst women's experiences build feminist knowledge, they should not take a woman's story of her own violation and repeat that to others. Rape Crisis has always taken the sum of what is known from the work and used it in education (that only a small proportion of those who call Rape Crisis have ever reported an incident to the police, for example). To repeat an individual woman's account of her rape would clearly be to steal her autonomy again, and so has to be avoided. In more recent times this has met with particular challenges as the law has tried to access Rape Crisis records of individual cases, to use as evidence in court. In 2003 in the US, a Rape Crisis centre in Salem Massachusetts was ordered by the court to turn over the records of a young woman it had supported. The centre refused:

> The law in Massachusetts, as is the case in almost every state around the country, is that when a victim who has been sexually assaulted needs help afterwards, they're entitled to seek confidential counseling, whether it's a therapist, a psychiatrist, or a Rape Crisis counselor. They can't get better unless there's a meaningful promise of confidentiality. Unfortunately, defendants and their attorneys across the country are asking and receiving production of these records. They're getting court orders to require these records to be produced either to the judge in some instances or directly to the defendant in other instances. And the defendants really don't have any explanation for why they want the records. They just want to fish through and see if they might be able to find something.
> (CNN news report, http://edition.cnn.com/ TRANSCRIPTS/0301/21/tl.00.html last accessed 20.07.07)

In the US, similar to the UK and in other jurisdictions across the world, the decision on whether to request Rape Crisis records invariably rests with the judge (see Coussins, 1998: 94–106). Happily the UK government does appear to consider that these records should not be considered material evidence (Department for Constitutional Affairs http://www.dca.gov.uk/criminal/auldcom/ar/ar5.htm last accessed 20.07.07). Hopefully, this infraction of Rape Crisis core values can now be resisted.

Rape Crisis developing

As this chapter has already shown, the original London Rape Crisis was quickly joined by other groups, around Britain and at the same time, the nature of the work also developed. It was always true that the 'crisis' within the name Rape Crisis was for the woman caller to define. Rape Crisis has never turned women away simply because their rape happened some time ago, or even some decades ago.

> Initially . . . it wasn't atypical to get women who were raped 40 years ago ringing – we had lots of women who had been raped during the war ringing us.
> (Bowen et al., 1987: 50)

However, over time the breadth of the work also developed, partially as the skills of the women workers within the collectives developed, enabling women to speak of different forms of violation. At the same time, there were changes in Britain more generally, with a 'coming out' of feminism, which meant that the word 'rape' could be spoken more freely (see for example the setting up of the first SARC in 1986, discussed in Chapter 2) again creating the possibility for women to seek support in relation to experiences in their past. The core values discussed above included the understanding that women who called who had experienced sexual assault, sexual humiliation, flashing or being followed would receive the same support as those wanting to discuss rape. However, over time the range of experiences being discussed with Rape Crisis workers changed in other ways. So it was that Rape Crisis began to talk to women who had been raped in marriage, or in relationships, as a particular form of what we now name as 'domestic violence'. During this period, knowledge about physical violence within

marriage was already being developed within the refuge movement in Britain. By the time the first Rape Crisis centre opened in London, the National Women's Aid Federation had already been in existence for two years (there were 40 refuges in existence when the federation was formed in 1974; see http://www.womensaid.org.uk for details of this history) the refuge movement having been founded in England, a few years earlier (Hanmer, and Sutton,1984). However, knowledge about sexual violation within relationships was slower to develop and came, in part, out of women's stories as told to Rape Crisis workers. Over the years the working relationship between Women's Aid and the Rape Crisis movement has varied from place to place, but it can be argued that closer alliance might always have served women better, and we return to investigate this theme, in later discussions.

Another way in which the violations that women spoke of changed was in discussions of pornography. Women also began to speak to Rape Crisis workers of their experiences in relation to porn. They began to talk of being forced to make pornographic images or of being expected to copy scenes from pornography, in similar ways to the women quoted in Liz Kelly's research:

> We used to watch films and he would want me to do what . . . He said that anything that turned you on and involved two people was alright, but I didn't feel alright.
> (Kelly, 1988: 110)

At the same time as they were working within Rape Crisis centres, a number of activists were also involved in the more radical action groups, Women Against Violence Against Women (WAVAW, this connection is mentioned in Bowen et al., 1987: 56). This work would allow women who were engaged in support work to also become involved with campaigning for change and with forms of direct action against pornographers and others, via sex shops (see Chapter 6 for more on campaigning). It might be suggested that such tactics did little more than create resentment and hostility within mainstream organisations (such as the police) which have a continuing legacy today. Writing in 1985, Ian Blair (who was to become Commissioner of the Metropolitan Police) claimed that although the establishment of Rape Crisis centres in the US led to co-operation with the police, in the UK:

... shortage of finance, lack of appropriate training and continuing differences in philosophy between police and Rape Crisis personnel will inhibit, if not prevent, the future growth of the Rape Crisis centre movement and its relationship with the police in the United Kingdom.

(Blair, 1985: 84)

We return to the links between Rape Crisis and policing in the next chapter; however this comment serves for now to highlight the gap in understanding between the mainstream of provision and the growing knowledge of the Rape Crisis movement. Understandings of the connections between rape and pornography, and between physical and sexual violence added to the knowledge that was already growing about rape and sexual assault.

One of the most prominent set of events organised to protest against violence against women in the 1970s were the Reclaim the Night demonstrations. These were overtly physical manifestations of movement thinking. Begun in 1977, the first march was planned in Leeds and others were held on the same night around the country. These were intended to be joyful demonstrations against the limita-tions that women faced; women dressed up, sang songs and danced through the city streets, often through red-light districts. But the third London march through Soho in October 1978 had a different outcome and consequently gained most publicity. At this march police moved in to prevent women from defacing a sex shop with stickers, beat marchers with truncheons and arrested sixteen of them.

(Setch, 2003: 64)

Women's knowledge about violence against women continued to grow, through all of these experiences, and Wilson (1983: 12) theorised that women's sexual lives exist on a pleasure/danger continuum:

Men whistle and call after us on the street. This is at the other extreme of the pleasure/danger continuum and is a more contradictory experience than the sheer terror of rape and mutilation ... Yet the daily control of women by sexual innuendo is not trivial.

Radical analyses of the violence perpetrated against women helped to identify a continuum of violence (Kelly, 1988) placing 'everyday' violations (Stanko, 1990) within a structural context. This model sees all the forms of male violence as connected. The myriad forms of violation can all be understood as parts of a patriarchal structure which ensures women's continued oppression. So not just rape, but harassment in the street and at work, domestic

violence, pornography and many other types of violation are seen as connected to one another. This model was seen as very important in Rape Crisis and associated fields, as the groups developed and grew through the 1980s and into the 1990s. It was also seen as helpful in understanding another key area, that of sexual abuse of girl children:

Also as our counselling got better and we began to offer women a bit more in terms of counselling skills, women began to tell us about being raped as children as well as adults.

(Bernadette Manning, in Bowen et al., 1987: 50)

Liz Kelly reports that the topic of child sexual abuse, or 'incest' as it was often termed at the time, was explored by the Kinsey researchers in the 1950s. However, she goes on to say that it was not until the birth of the women's movement in the 1970s that research into the scope of sexual abuse began to be undertaken in the US (1988: 59). Louise Armstrong, herself a survivor of abuse, was an early example of a woman who spoke out about 'incest' in the United States, when she published her important text, *Kiss Daddy Goodnight* (1978). Work on child sexual abuse (CSA) also began in Britain, and a number of specialist agencies grew out of the women's movement, which catered specifically for women who were survivors of CSA. For example, in Manchester there was a group named 'Taboo' (originally named Manchester Support Group for Incest Survivors) who ran a refuge for survivors of sexual abuse and which finally closed in 1991. In Cambridge, collective members from Rape Crisis 'felt frustrated by the knowledge that there was nothing practical we could do to help young survivors of "incest" who were being faced with the choice of staying with men who have abused them in the interests of 'keeping the family together' or [being] placed with foster parents where the foster father may hear of the abuse, and repeat it, or [being] put into institutional care, often with boys who have been sent there for assault and violent behaviour' (Jenny for Choices: c1986). These women, together with sisters from Women's Aid and Incest Survivors' Self-Help Group, went on to found Choices Refuge, which still exists as a counselling service today (http://www.choicescounselling.co.uk). These are just examples of work which often involved Rape Crisis centres working with their local incest support groups, which also tended to draw on a straightforward feminist approach to support work. In many ways then, the early Rape Crisis centres are best understood as groups which were part of a wider network of feminist organisations. Sadly, the landscape has changed in the intervening years, so that the surviving centres often exist now without such stimulating and supportive networks.

Conclusion

Altogether then, it would be fair to say that the anti-rape movement had founded an important agency which started out in the US but then took shape in various countries around the world, including in Britain. This 'Rape Crisis' idea quickly caught on and went on to develop a range of working methods to allow for support to be offered to women who had experienced abuse from anywhere within the continuum of violence.

At the beginning, the idea of Rape Crisis was closely linked to a wish to end the patriarchal society, and this can be seen in the involvement of women in a range of related, and sometimes much less public, forms of activism. The groups began as collectives and did so in a wish to prefigure the type of society in which feminists wanted to live. This was a non-hierarchical world view, which wanted to eliminate power imbalance in all forms of human relationships. The Rape Crisis work was fluid, there was no talk of 'boundaries':

> When I first worked at a Women's Aid refuge it was the same – women workers visited the refuges in the evening and had tea and watched TV. We worked on the principle that the line between those of us who worked there and those living there wasn't there. We tried to run the refuge like a community and survivors of DV got jobs and we never thought in terms of boundaries and supervision etc. (Comments from Jude Boyles, former collective member at Cumbria Rape Crisis and Women's Aid)

Gradually all of these groups began to seek more funding to help them to carry on with the support work, which was proving very demanding. There was a sense that agencies and government *should* support this work, though there were also debates about the dangers of co-option inherent in taking money from the patriarchy. The wish to engage with wider society in these ways did indeed prove challenging to Rape Crisis centres and Chapter 2 picks up this story, showing how the groups developed and changed through the 1990s.

The Centres: Change and Challenges

Introduction

This chapter provides a starting point in investigating the work of Rape Crisis centres as they have developed from their founding days, back in the 1970s and 1980s. The chapter outlines some specific stories of individual groups but also draws on what we know of others. It analyses some of the issues that show how the groups have moved on from the early beginnings described in Chapter 1. Drawing on the contributions we have received from existing groups, the chapter considers the complexities of Rape Crisis work, both for the groups and the individuals involved. It looks at a concept named here as 'the living dynamic' which is a tool to describe some of these challenges. We then profile three Rape Crisis centres, with a brief outline of their stories, from their inception to the present day, to give some idea of how this dynamic operates in individual groups.

Chapter 1 has already referred to the rather awkward relationship between the feminist Rape Crisis centres and organs of the state such as the police. These difficulties should be no surprise, given the willingness of feminist anti-rape theory to challenge the status quo. However, they have produced a number of problems which Rape Crisis continues to tackle to this day. In this chapter we examine some of these difficulties in considering the widespread shift from collective structures towards hierarchies; the tendency to drop the 'Rape Crisis' name; and the linked topic of the ongoing struggle to find and maintain funding. This has also been affected by the challenge posed by Sexual Assault Referral Centres (SARC) which now appears to be the government's preferred model of support for rape survivors. This chapter also examines the beginnings of these SARCs, and their current work, in order to draw comparisons with Rape Crisis. It begins, however, by introducing the questionnaire and interviews that we have conducted for this book.

Collecting knowledge

When we began this project we knew of various printed and online sources of information about Rape Crisis, and we have drawn on many of these in writing the book. However, we were also already aware that Rape Crisis was under threat. We knew that a number of centres had closed at the end of the 1990s and we wanted to try to get an up-to-date picture of the centres surviving. We therefore made an attempt to collect some further information about some of those existing groups.

This chapter (and some of those that follow) draws on the data collected within the questionnaire sent out to Rape Crisis centres during 2005. A total of 38 centres were contacted for this research, identified using the Rape Crisis website (http://www.rapecrisis.org.uk). This site belongs to the Rape Crisis co-ordinating group which was the successor to the now defunct Rape Crisis Federation and the role of this group is discussed further in Chapter 4.

Of the 38 centres initially contacted, 25 responded to our questionnaire. This asked for some basic information about their organisation, its age and name, its structure and work. A copy of the questionnaire is included in Appendix 1 of this volume, together with a list of those who responded. A further three centres (in Merseyside (RASA), Cornwall (WRSAC) and South Essex (SERICC) then took part in detailed interviews during 2006. In addition, a number of ad hoc conversational interviews have been conducted with women working in Rape Crisis, in recent years. Where those women have given permission they are quoted here to give further voice to the wider movement.

The questionnaires and interviews have enabled us to write a book which, we believe, is in the spirit of consciousness-raising. We have used the voices of the women working within Rape Crisis to illustrate the issues we discuss and to inform the conclusions we reach. Rather than simply describing the centres and their evolution, we have created a book that should allow others to understand enough to become involved with Rape Crisis.

Feminism and the 'living dynamic'

Chapter 1 has already identified a number of key aspects of the Rape Crisis approach to support work and we know that assumptions are sometimes made about the therapeutic nature of Rape Crisis work which can render invisible the other valuable efforts that centres undertake. It described how the early groups were a part of the wider network of feminist activism but there are also other important facets of the work of Rape Crisis, which deserve further attention here. We have already seen that within radical feminism and Rape Crisis work, the personal truly is political, and the reality of the work is such that the complexity of this (apparently simple) statement has only increased over time.

Today, it is clear that the central work of Rape Crisis is in supporting women. However, women in the centres also have a campaigning profile and they contribute to relationships within the group, within the larger network of Rape Crisis and within the yet wider group of agencies working with survivors of sexual violence. One important aspect of the independent nature of Rape Crisis is in the belief that women who use the service should be permitted the space in which to 'self-refer'. In other words, Rape Crisis has always preferred that women have chosen to call and have not merely been passed on by some other agency or individual who believes it is time for her to speak of her violation. This can lead to some conflict when trying to work with other agencies who can view this approach as lazy, or lacking in direction, instead of understanding it as an attempt to value women's autonomy and self-determination. On the other hand:

> For many women it is not culturally familiar to just pick up the phone and self refer – that's when we have a responsibility to try to reach those women. We were right to be challenged and I have experienced this a lot in my work with refugee women.
> (Jude Boyles, former collective member at Cumbria Rape Crisis)

This then is just one example of the many intersections of the national, the local, the personal and the interpersonal perspective which Lee Eggleston at SERICC calls the 'living dynamic' (a term originally coined with Zena Barnacca). This term was developed as a way of conceptualising the competing pressures between radical activism and service provision. These

pressures drive the organisation, and so staff and volunteers have to negotiate and manage them every day. We have borrowed this concept of the 'living dynamic' as useful shorthand for discussing an even wider range of pressures. The living dynamic includes trying to work with social care agencies, even when they fail to understand our reasons for wanting to wait for 'their client' to call the line herself. The living dynamic also consists of many other issues that may test the feminist principles and ethos of Rape Crisis centres including: changes to core values which need to be developed to respect the position of refugee women; landmark cases which have sometimes stretched the breaking point of individuals and the organisations; developing knowledge of the law; striving for qualifications and encountering new aspects of our own and others' experience. The following discussion begins to unpick some aspects of this dynamic, but this is a theme we return to often, as we paint a more detailed picture of the changes and challenges faced within the Rape Crisis movement.

Most centres are (and generally have always been) run by a mixture of paid and unpaid (volunteer) women. The largest centre responding to our questionnaire has 45 while the smallest has just eight women workers. Some centres are run entirely by volunteers. Whilst in some places the time given by individual volunteers may be extensive, in others, women may work just a few hours a month. All but one of the centres surveyed operate on a women-only basis and even that one centre has a telephone helpline that is staffed exclusively by women. Most centres self-define as feminist organisations and declare feminist beliefs about the causes of rape as rooted in the patriarchal structures of society:

> We use the terms feminist and woman-centred. When we recruit for new volunteers we are very clear in the training packs that our services come from a feminist perspective. Very clear and upfront. In a multi-agency setting we'll use woman-centred. Women don't have to be feminist to work here but they have to understand that this is our underlying ethos and working practice. It's our baseline. I can't imagine not having a theoretical perspective to take the work from because if you don't have that, you are in a maze.
> (Cornwall)

Indeed, as this worker indicates, it is the feminism which makes Rape Crisis work manageable for most of those who work in the area over the long haul. Yet immediately the complexity of the 'living dynamic' peeps out in this comment. 'In a multi-agency setting we . . .' use another term, presumably to make the message of Rape Crisis easier to absorb. Similarly, not all of the centres do describe themselves as feminist; again this can stem from concern over the way that feminism is perceived, 'It is not always a key thing to talk about feminism partly because feminism doesn't seem to be understood anymore. We are definitely woman-centred' (Merseyside). Whereas in truth it is feminism that keeps Rape Crisis dynamic. Feminism provides explanations for the horrors that women tell us about and allows us to put them into a context for the women we work with and for each other. Feminism also creates the commitment to women which enables us to continue to want to do this work. Finally it also provides the motivation to continue to work with women (be they colleagues, callers or the professionals we encounter) even when they appear to want to obstruct our every effort. This form of commitment to a woman-centred view is part of the living dynamic and it is a sad comment on the co-opting nature of multi-agency settings that they encourage women to deny this.

This living dynamic also takes Rape Crisis out into the world. RASA in Merseyside makes the point that although 'we are easier at talking about rape in society today than 20 years ago and more women are coming forward either to the police or to us to talk about what happened to them, this is still difficult and is particularly so in relation to the abuse women suffer in their early lives'. Whilst rape is now reported to the police much more often than it was in the 1970s, all of the estimates are that it remains a largely unreported crime. It is also clear that it is particularly complex to try to retrospectively report abuse which took place some years ago. Home Office research shows an ongoing decline in the conviction rate for reported rape cases, with an all-time low of 5.6 per cent (Kelly, Lovett and Regan, 2005). Campaigning on this issue is therefore a central part of the 'living dynamic' of Rape Crisis work. Rape Crisis centres are often the only people that women tell their experiences to. It is therefore the responsibility of the workers to continue to speak of the lessons learned from the CR process which is Rape Crisis work.

Rape Crisis is also in a unique position in terms of its ability to challenge men's explanations for their behaviour. Again, drawing on feminist anti-rape theory, Rape Crisis workers hear women's attempts to articulate what happened to them. Elizabeth Stanko discusses how women plan their lives around the unpredictability of men's behaviour and how men's 'physical and sexual intimidation towards women' (1985: 72) operates on two levels, within individual reactions and wider societal reactions. Both levels act to deny the impact of male violence on women. There are so many types of male violence against women, and men make so many justifications for their violence, that women cannot be expected to immediately understand or know what these reasons may be (see Figure 2.1).

It has been argued that abusive male behaviour is no more than an extension of typical male behaviour (MacKinnon, 1987; Kelly, 1988; Stanko, 1990) and because of this it is often difficult for women to acknowledge. This affects how violence is defined. It might once have been suggested that these behaviours were individual pathology or a feature of dysfunctional families, but thanks to feminist anti-rape theorists such as Brownmiller, Griffin and MacKinnon it is now easier to see that abusive behaviour is something which is socially normalised (see also Schechter, 1982). Extreme violence is nothing more than the most distant end of the continuum of male imposed control under which all women live (Kelly, 1988). This knowledge began to grow from CR and has continued to change and evolve through the process of Rape Crisis support.

Coming together: starting a centre

The 'living dynamic' of Rape Crisis work is illustrated in the following stories of the individual Rape Crisis centres where workers participated in lengthy interviews for this book. In dealing with the competing pressures which centres negotiate and manage every day they develop their own strategies and responses to the challenges they meet. Chapter 1 provides the story of the beginnings of Rape Crisis at the national level but at a more localised level it is informative to look at the similarities that underpinned the emergence of centres in different parts of the country. Very few centres have a written history and for some centres their history has been lost because founding members are no longer around to maintain the oral history of the service. What follows then are three

Types of violence	Justifications for violence
Rape	Revenge
Date rape	Punishment
Marital rape	Displaced anger
Gang rape	To feel superior
Drug rape	In addition to another crime
Child rape	Easy target
Incest	As a means to sexual access
Pornography	To take what is denied
Dogging	As male entitlement
Sexual harassment	Avoidance of intimacy
Murder	Denial of emotions
Battering	Dominance
Prostitution	Control
Genital mutilation	Excitement
Stalking	Fun
Abusive telephone calls	Recreation
Silent telephone calls	To prove themselves as men
Unnecessary surgery	To 'beat the system'
Wolf-whistling	Sense of achievement

Figure 2.1   Range of 'violences' and 'causes' identified by Rape Crisis volunteers at a training session

different stories but they are stories with similar themes of hope, struggle and success.

South Essex

This group was formed quite early in the history of Rape Crisis in the UK. They have continued to be involved in work at all levels, local, regional and national, over a 25-year period. Their experiences help to illustrate some of the themes discussed later in this chapter, of the evolution of the structure of groups; of name changes; the struggle for funding and of the pressure of the SARCs as an alternative model of support. In addition though, the story of South Essex Rape and Incest Crisis Centre (SERICC) also tells us something about the ways in which the work of Rape Crisis broadened during the 1990s and of national lobbying in the ten years following the Labour party success in 1997.

In 1981 Thurrock Women's Action Group (TWAG) was formed (see glossary). This was a group of around ten local women who came to define themselves as feminist. Included in this group were Lee Eggleston and Sheila Coates, who both work at SERICC today. The TWAG women had backgrounds in the social political movements of the early 1980s (for example, CND – the Campaign for Nuclear Disarmament – and Greenham Common). The move towards providing services emerged during a meeting

when the issue of rape was raised and the women found that most had experienced sexual violence of some sort. Here then was CR in action. Some of the members had heard of London Rape Crisis Centre (LRCC) and a meeting was arranged where, after conversations with Bernadette Manning of LRCC, it was decided to start a line.

In 1983 LRCC offered training, a constitution was drafted and they registered as a charity and so in early 1984, Grays Thurrock Rape Crisis Line was opened. At the same time, this group of women opened a refuge – Thurrock Women's Aid – and the two organisations shared everything, even having a joint letterhead. The Crisis Line was completely staffed by volunteers, the organisation was run as a collective and their first income was £64.30, the proceeds of a jumble sale.

In 1985 the Crisis Line changed their name initially to Grays Thurrock and North Kent Rape Crisis Line and then in 1986 to South Essex Rape and Incest Crisis Centre (SERICC), the name still used today. In 1988 the first local government funding was secured from the joint finance budget (social services and health authority) and this amounted to around £8,000 for a one-year period. The renaming was also part of a more general process of change including a restructure and geographical shift to the South Essex catchment area, to ensure the survival of the organisation. The needs of the organisation were however never put above the needs of service users as when these organisational changes took place, Canterbury Rape Crisis was able to cover the residual areas and so the needs of local women were not abandoned. In addition, the Thurrock refuge also continues independently to this day, now inhabiting purpose-built premises.

During this time the organisation continued to be run as a collective but in 1988 a management structure (consisting of around six women) was adopted. Another six (more or less) volunteers were involved in the core service provision. There was one part-time paid worker (Sheila Coates) who also worked part-time at Women's Aid. Despite the formalised structure of the management group, most of the decision-making was still conducted along collectivist lines. Those who had been with the organisation from the outset instinctively worked in a collective manner but other volunteers had experience of hierarchical working models from within the statutory sector. As time went on tensions between these two different models became progressively more heightened.

While funding was secured on a year-to-year basis, the women of SERICC developed the skills and knowledge necessary for the survival and development of their organisation. From 1988, the group experienced a five-year learning curve where they had to struggle for the right to participate in local networks. Determined to raise awareness about the issues the worker joined every committee and multi-agency partnership possible, all whilst fighting against the negative label of 'man-hating, radical, lesbian feminists'. The worker gave talks everywhere she was invited. The key messages were about the nature and extent of sexual violence, and what sort of services women needed.

This period was not just characterised by structural change and skills development. It was also a period when the nature of the continuum of violence was further highlighted. In 1988 SERICC faced the issue of ritualistic abuse. Ritual abuse or 'satanic abuse' as it was also named was causing concern around the nation at that time and views were widely split, within and outside of the Rape Crisis movement, as to whether it actually existed (see DoH, 1994; Campbell, 1997; Scott, 2001). One way of understanding this emergence is that the women (working in Rape Crisis and elsewhere, such as in social work) had

learned enough to be able to 'hear' these stories. It had already become apparent that feminist knowledge of male violence was still growing and that this knowledge could only develop further once women heard more about the forms of violation that men are capable of committing. This is illustrated by the development of key services. When Rape Crisis services first began, the women who called spoke of rape. Before too long however, women began to talk about child sexual abuse and rape within marriage, and centres responded, as SERICC had, not only in expanding the services but also in changing their name (with the shift from 'Rape Crisis' to 'Rape and Incest Crisis'). Ritual abuse came to be understood as another form of sexual violence, amongst the continuum of abuses. It has much in common with the persistent humiliation and violation of women within family relationships or in enclosed communities such as hospitals or prisons. The differences here though were that in ritual abuse the women being violated appeared to be free to leave and that they were also being abused by other women. Both of these aspects caused tensions (and scepticism) within Rape Crisis and around the country.

Women survivors typically spoke of ongoing abuse which had begun when they were very young and where their very coping strategies were used to keep them trapped in an ongoing cycle of horrible degradation. Nationally a number of Rape Crisis groups became involved in supporting ritual abuse survivors and women at Manchester Rape Crisis began to emerge as having the knowledge and confidence to advise others, in particular, Sara Scott provided training and consultation to a number of agencies. Lacking expertise, SERICC liaised with Sara Scott at that time and was then able to develop its own practice in this area.

Moving on from this experience, in the early to mid-1990s other Rape Crisis groups emerged in the local area – including Colchester, Chelmsford and Harlow – and the existence of these groups did help to ease SERICC's feeling of political isolation. However, at the same time, the number of calls to the service continued to increase and the concerns about funding instability also persisted. The number of paid staff members increased, so that by 1991 there were five paid workers, a mixture of part-time and full-time.

SERICC also had a problem with office space and, despite having a satellite office in Basildon from the mid 1980s to 1995 they began to grow out of their available space. As result of their unfailing determination to attend every possible meeting in the local area, they met a supportive woman who offered the space above the church hall. SERICC refurbished the space and constructed offices and counselling rooms. They expressed their thanks by assisting at the woman's ordination ceremony when she became one of the first female ministers in the country.

SERICC believed that the 1997 New Labour government would deliver on the issues. A Women's Unit was announced with a Minister for Women and, indeed, SERICC's first foray into national politics was to telephone Joan Ruddock on her first day in office as Minister for Women. They managed to secure a half-hour appointment with her and then talked for two hours about the needs of adult survivors and SERICC's struggles against funding cuts. Sadly, the subsequent move towards a national focus on the issue only served to show the women of SERICC just how little knowledge existed about sexual violence and also just how powerless this new Minister really was.

SERICC was later invited to participate on many government steering groups, committees and panels. One example of this was their participation in the *Living Without Fear* programme which was headed by Margaret Jay (Cabinet Office, 1999). The programme developed a funding stream for 'partnership' organisations working on issues of violence against women and SERICC secured a project in partnership with the Zero Tolerance Trust. The *Living Without Fear* document contains the following comments about Rape Crisis:

> *Over the last 25 years the voluntary sector, and more recently many statutory agencies, have achieved an enormous amount. We pay tribute to them. It is thanks to them that there is so much from which to draw in setting out an agenda for the future. But provision is still patchy (see map of distribution of Rape Crisis centres . . . Our goal is that within five years there will be effective multi-agency partnerships operating right across the country, drawing on the experience and good practice in this report.*
> (http://www.womenandequalityunit.gov.uk/ archive/living_without_fear/images/03.htm last accessed 20.07.07)

The map provided in this document showed a distribution of over 50 centres around the UK. Sadly, and despite the grand goals of *Living Without Fear*, there are fewer centres today than

there were when the Labour government took office in 1997. This trend is explored in a number of different ways within this volume, including in the challenge presented by Sexual Assault Referral Centres in this chapter, and in the story of the Rape Crisis Federation in Chapter 4.

Looking back now on the *Living Without Fear* initiative it is easy to see that the position of Rape Crisis within the national strategy on violence against women was never properly established (see also Jones, 1999). Refuges were formally part of the 'Supporting People' framework (though Kate's ongoing contacts in Women's Aid report that this has created real problems for them in practice). Services for rape survivors were, however, centrally positioned within SARCs; the comment on Rape Crisis was simply:

> *Along with other sources of funding, the new arrangements [referring to 'Supporting People'] could also contribute to funding crisis help for rape victims, such as services provided by Rape Crisis centres.*
> (Cabinet Office, 1999: 26)

As ever, Rape Crisis was not positioned as an essential service, despite the hard work and diplomacy of women such as those at SERICC. Thankfully, SERICC has survived and was lauded as a 'good practice' model in the *Living Without Fear* document (Cabinet Office, 1999: 29). The relationship between SERICC and the Home Office has developed year on year. In 2003 the Home Office increased funding for SARCs and Essex police have been informed of the intention to locate a SARC in Thurrock but only if SERICC is part of the partnership.

At the time of our questionnaire, there were 13 women working within SERICC (consisting of project workers, managerial and counselling staff) and seven on the management committee. They open a phoneline three times each week and take around 100 calls each week. They also provide around 30 face-to-face support sessions each week and continue to be involved in a number of other activities. SERICC are currently funded by South West Essex Primary Care Trust; Thurrock Council; Essex Social Services (Mental Health Services); Thurrock Supporting People and the Home Office. Finally, members of SERICC are active within campaigning organisations such as the Campaign to End Rape (CER, discussed further in Chapter 6) and they also continue to undertake the local and national lobbying work we have already mentioned.

Merseyside

The Rape Crisis centre in Merseyside was founded a little later than SERICC but also came out of a group of women meeting together and wanting to make a difference. Again, this story demonstrates the reality of changing name and structure. This group has also had good links with other women's groups locally but has not had quite the same national involvement, probably simply because of their geographical location. In addition, this group has received funding from a range of sources over the years and has taken on counselling students, as part of the group, to help provide services to women callers.

RASA (Rape and Sexual Abuse Counselling Agency) was formed in 1986, originally called Wirral Rape Crisis Counselling Service (WRCCS) and the helpline opened in July 1987. Little remains of the early history of the centre but it is possible to glimpse something of the pioneering spirit from their library of annual reports and the memories of women who joined the service in the early years.

The group grew from the interests of a small group of women who had grown friendly during their participation in a college class on Women's Studies. Politicised by their studies, they had learned of the effects of sexual abuse on women's lives and 'were concerned that other local Rape Crisis centres were receiving many calls from the Wirral area' (Annual Report, 1989). The nearest centre was in Liverpool and after visiting the women at that centre they decided to start a Rape Crisis group in Birkenhead on the Wirral. Their first task was to register as a charity and to set up the phoneline. Established as a collective, the women set themselves the following aims:

1. To offer a free and confidential service to women and girls who have been raped, sexually assaulted or sexually abused, either recently or in the past.
2. To provide both telephone and face-to-face counselling that is accessible to all women.
3. To provide practical information and support concerning legal and medical issues.
4. To educate the public (particularly young people) about sexual violence with the aim of increasing awareness.
5. To provide training for other agencies.
6. To strive to work in an anti-oppressive way. We will actively oppose racism, classism, misogyny and discrimination against women because of age, disability or sexuality.

7. To make links with other organisations, Rape Crisis centres and campaigning bodies that share a similar philosophy.

This list of aims was similar to that of other groups at the same time and, crucially, involved a commitment to a range of anti-oppressive practices. In trying to ensure that the work and culture of Rape Crisis was working against dominance in human relationships, the groups were following the blueprint that the American sisters of the Women's Liberation Movement had originally outlined. Just like SERICC, the RASA group grew out of consciousness-raising and was formed on feminist ideals.

By 1989, thanks to a grant from the Local Authority Inner Area Programme, the group was able to employ a full-time worker whose tasks included office administration, service co-ordination, publicity, fundraising and liaison with outside agencies. This list again brings out that living dynamic, the struggle to balance an astonishing range of tasks, in one paid worker's post. In the 12-month period to September 1990 the centre received 503 telephone calls, less than they now receive in a month, but this confirmed the need for the service in the area.

Even at this early stage the women who had come together were aware that the title 'Rape Crisis' could be misleading 'as it implies that we are only available for women who have been raped recently and are in crisis' (Annual Report, 1989). From the start, the service saw self-referral as an important step for women regaining control over their lives: control that sexual violence takes away. At the same time they acknowledged that for a variety of reasons some women are unable to refer themselves and so the centre took on a considerable amount of inter-agency liaison work right from these early beginnings. The centre's involvement in the local community also included sending representatives to speak at domestic violence conferences, the Well Woman Centre and Women's Aid, providing training to outside agencies and sending volunteers on fundraising courses. They also had input into the local police 'Sexual Offences' course and attended the local Voluntary Services Charity Fair and local community open days. In 1989 they provided workshops to five local schools and colleges and this was at a time when sexual violence was still a difficult subject to cover in school education (arguably it still is).

The service began to grow during the early 1990s as grants from the 'Local Authority Community Chest Fund' and the local 'Sheila Kay Fund' enabled them to purchase publicity materials and conduct training courses for new volunteers. These early courses spanned ten sessions and included developing listening skills, examining the myths and facts of sexual violence, equal opportunities, and legal and medical issues. They also took on placements for social work students and trainee counsellors.

One issue which has challenged many groups has concerned women who are training as counsellors, wanting to get involved in the work. Some groups have taken the view that these women are not sufficiently committed to Rape Crisis and so should not be welcomed into the groups. RASA has developed a different response and continues to provide placements for trainee counsellors today:

> Students who get their placements here have already completed two years at college and they have to undertake our training. So I have no problem with students gaining experience here because it is making them better counsellors, more skilled, more knowledgeable and they are going to take that experience out with them when they become full-time counsellors.
>
> (Merseyside)

So RASA sees part of its 'living dynamic' as helping trainee counsellors develop their skills in a Rape Crisis environment, so that they can better support women in the future. Honesty is a core value and so: 'survivors are told that their counsellor is a 'counsellor in training' and they discuss this together before the beginning of the counselling'.

To bring the picture of RASA up to date, the group consisted of 32 women at the time of the questionnaire and has recently shifted back towards a more collective decision-making process (further discussion of these changes in structure follows). They still run a helpline, which is open two evenings and two afternoons per week and each week they take around 40 calls on that line. In addition, the group run face-to-face, individual sessions for around 36 women at any one time. RASA also provides support via outreach and home visits, visiting women in hospital and accompanying women to the police and courts. The group had no active campaigning profile at the time of the questionnaire.

Cornwall

Finally then, we profile the Cornwall group, which is a newer venture than SERICC or RASA. This group did their groundwork carefully so that when they launched the line, they were ready to receive calls. Initially however, their funding position was extremely precarious. They have now moved on though, to broaden out their service provision to a much wider range of services than the previous groups profiled. Here then is an attempt to create services for women across a wider range of forms of abuse.

As with so many women's groups, this group started around a kitchen table, becoming a Rape Crisis centre in the early 1990s. There was no intention to launch the helpline for a year or so. Instead the women who met started by having public meetings. Their first work was to become registered as a charity, draw up the policy documents together, put the constitution together – basically to get it right.

The key organiser had come from Worcester – where a Rape Crisis group had launched in 1987, and she had become part-time co-ordinator for that. After moving to Cornwall in 1991 and being involved in a lot of creative projects including editing a women's magazine, she found she missed contact with other radical feminists. 'I'd been involved in Greenham and thought I would always find radical feminists in the world but being down in Cornwall I didn't'. But after meeting up with a woman who was doing a Women's Studies course at Plymouth University, she then met others: 'there were about six of us, youth workers and other people on women's studies courses. Women who were very committed to working with other women – there was a real political drive'. Like the other groups profiled, Cornwall's founding women met through their wish to learn more about women's lives. In a sense then, each of these groups grew out of a pre-existing concern with consciousness-raising.

The 18 months of groundwork culminated in a public meeting in 1994 at Bodmin Community College. The plan was to show a video of Birmingham Rape Crisis (produced by Central Independent Television in the mid-1980s) and they expected to attract about 20–30 women. As it turned out, 60 or 70 women turned up. 'There were women standing around the room – there is one bit in the video where the Rape Crisis worker says ''no group has ever handed over power,

power has to be wrested from the powerful''. That really went to the heart of what Rape Crisis was all about.' From that meeting the first training group was recruited. The training took the form of a 12-week course with a residential weekend in the middle. 'We still do a 12-week with a residential at the end of the 4th week. Early spring and late autumn, we run it each year.'

So the Women's Rape and Sexual Abuse Centre (WRSAC) began, with the phoneline launched in 1996. Their total possessions amounted to a filing cabinet in a local community centre, and the Rape Crisis line was open one night per week. It was all voluntary – no-one got paid and funding consisted of a donation of £1,000 which had been given by the tutor from the women's studies course where founding members had met. From those beginnings face-to-face work and outreach developed. The first funding bid was not successful; 'We put in a **huge** lottery bid for something like £280,000. The Lottery were very impressed with the bid and came down to see us but we really were not going to go from managing £1,000 to £280,000 overnight!' They were successful with an 'Opportunities for Volunteering' grant in 1998 which paid for one full-time co-ordinator and eight hours of admin per week (these grants are distributed by the Department of Health). Then an organisation called Community Projects Trust offered a free room in their building in the centre of town:

There was a tiny window backing out onto a brick wall which the volunteers painted custard yellow. By then we had a committed group of 12–15 women and we did our first successful Lottery bid in 1999. The next Lottery bid after that was much bigger, around £260,000 and that gave us funding for the posts of Agency Director, Volunteer Co-ordinator, Project Development worker and an admin worker. These felt like the golden years.
                                                      (Cornwall)

The 1999 *Living Without Fear* initiative was also a key point for WRSAC. 'All the time I was working really closely with the Domestic Violence Officer, in St Austell police station, called Lisa Willis. There are six districts in Cornwall and we cover three of them. One of these district councils had a launch of the community safety strategy and DV, rape and sexual abuse were not included'. Women from WRSAC and from the local refuge pointed out to the organisers that there was no mention of violence against women. 'So someone said, right,

let's start a DV subgroup. We put in a bid to get some workers. We still do that work; we got a service level agreement with a statutory agency and got invited to all sorts of tables we would never have got invited to'. Clearly then, with the right local will and with a clear voice, the *Living Without Fear* publicity could make a difference on a local level, even if it has failed for Rape Crisis on a wider stage.

WRSAC started out as a collective, but like the other groups profiled have felt that this could not continue:

The structure changed in 1998 when funding/funders required us to have a Management Structure and 'a Manager'. Now, due to the size of the organisation, it is clear that we need 'leadership' however this is defined.
                                                      (Cornwall)

The group continues to open a phoneline five times a week and to take 30 to 40 calls each week. They also provide face-to-face sessions, run a self-support group and a young women's network group. Unlike RASA, WRSAC does not take counselling students as volunteers: 'we made a policy decision many years ago not to use counselling students. We felt our agency isn't here to test our women on students so we have always implemented that'.

WRSAC also 'provides women and teenage girls with Domestic Violence Support Services. We have two full-time DV support workers and one part-time worker providing services alongside a male perpetrator programme'. In addition to this pioneering work, WRSAC is also involved in local groups and partnerships and has some involvement in national lobbying. Alongside SERICC, this group was represented at the founding meeting of the Truth About Rape Campaign (discussed further in Chapter 6) and continues to organise local events such as Reclaim the Night marches.

These three short outlines cover a multitude of women's work, over a wide geographical area and across a period of many years. It is almost impossible to do justice to the effort and enthusiasm poured into this, from all of the centres. Nevertheless, we hope that these stories can give some idea of the commonalities of the centres as well as of some of their differences. Chapter 3 continues to paint a more detailed picture of the services provided by the centres, but in this chapter we want to take the time to draw out some of the themes from these stories, which have also affected many of the other groups, across the years.

Changes (1): collective to hierarchy

This discussion concerns the way that the centres have been structured and why they were built that way. As Chapter 1 has shown, the original model for a Rape Crisis centre was of a non-hierarchical organisational structure based on the concept of collectivity. Although, as the case studies demonstrate, many centres have ceded this organisational structure for a more mainstream style involving some form of management committee, many centres have still retained a feminist ethos of equality (Charles, 2000). We have already outlined the importance of the collective structure in the foundations of feminism in Chapter 1 but this section attempts to build on that introduction before moving on to explain the decline in collective structures, which the stories above have already illustrated.

The use of the collective is linked to the wish to build practice and theory from women's lived experience and to the desire to create a world where human relationships are built on mutual respect and not on dominance and submission. In order to try to bring this imagined world to life, the original groups coming out of Women's Liberation all tried hard to work in a non-hierarchical manner. Chapter 1 has already shown that this could create complex and exhausting structures. At times, collective meetings within Rape Crisis would run long into the night, in order to try to resolve difficult issues by consensus, not by simple majority. When the decision to be dealt with was hard (if it involved limiting the service; or forging relationships with patriarchal agencies; or responding to charges of discrimination or bias within the group itself), then the possibilities for strife were legion. Collectives are also often open to caucus formation or 'you lot' as such cliques are often termed in real life. They are also vulnerable to the driving will of the middle-class and educated white women who may well have more time and energy available to give to the group, by virtue of their privilege and associated (relative) wealth. Equally though, they have also been hampered by agendas built on 'identity politics' which are perhaps best understood as expressions of fear, at working in new landscapes. Sometimes then, collectives have been seen as problematic

structures which hamper the work of Rape Crisis more than they help it. However, we would like to posit the alternative explanation, that collectives appear difficult simply because they are revolutionary.

We inhabit a world which is built on hierarchies. Our schools, hospitals, police forces and even families are built on the notion of a pyramid of power, with those at the bottom (the children, or patients, the public, the constables or even the criminals) having the least access to decision-making and to making change within the structure. This is generally a larger group and power is gradually filtered up through the hierarchy into fewer and fewer hands, until the small group at the top (the head-teachers; the hospital consultants and directors; the chief constables; the parents and grandparents) are the people who can truly make decisions and effect change. From a feminist perspective this is often seen as being problematic because within many organisations those at the top are more likely to be white, middle-aged and middle-class men who are therefore likely to resist the feminist call to change. This equality of opportunity based challenge is familiar to all but is merely a side-effect of the resistant nature of hierarchies and is not what we are centrally concerned with here. Collectivity confronts another problem with hierarchies and therefore makes a different challenge to their power. The collective identifies a problem which is inherent in the very being of the hierarchy. This is the problem of dominance and submission which all hierarchies need to survive. No structure can continue using this pyramid shape without the permission of the many at the bottom to the holding of power by the few at the top. This structure is viewed as a problem by feminism which wants to struggle towards a world where human relationships are built quite differently. Instead of simply ceding decisions to a few and, in doing so, laying ourselves open to misuse of the power we have given to the leaders, feminism wants to find ways for all people to take part in decision-making, at different levels.

This then is the true revolution of collective working and this is also a response to those arguments that collectives are difficult and time-consuming. Collective working is bound to be a struggle, since it is part of creating a different world. It involves giving power to those less skilled in equal measure to those with clear advantages. The collective can be understood as

Collective membership entails sharing responsibility for the whole service including:

- Keeping the phoneline open.
- Making decisions at Monday meetings.
- Raising funds.
- Paying bills.
- Selection and training of new members.
- Housework.
- Publicity.
- Providing support and supervision, etc.

Figure 2.2   From Manchester Rape Crisis – Policy Document, circa 1990

anti-oppressive working brought to life. Collective working strives to ensure that the white, heterosexual, non-disabled, middle-class, educated women *do* share their expertise and energies with everyone else, regardless of previous experiences. However, within this is also the key problem which collectives are bound to encounter. Being a part of a collective requires everyone being willing to work equally. It means that nobody can just do their bit on the phoneline and then go home. All of the members of a collective are responsible for painting the walls and buying the tea. This does not mean that everyone has to do the same tasks but that everyone is responsible for them being done. Similarly, everyone shares responsibility for paying the bills and developing policy (see Figure 2.2). Often then, collectives are inconvenient to maintain as it is difficult to find a supply of individuals willing to take on this level of responsibility. The following extract is from a notebook Kate kept during her training as a Rape Crisis volunteer, in 1990 (see Figure 2.3).

It is interesting to reflect on the impact of this imperative on women from different backgrounds and with differing lives as differences 'between women have led to fears of fragmentation of the women's movement' (Lupton and Gillespie, 1994: 33). A Black single

Why work collectively?

- To distribute power
- To share responsibility
- To make the most of different experiences/skills
- To avoid hierarchies
- To have a common aim
- To give support

Figure 2.3   Notes from Manchester Rape Crisis training

parent; a lesbian bank manager; a 21-year-old college student and an Asian advice worker may all have differing abilities to offer and are also likely to experience the stresses of collectivity differently. Yet, each of these was present on that Rape Crisis training course, back in 1990. At the same time as collectivity strives to create a post-patriarchal oasis, it is 'naturally' hampered by the realities of existing within a post-colonial, ableist and capitalist patriarchy.

The Rape Crisis groups in Britain set out to create these idealistic collectives but the stories of individual groups in this chapter have already illustrated a trend away from collectivity. SERICC were early adopters of a new style of working, changing to a management structure in 1988. The change was adopted to address two different but important imperatives:

- To resolve internal differences related to rights and responsibilities.
- To simplify funding applications.

Within SERICC the stresses of holding collective responsibility were seen as too great to overcome. But the outside (hierarchical) world was also intruding into the structures of Rape Crisis groups. Of the centres who responded to our questionnaire all but four had formerly operated as collectively structured organisations. However, only six retain this structure today (another one defines itself as a co-operative and one other said they are not officially a collective but debatably they could be considered so). Many of the centres that changed their organisational structure in the 1990s cite 'pressure from outside funding bodies' (Bradford) and specifically mentioned the changing requirements of 'the Charity Commission' (Colchester) and the National Lottery (RASA and Wycombe). Peterborough's statement exemplifies this 'We changed to have a Board/Trustee structure to ease filling in funding forms, etc. We are still run by the volunteers though' and Wycombe insist that whilst the stated structure may change because of outside pressures, '. . . many of the principles we apply in running the organisation today are based on the early days of collective working'.

Clearly though, despite such reassurances, the early ethos of collective working was lost in transition. The wish to work in a democratic manner and with an emphasis on equality of opportunity may survive, albeit the challenge to the hierarchies which abound in our society has gone. Also lost are the drive to ensure that work is shared equally and the structural reminder of the risks of dominance and submission within hierarchies. It would be an oversimplification to suggest that the older collective structure ensures that such dominance cannot occur but it does create the possibility of challenge, which is much harder to sustain within a hierarchy. Whilst a well-meaning and democratic hierarchy can fulfil some of the aims of collectives, it cannot do all that they entail. It is also arguable that the shift from collective to hierarchy has been accompanied by a more general co-opting of Rape Crisis into the mainstream of service provision, and away from that original vision of radical support work, and this theme is explored further throughout the remainder of this chapter.

There are other related issues of power imbalance, not discussed here in detail, which are not linked with the collective or hierarchy debate, but which are sometimes confused within this discussion. A key issue in many voluntary groups are the problems raised by the differences in power between the volunteers, the paid workers and the management group. These splits also exist in collectives, though clearly the groupings are different, since everyone is part of the management. In a hierarchy, the workers and volunteers occupy a position of structural inferiority, by comparison to the management group, at least in theory. In reality however it does not always play out in this fashion. Where the management group is made up of volunteers from outside the organisation, it often meets once a month, or less frequently. The group is clearly reliant for making decisions on the information given to them by women within the main group, and in such situations the practical power is often in the hands of one or two workers, perhaps the salaried women, who have the most access to knowledge, simply because they are most often at the centre.

This short outline serves to demonstrate that the hierarchy can create more problems than it solves, since it adds an extra layer to the organisation, which is then capable of exerting undue dominance, or being dominated by workers, either of which can be quite problematic in terms of decision-making and strife. The collective is still at risk of dominance by white middle-class women, by paid workers, or by anyone else who assumes power but it is less formalistic as well as more capable of questioning such power swings.

This then is another aspect of the living dynamic. In order to continue to survive in a patriarchy, groups have felt that they have needed to let go of some of the early ideals. There were other pressures at play here too, such as the perceived need to become more 'professional' in the style of work undertaken. This involved the creation of other hierarchies in the importation of ideas from counselling, such as 'boundaries' and 'supervision' (see Glossary for a little more on this trend towards *professionalism*). However, it is possible too that there is a shift back towards collectivity in some groups. The counselling co-ordinator at RASA in Merseyside has seen both types of structure:

> *RASA used to be a collective but is now a management structure. I was against this change when it was first suggested because women thought it was going to be a utopia. The main reason for the change was to satisfy the Charities Commission and funding bodies. I always much preferred a collective, okay it didn't always work but at least we were all in it together. Yes, some women had louder voices than others but they still do, the change of structure was never going to change that. We have recently returned to a more collective style of working. We need to hold onto the fact that this organisation has been running successfully for 20 years and really does not need sweeping changes.*

(Merseyside)

Changes (2): leaving 'Rape Crisis'

When women in Washington came up with the 'brand' name of 'Rape Crisis' they created an idea which has now traversed the globe (Brownmiller, 1999). For example, there are Rape Crisis centres in Tokyo and Sydney as well as across Europe and America (http://www.tokyo-rcc.org/center-hp-english; http://www.nswrapecrisis.com.au; http://www.rcne.com; http://www.rainn.org; last accessed 20.07.07). These pioneers created a blueprint for a service which has grown in ideas as well as locations. Part of that knowledge has, however, led to an increasing tendency to abandon the 'Rape Crisis' label, although some groups have stuck to the tradition. Watford Rape Crisis, formed in 1988 and still with its original moniker is just one example. However, two of the case studies have already provided examples of name shifts and this section examines the reasons for this trend away from 'Rape Crisis', looks at some of the replacement names developed and considers whether there are disadvantages to these changes, alongside the clear rewards that the groups perceive.

In her elaboration of the continuum of violence, Liz Kelly considered services for women and the nature of 'Rape Crisis'. Within the groups themselves there was generally an understanding that a 'crisis' could be defined as whatever had precipitated a phone call from a woman. In other words, it was not limited to the immediate aftermath of an incident of violence but was left to women to self-define. According to Kelly's research however, this was limiting uptake of the services:

> *Evidence from the interviews, however, suggests that some women may not even consider contacting these services because they define their own needs as falling short of a 'crisis'.*

(Kelly, 1988: 233)

So, one impetus to change name came from this wish to encourage women to access the service at any time they wanted support. Sheffield Rape and Sexual Abuse Counselling Service demonstrate this with their comment that the name change 'acknowledged that we didn't do much crisis work and did work significantly around sexual abuse and incest'.

A second issue is also spotlighted by Sheffield's comments and concerns the range of 'rapes' being reported to Rape Crisis centres. As women's knowledge of the continuum of violence grew and a wider range of survivors of different forms of violation got in touch there was a concern that the inclusion of 'rape' in the name might discourage some callers. Many groups, such as Barnsley, fore-grounded 'Sexual Abuse' in their new titles (Barnsley Sexual Abuse and Rape Crisis Helpline – BSARCH) as a way of dealing with this: 'we wanted to make the service more relevant to survivors of childhood abuse who are a significant proportion of our client base'. In Merseyside the name change occurred in the late 1990s, 'to acknowledge the fact that we work with a wider group than women who have been recently raped' (RASA). So the organisation changed from being Wirral Rape Crisis Counselling Service (WRCCS) in 1998 to the Rape and Sexual Abuse (RASA) Centre to acknowledge the fact that many women needed the service to support them due to historic child abuse and other forms of sexual violence. Around half of those who contact RASA are adult survivors of child abuse and 76 per cent of all their callers

knew the man who had assaulted them (RASA, 2000). Similarly, many other groups changed from a simple 'Rape Crisis' name to something that included words like sexual violence, sexual abuse or incest – for example 'Bradford Rape Crisis' became 'Bradford Rape Crisis and Sexual Abuse Survivors Service' and 'Rape Crisis (North Staffs and South Cheshire)' became 'Women's Rape and Sexual Violence Service'.

Finally, there were more pragmatic concerns involved in some of these name changes, to do with obtaining support from funders. Once groups began to receive funding from local councils it became apparent that there could be tensions if the name of the group did not reflect the geographic location of the council. This influence was apparent in the story of SERICC examined earlier. Additionally in Worcester, the group changed from 'Hereford and Worcester Rape Crisis' to 'Worcestershire Rape and Sexual Abuse Support Centre' to reflect a wider area and make the range of provision more apparent. Again, in Merseyside the move from a name beginning 'Wirral' to one beginning 'rape' was useful as: 'In directories we'd be R not W. We cover Merseyside and beyond not just Wirral, (and so the change could) encourage Liverpool/Merseyside to fund us'. Here then another concern to be as accessible as possible was coupled with a wish to capture the interest of potential funders.

Just over half of the centres surveyed had a change of name between 1986 and 2004 with most changes occurring in the mid 1990s. Clearly then the 'brand' of Rape Crisis has been diluted considerably through this process. Whilst the reasons for the changes are entirely sensible this shift can only make it harder for groups to see connections that allow for strong networking and the changes also make it harder for the public to understand the 'Rape Crisis' idea. A key issue is that there is no new name, uniformly adopted, to replace the 'Rape Crisis' label. We have already remarked that the names adopted by the centres do have something in common yet there is no replacement phrase which can be used to identify them clearly. All of this is examined further in this volume, as we progress to look at the services provided within 'Rape Crisis' and at the attempts to create national networks. Despite acknowledging a widespread shift away from the name 'Rape Crisis', many groups refer to themselves as such (even if just informally) and we do continue to use it within this volume precisely because there is no consensus as to how to replace it.

The discussion here on structure and naming are internal changes which have affected a number of the groups over the years since their formation. Next we focus on challenges from the outside, in the form of funding crises and competition from Sexual Assault Referral Centres.

Challenges (1): funding – a structural inequality

This volume has already made mention a number of times of the problem of funding and this is because finding and keeping enough money is arguably the biggest challenge faced by Rape Crisis centres throughout their history. Indeed, concerns over finance have been factors in both of the 'changes' we have already surveyed in this chapter. In this part we develop the discussion of funding a little further by looking at the kinds of finance available to the groups and at the tensions that each brings with them. The position of centres in the UK is contrasted with those in Ireland where there is some state funding of Rape Crisis centres.

At the beginning of the Rape Crisis story here in the UK there was considerable concern about taking money from organisations seen as being entwined with the patriarchy. The view was that for Rape Crisis to remain radical, it needed to stay independent. Over the years however, this approach has gradually been eroded by the demands on groups to provide a service. Almost as victims of their own success, the feminist challenge created greater knowledge of rape and as public awareness increased, demand for services also went up. Rape Crisis centres found they were moving 'from Women's Liberation groups, to service providers, with workers and management committee members' (Foley, in Hester et al., 1996: 168).

Marian Foley's comment here reminds us that the changes and challenges we are examining in this chapter are in fact intertwined. We analyse them separately, to give some space for reflection on the pressures Rape Crisis endures but in lived reality they interact and reinforce each other. As centres have shifted away from collective structures so the possibility of raising funding from a wider range of sources increases and so the move away from feminist anti-rape roots is

reinforced. Indeed, Charles (2000: 150) has questioned whether it is 'possible to retain feminist values and political principles' following such shifts.

Most centres have been funded partly through private monies, via charitable trusts and individual donations, and partly through local government, social services or health authority grants, though this is usually the much smaller part:

> Funding has been an ongoing problem, some local authorities have provided (limited) funding to their RCC, but others consistently refuse to, and there is no statutory requirement to provide support to rape victims.
>
> (Cook, 1997: 24)

Secure funding would permit the Rape Crisis movement to expand and improve the quality of existing provision. Without adequate funding, most centres find that they are limited to focusing on service provision and are constantly struggling to provide a very limited range of services. As the case studies have illustrated, centres do not provide 24-hour phonelines but open when they can, creating varied provision in different areas which is, doubtless, annoying and frustrating for potential callers. Working in such an atmosphere is draining and creates feelings of powerlessness in workers, an issue that we discuss further in the next chapter. Having workers overwhelmed is counter-productive since it tends to mean that the turnover of volunteers and paid staff increases. The original vision of Rape Crisis was of taking power for women (not increasing a sense of helplessness) and one key way to achieve this is to be involved in campaigning work as well as service provision. Combining campaigning against male violence against women with providing services to women is part of the 'living dynamic':

> We think it is really important to us, you know as feminists, to speak out about male violence. Otherwise all we are doing is playing nursemaids, making women better for, who knows, more abuse.
>
> (Merseyside)

Lack of funding therefore marginalises Rape Crisis, makes sure that it cannot keep up with demand and increases a sense of powerlessness. For all centres, fundraising tends to be a driving force. There is rarely a sense of having sufficient money and what funding the centres do have is not generally guaranteed beyond the next two to three years. Typically centres may receive some finance from the Victims Fund (discussed further in Chapter 5) or their local council and it has been argued that such local level funding was preferred to more centralised national funding: 'feminists have turned to local councils for funding, access and space in order to maintain their activities, and (fearing hierarchy and male co-option) have tended to prefer local-level dialogues' (Gelb, 1986: 117). At one time this was grant-aid and could generally be relied upon to continue. However, when cuts have been threatened, one benefit of council funding is that it is susceptible to public pressure and so, at various times, Rape Crisis centres have been able to fight local campaigns to retain funding, in the face of threatened cuts. For example in 1991, Manchester mounted a successful campaign against a proposed 'review' of council funding, involving a candle-lit vigil and a letter-writing drive.

Nowadays council funding tends to be governed by more formal service-level agreements and the terms of these are naturally dictated by powerful councils and imposed upon the less powerful Rape Crisis centres. In other words, these have tended to increase financial uncertainty and the bureaucratic burden upon centres. In addition to this, some centres have received funding over the years from the Lottery, Comic Relief, or other charitable foundations. Sometimes, as our case studies illustrate, there are particular local charities that will provide some assistance. Crucially though, every grant tends to come with its own form-filling burden and no money is given indefinitely.

Information sharing is another related issue. Funders usually require outcomes and performance indicators based on data collection and record keeping. Traditionally Rape Crisis centres have been reluctant to keep and share records. In the early days of the Rape Crisis Federation (discussed in Chapter 4) even the collection of data for their annual 5-point monitoring exercise was found to be difficult. Centres were using a diversity of different systems to collect data and this led to problems of comparability on a national basis. To bring consistency to the issue of data collection and analysis, a database consultant was employed by the Rape Crisis Federation to design a system specifically for the movement. The database expert, Sue O'Rourke, designed a system that

proved extremely effective and which was also subsequently commissioned in Scotland. However, funding constraints meant that the system could not be sustained and many groups have lost the workers who were trained on the data system, leading to these centres returning to ad hoc methods of data collection. A perennial problem has been that some workers see the issue of data gathering and information sharing as a form of state control and consider that the purpose behind such exercises is not always clear. Unless it is seen as strictly necessary, Rape Crisis workers will not prioritise it because rape work is time-consuming, demanding and emotionally intense. Collecting seemingly irrelevant information from callers is a point of contention for many workers:

So you are supposed to ask her about her age, ethnicity, where she lives and so on and this is in the middle of a call where she is pouring her heart out to you. Sometimes you can tick the boxes just out of what she has told you but I'm not going to end the call by going 'by the way can you tell me what your racial origin is'.

(Volunteer)

Altogether then, fundraising is an ongoing struggle and money not routed through mainstream funders has always been extremely valuable. During the 1990s, Manchester Rape Crisis had an affiliated support group 'Friends of Rape Crisis' which existed outside of the collective and worked to raise money for the group by running raffles, events such as women's discos and even a lottery. At other times other groups have also worked to obtain their own stream of independent funding, however small. Nevertheless, it is more formal aid which is generally seen as the likely saviour of centres:

A lot of it is down to personalities – finding people who care and have influence to make changes. What I'm working on at the moment at county level is to establish secure core funding. My argument is that we've been here for ten years, we've brought money into the area, we provide employment, we provide the most incredible services for women and it's about time you provided core funding. I've just heard that we might be getting some small amount of core funding (around £17,000) but in the meantime we continue to put in bids to many funders.

(Cornwall)

Many centres argue that guaranteed funding is the single most important thing that would help the successful operation of their agency and this is endorsed by WRSAC in Cornwall: 'As a manager I don't have enough time to do real grassroots work. I can bring money in for projects but just give me the basics – we are probably only talking £70,000 – it is not a lot to ask'. This would allow centres to manage and develop the services they provide. However, there is a key dilemma here. Rape Crisis centres want secure funding to enable them to continue to work in a radical way, which allows for ongoing campaigning, as well as support work. It is reasonable to suggest that funders able to provide long-term financial stability are unlikely to be those who would support a radical position. Secure funding is therefore likely to mean a surrendering of the more radical aspects of Rape Crisis work. This is illustrated by the experience of Irish Rape Crisis centres. These centres receive financial support from the state, although they argue that funding levels are inadequate and that this money comes with strings attached:

> Meaningful participation of any NGO (non-governmental organisation) in partnership and consultation with the state is labour intensive. It requires that resources are available to train staff, and then staff must be available to attend meetings, attend seminars, build relations with civil servants, read national and international reports, research the experiences of other NGOs, research the experiences of other countries, and travel abroad for seminars. Without the funding to employ staff in this role an NGO cannot participate in meaningful partnership with the state.
> (Rape Crisis Network Ireland, 2000: 5)

Perhaps because of such limitations, Dublin Rape Crisis Centre (DRCC) began charging for counselling to help alleviate financial problems:

> Women are offered six free counselling sessions here and then we ask them to contribute something. There is a sliding fee-scale depending on their means. We don't want to exclude anyone.
> (Interview with Dublin Rape Crisis Centre Counsellor, June 2000)

This allows Dublin to work with a large number of clients, as illustrated by their annual statistics. For the 12-month period ending June 2000, DRCC took 29,643 telephone calls and counselled a total of 703 women and men. The phoneline is a freephone number and is open 24 hours a day, seven days a week; the centre has 30 paid staff and 70 volunteers. In comparison with British centres, this is a huge organisation. However, Ryan-Flood (1998: 106) has expressed concerns about the 'increasing professionalisation of services' and cites the example of DRCC as an originally feminist-inspired organisation which has now moved to a more 'professional' image and a hierarchical organisational structure as a way of securing state funding. One woman spoke of how forbidding she found DRCC:

> I could barely bring myself to walk up the steps. There is the banner above the door and it feels like you've put yourself on display for all the world to see walking up them steps. Then it was explained that I would have to pay for the counselling. So where is the point of me going back? It's not for the likes of me that place. It might be okay if you're earning, you might like it. But I didn't.
> (Interview with female survivor of rape, June 2000)

Fortunately, this woman had later been able to access a centre that did not charge for their services. Clearly then both mainstream funding and charging for services carry their own challenges:

> There has to be an acknowledgement that if a funder is providing money to a service then they will want input as to where that service is located, how it operates and the quality of the service provided.
> (Interview, Irish Department of Justice, Equality and Law Reform, June 2000)

For all Rape Crisis centres, including the Irish centres, funding remains a major challenge. In addition to the levels of paperwork already alluded to, another drain on resources is the drive towards 'partnership' models of working. Whilst these can mean that the agenda of the voluntary sector, including Rape Crisis, is brought into mainstream organisations, there is no real recognition of the cost of all of this to the individual groups concerned. Witness the levels of work put in by workers in our case studies and yet no funding is provided to cover the costs of this worker time.

> Multi-agency work is a massive drain on the service – it's all I do. I fundraise and go to multi-agency meetings to fundraise. The whole focus of what I do, we have all these projects and I just run around keeping them afloat. We get no money from health, no money from social services.
> (Cornwall)

This pressure is always in the minds of women working in Rape Crisis centres and formed one of the pressures that affected the former Rape Crisis Federation, which is examined in Chapter 4 of this volume. The reality for most groups today is that they survive by accepting some level of co-option into mainstream agendas whilst trying to stay involved in grass-roots activism where they can. All of this contributes to a tendency for Rape Crisis to lack a national voice with which to tell the public of the problems that the centres encounter. This, in turn, also leaves space for a challenge by another form of agency, the sexual assault referral centre, or SARC.

Challenges (2): SARCs

Within the *Living Without Fear* exercise already discussed in this chapter, it became clear that Sexual Assault Referral Centres (SARCs) were to be the dominant state-sponsored answer to the question of support for women who are raped. The public can be very vague about the difference between Rape Crisis and SARCs, to the degree that it has been commonplace for Manchester Rape Crisis to receive calls from women who were being supported by the local SARC. In fact these centres are not services for women-only and they occupy a very different theoretical and practical position to Rape Crisis, in terms of their responses to rape. This discussion looks at the work of these centres and at their development over a 20-year period. We outline key distinctions between Rape Crisis centres and SARCs in an attempt to consider whether they can continue to co-exist successfully. However, the discussion begins with a brief reflection on the role of the police in responding to raped women.

Chapter 1 has commented on the likelihood of Rape Crisis having a fraught relationship with the police. In the early days of London Rape Crisis the Metropolitan service would not recognise the group as an 'official organisation' (Bowen et al., 1987: 54), and it was said that a memo was issued instructing officers not to cooperate with Rape Crisis in any way. As the first centre developed, workers began to collect knowledge on the ways that the police treated women reporting rape:

> We discovered all kinds of appalling things like women being left with no clothes, being driven home with only a blanket round them, being taken around the streets immediately after the rape to look for the rapist.
> (Bernadette Manning, in Bowen et al., 1987: 54)

The consciousness-raising process of Rape Crisis was at work once more, allowing women to understand why the police might be so very hostile to Rape Crisis. Not surprisingly then, Rape Crisis developed a position which argued that it is important to inform women of the reality of reporting rape, rather than try to persuade women to go to the police. Any woman who contacts Rape Crisis and wants to make a report will be supported but no woman would be told that it is her duty to do so.

In early 1982 the whole country was alerted to the problems of policing rape when Roger Graef's television documentary about Thames Valley Police showed unkind and demeaning questioning of a woman reporting a rape. This led to then Prime Minister Margaret Thatcher criticising police treatment of women reporting rape and to the establishment of the first 'rape suites' (from http://www.rapecrisisscotland.org. uk/about_us_1.htm last accessed 20.07.07; also see Foley, in Hester et al., 1996 for more on rape suites). In 1983 the Home Office responded by recommending that women should be able to request female doctors and utilising this recommendation, Tyneside Rape Crisis Centre and Northumbria Police established the 'Tyneside Women Police Doctors Group' (Campbell, 1997). Their first conference invited a Manchester-based female doctor, Dr Raine Roberts, who, sufficiently distressed by the Graef documentary, went on to start the very first SARC, properly titled the St Mary's Sexual Assault Referral Centre. Dr Roberts set up the service within the local maternity hospital and her vision had great impact on the model of centre adopted:

> The Centre was established in 1986 to provide a comprehensive and co-ordinated forensic, counselling and medical aftercare service to adults in Greater Manchester who have experienced rape or sexual assault (whether recently or in the past). Dr Raine Roberts MBE was instrumental in establishing the Centre and was the Clinical Director from the start in 1986 until she retired in 2003. The first service of its kind in the country, the Centre is nationally recognised as a model of good practice in providing immediate one-stop services to both female and male victims and to date has provided services to around 10,000 clients.
> (http://www.cmht.nwest.nhs.uk/directorates/ smc/about.asp, last accessed 20.07.07)

From the beginning then, this centre provided services to men as well as women and was based on a counselling/medical model of rape. SARCs have attracted sustained criticism for this tendency to 'individualise and depoliticise the issue of rape and men's violence by placing it within a 'medical' context' (Lupton and Gillespie, 1994: 8) and for perpetuating the associated marginalisation of the expertise of Rape Crisis services. There has also always been an impetus to encourage clients to report rape to the police (typically the largest funder of the SARCs). In the Manchester area anyone reporting rape or sexual assault to the police is supposed to be taken to the St Mary's Centre once they have made the initial complaint. However, there continue to be doubts as to the implementation of this procedure.

At the centre clients are given clean clothing, a forensic medical examination and offered support from a crisis worker. This is a useful model of support for women who go to the police and offers a massive change from the treatment of the women in the 1982 television documentary. However it is also a long way removed from the Rape Crisis model of support and the philosophy inevitably affects the approach offered. Crucially, there is a chronic conflict of interest between the criminal justice and forensic impetus and the needs and wishes of women attending the centre. It cannot be possible for SARCs to ever respect the autonomy of survivors in the manner of Rape Crisis, since they are always beholden to their funding body, the police:

> *SARCs – these are police-led initiatives and because of this they may not offer exactly what a survivor needs because the survivor is not at the centre, the demands of the Criminal Justice System is at the centre of a SARC. The priorities of the criminal justice system means that certain boxes have to be ticked. So while part of me thinks it is good that all these services are in one place in a SARC, especially the forensic examination, yet part of me thinks it is not enough, it is just a part of the solution. So much of it comes down to the individuals involved in the running of a SARC. Policing rape is still very hit and miss. A lot of it comes down, still, to the first police officer the woman sees. And there is too much at stake to risk that going wrong.*

> (Merseyside)

Today the St Mary's Centre has developed and is used as a model for the formation of others and has some particular areas of strong practice, for example in working with refugee women. Two SARCs were set up in the 1990s, REACH in Northumbria and STAR in West Yorkshire, and others have now followed. Research by Lovett, Regan and Kelly (2004) is the most extensive and thorough examination of SARCs to date. They

demonstrate that the establishment of the early SARCs was due to a range of criticisms of police responses to rape victims including:

- Low reporting of rape.
- Delays in locating a forensic doctor.
- Lack of female forensic doctors.
- The environment in which forensic examinations took place.
- The manner in which examinations were conducted.
- Inconsistency of evidence gathering.
- Absence of medical follow-up and support.
- Lack of co-ordination between agencies.
- Limited support services for victims/survivors.

> (Lovett, Regan and Kelly, 2004: 6)

Today, services to survivors of rape are also provided by Victim Support and other agencies in different locations. However the SARC model is clearly the current government favourite and there are now 15 SARCs in the UK with a government target of 30 centres in total. Even the SARCs are critical of this agenda however, as there are some 43 police services in England and Wales alone and so the government target does not even aim for one centre per force (Dr Cath White, Clinical Director of St Mary's, 9 May 2007, talk at MMU).

From the beginning, the relationship between Rape Crisis and the St Mary's Centre was difficult. Foley (in Hester et al., 1996: 169) documents that the Manchester Rape Crisis collective were not invited into the process by which the SARC was created and to this day the two centres tend to exist very separately. Although there are exceptions, the SARC clients have generally come via police referrals and have, by definition, reported the crime to the police. By comparison, Rape Crisis generally deals with women who have not reported to the authorities:

> *You know, SARCs are all about women who report to the police, its all to do with the criminal justice system. Most women never touch the criminal justice system.*

> (Cornwall)

At a European conference held in Dublin in June 2000, delegates from 20 European countries gave evidence to suggest that no more than ten per cent of rapes are ever reported to the police. The Rape Crisis Federation of Wales and England argued that only seven per cent of service users typically report to the police (archive material) and local groups suggest the figure could be even lower:

> *Some estimates say that between only 2–10% of these crimes of sexual violence will be reported, because of the fear of not being believed, being blamed, other repercussions and embarrassment or racial/cultural issues associated with these issues.*
>
> (Manchester Rape Crisis, 2000 Archive materials)

Since the emergence of the Rape Crisis movement in Britain, there have been 'changes in police policy and practices, together with ad hoc reforms in the treatment of rape victims in the wider criminal justice system' but it is argued that these 'emerged as a result of successful public campaigns by feminist action groups' rather than through the efforts of the police as an organisation (Lupton and Gillespie, 1994: 25). Just as women tend not to refer to the police, so very few referrals to Rape Crisis are made by the police or other statutory agencies. Just ten of the 354 'new' female callers to RASA in 1999 were referred by the police, less than three per cent.

> *RASA annual figures show that more women obtain the number of the service from telephone directory services than from the police. Stranger rape has been the category focused on by the police. When a woman is raped by a man she knows, her status as 'victim' becomes, for the police, somewhat muddled. The closeness of the relationship may therefore make the task of reporting the rape all the more difficult. If police have difficulty in recognising the event as a rape, that has implications for how the woman is treated.*
>
> (Merseyside)

So Rape Crisis tends to support women who have been raped by men they know, where it may have happened some time ago and where they are less likely to have reported to the authorities. By contrast, just eight per cent of St Mary's clients are self-referred (Dr Cath White, 9 May 2007), although the Lovett, Regan and Kelly study suggests a higher rate of self-referral. 'Almost a quarter were self-referrals, especially at REACH and St Mary's' (Lovell et al., 2004: Executive

Summary page x). The remainder come to the SARC via other agencies, generally the police. The SARC model and its Irish cousin the SATU (Sexual Assault Treatment Unit) is discussed further in Chapter 5. For now however, it is safe to conclude that this state-sponsored model of support is only available to a limited range of those who experience rape and it is important that both groups publicise this reality. Only when a distinction between SARC and Rape Crisis is more widely appreciated by the public and this type of information is available can Rape Crisis begin to find the type of security of tenure that it surely deserves.

Conclusion

This chapter has begun the process of reflecting on the progress of Rape Crisis from its early beginnings to the present day. It surveys just some of the major issues that appear to us to have driven these changes, but alludes to a number of others. We have outlined the complexity of Rape Crisis work, using the tool of the living dynamic to help to show how fundraising, campaigning and support work are interlinked and how all are fed by the feminist ideals that still underpin the heart of this movement.

Rape Crisis continues to face challenges, most notably from the ongoing struggle to find enough money to survive and from the force of the SARC model which is increasingly put forward by government as the best strategy for support of survivors. In fact, and somewhat ironically since its gender-neutral appearance can give the impression of inclusivity, the SARC model fails to support all women. It serves too many 'masters' to maintain the independence necessary to allow support for the women trapped within a mental institution or prison; to support women working within prostitution and to support women raped in relationships and women raped as children, who have no wish to get involved with statutory agencies. All of these women have real support needs and they are ignored only at tremendous costs to society, as later chapters show.

CHAPTER 3

Sticking Plaster or Survival? Defining the Work

Introduction

This chapter is about the services the Rape Crisis centres provide and the types of work involved after a woman has contacted the centre. We review the types of services currently provided by the centres and the evolution of these services since London Rape Crisis first opened in 1976. The chapter considers which women get involved with Rape Crisis work and what transformations they have to undertake to become Rape Crisis workers. As with the last chapter, our discussion here draws upon the interviews and questionnaires completed for this book, as well as on other sources. We also continue to use the concept of the living dynamic to explore some of the tensions within Rape Crisis work today and in particular we consider the pressures brought about by involvement in 'partnership' work with external agencies.

Rape Crisis centres continue to have a profound effect on women's lives:

> Continually confronting and re-interpreting the issues of power, centralisation, professionalisation, voluntarism, and financial support, though often a painful and conflictual process for individuals and organisations, has contributed to dynamism and maturity in the movement as a whole.
>
> (Gelb, 1995: 130)

However, it is also useful to acknowledge that not all Rape Crisis centres today have the same philosophy. As discussed in the opening chapters, the groups studied here come from the women's movement of the 1970s. Such Rape Crisis centres have been depicted within some literature as:

> ... extreme feminist organisations, anti-police, anti-men and more concerned with 'radical feminist politics' than providing effective support services for women who have been raped ... This is a misrepresentation of RCCs based not on any systematic evidence, but rather on commonly held misconceptions about autonomous women's groups.
>
> (Lupton and Gillespie, 1994: 19)

Other groups have developed from the emerging victims' movement (Williams, 1999). Where the first groups were feminist-based and run by women, for women, others such as Wiltshire Rape Support Line provide services for women and men and encourage participation from male volunteers and counsellors. These other groups clearly have different philosophies and aims from the original Rape Crisis centres and they are not our focus here. Although Rape Crisis centres vary in ideological perspectives and organisational forms, centres which remain committed to feminist understandings of sexual violence provide evidence of the movement's goals, ways of working and sense of purpose. The processes of change and the maintenance of the work within these groups can lead to difficulties for individuals involved, so that not everyone who contacts or works in a Rape Crisis centre leaves with a sense of having achieved what they came for. This chapter also tries to explore some of the difficulties within the work which can lead to these problems.

Of course not all survivors of rape contact a Rape Crisis centre. Indeed, as Chapter 2 has shown, there are still many women and girls who are raped and who tell nobody of their experience. However, some women also contact the police or other services before, after or instead of contacting Rape Crisis. As the foregoing chapters have begun to indicate, other agencies approach the topic of rape in different ways. In this chapter we outline the services offered by feminist Rape Crisis centres but we begin by looking at the language used to describe women, rape, and those who call Rape Crisis.

Talking about the services

Chapter 1 has already indicated that there was a concern with language from the beginning of the Rape Crisis movement, as part of an acknowledgement within feminist theory more widely, of the power of naming. As the introduction to this chapter has commented, women who are raped may contact a range of different agencies and there are fundamental differences between the responses of these different avenues of support. Crucially, the identity of a woman who has experienced sexual violence will be constructed differently by the law, by health services or by Rape Crisis centres. Seen as a crime victim but also as the primary witness by the police, she may experience disbelief and harsh treatment (Lupton and Gillespie, 1994). 'How one treats a victim is different from how one treats a witness. The former requires empathy, comfort and support; the latter, strict questioning to assure the accuracy of their account' (Martin, 2005: 2). Likewise, within a health discourse she will be constructed as a patient but this identity will be compromised if she is not physically injured and so again she might be disbelieved and unsupported. 'Injustices like these harm victims but they also harm society. Officials who represent the common good yet treat victims as if they are suspects or pariahs perpetuate a second assault' (ibid.). Part of the work of Rape Crisis is to encourage mainstream organisations and agencies to improve their response to women who have experienced sexual violence. However part of the work of this volume is to clarify how Rape Crisis work is unique and also why it is constructed as it is.

Rape Crisis workers understand rape through their experiences of working with women, and by challenging mainstream myths embedded in dominant portrayals of women within society. One of the starting points for Rape Crisis work is continually thinking about how to talk about feminism, how to define rape and how to talk about the women who use the services. It is clear that the response to women by Rape Crisis must start from a different place than the problematic examples above. Chapter 1 has discussed the early use of the term 'survivor' in preference to the poorly perceived label of 'victim'. This continues to be an area for debate within the movement as these comments from the counselling co-ordinator at RASA in Merseyside show:

> We are definitely woman-centred and use the terms 'women' and 'survivors' – we do not talk about 'clients' or 'victims' unless it is appropriate. We get the terms used by the police and other organisations but it is rare that we use the term 'victim' ourselves. Sometimes we use 'service-user', again it depends on the context but even when the police use the word 'victim' I'm more likely to pull them up on the term rather than repeat it by using their terminology. In the context of the Home Office we have seen a move from them to using the terms 'victim' or

> 'survivor' and they seem to be understanding that more than they ever did in the past, so our language has made an impact on how sexual violence is understood by those government agencies and in their own writing.
>
> (Merseyside)

However, these are also some areas where it seems that the concept of 'victim' is being re-evaluated. Martin (2005) takes the view that the term 'victim' acknowledges the violating experience and that in the US, many groups who steadfastly used the term 'survivor' in the past are now using the term 'victim' more frequently. This change in terminology is also evident in the UK. Workers in Cornwall draw on their own histories and understandings, as well as the women they work with:

> We also discuss the whole language between the terms 'victim' and 'survivor'. When I came into this movement in the 1980s, everybody wanted to use the word 'survivor' – it was seen as empowering. Over the years things have changed. It's been interesting to see the language change. It's become important for women to see themselves as victims of crime. The Criminal Justice System has changed its view of the victim and although there is still a lot of victim-blaming, the term has changed and become more empowering. Women see themselves as victims of crime who deserve justice. 'Survivor' seems to have lost its power. Back when women were first breaking silence about rape, it was seen as very powerful.
>
> (Cornwall)

Adapting to changing sets of understanding, the Cornwall workers strive to use the right words because they understand that words are powerful. Whilst other groups might not adopt this model, it is interesting to see a different approach to a long discussed topic.

The Rape Crisis movement continues to search for a language that women can use to explain their experiences where existing language does not appear sufficient. It has been argued that 'some of the meanings which women may be generating to explain their existence could be literally 'unthinkable' to many men ... the patriarchal order has many tools for silencing women' (Spender, 1992: 74). Reclaiming the word 'victim' may be a small part of that process. Language matters because it frames action. Understanding the nuanced differences between 'victim' and 'survivor' and their changing meaning within the wider context creates a sensitivity to language which can result in sensitivity to the person. A woman should be treated with empathy and without blame, and such understanding and validation of her feelings will help to empower her.

Another topic mentioned in Chapter 1 was the preference for terms other than 'client' to describe those calling the line. The examples in Chapter 2 show, however, that some Rape Crisis centres are content to describe their work as counselling. In describing their services today, the Cornwall centre echoes the comment made earlier by RASA in their dislike of the word 'client':

> *It's in our policy document that we refer to 'women'. We don't use the word 'client'. I'll use the word 'service user' in multi-agency settings. We would say that we use a support and advocacy model. That's not to say we don't have counsellors working with us but we would say that counselling is much more a medical model and we don't want to medicalise women. We prefer to say that women are victims of crimes that have short- and long-term effects. If women ask for counsellors and therapy we would signpost them to that and support them in that choice.*
>
> (Cornwall)

In Cornwall then, there is still a concern to avoid the medical approach to rape and, with that, the label 'counselling' is seen as problematic. Here they aim to emphasise the positive aspects of established expertise and the provision of specialist services without medicalising or pathologising rape:

> *I started a counselling diploma many years ago and dropped out. I didn't find it too useful. It's only as good as the people who teach it and it's a bit like pyramid selling. It felt like, 'if you can afford to pay to become a counsellor, then you can become a counsellor'. There's something about it. I did a humanistic counselling course – Carl Rogers – watched a video and it didn't touch the power and abuse issues the woman obviously had. There's a level of counselling that I just don't get. Women have always listened to other women and there is a massive de-skilling exercise of that going on through counselling. It's a real dilemma. We have women with differing needs coming into the organisation and so it's, for me, about having good co-ordinators who do the matching. It's a dilemma and we need to have a dialogue about it within the movement. Maybe like with everything, our strength is in our diversity but we do need to be able to discuss it.*
>
> (Cornwall)

Chapter 2 has already illustrated that in RASA this is treated differently. The worker there also makes a distinction between support, counselling and therapy:

> *We use the terms 'counselling' and 'support'. Some women that we see – I couldn't put my hand on my heart and say it was counselling. It is support work. I do not use the word therapy because traditionally therapists, in the mainstream understanding, were male and took the role of experts, in a very superior way. Sometimes I will suggest to women that they need a different form of counselling (other than person centred) or therapy but here I mean the sort of alternative or complementary therapies that are available. These might be outside of RASA but also some counsellors here offer alternatives to person-centred counselling. Women need different things and one of the real skills of RASA is acknowledging and identifying these needs. We support all women, we do not turn women away. And so some women have mental health needs, others have learning difficulties and may not understand or be able to engage in the counselling process, so we try to meet these needs too as best we can. We liaise with a whole range of agencies too but we try to find out what support women need and this ranges from counselling, to accompanying women to medical or legal appointments and writing letters to courts, housing departments – whatever is needed really.*
>
> (Merseyside)

Consistently, in talking with Rape Crisis workers, the notion of 'the woman's choice' and 'whatever is needed' comes to the fore. This is not mere rhetoric but one of the guiding philosophies of Rape Crisis work. This brief discussion serves to highlight some changes since the 'core values' of the early days, discussed in Chapter 1. Within the Rape Crisis movement in its widest sense there would be greater variation of approach as some groups have consciously stepped away from their feminist roots. Across the range of groups who responded to our questionnaire it is clear that there is divergence in the approach to terms such as 'counselling' or 'support work' and 'victim' or 'survivor'. One thing these groups do tend to have in common however is an awareness of the need to consider what language they use in the course of their work and some willingness to enter into debate about terminology. To this degree then the original concern with language clearly remains within Rape Crisis.

Types of services

As this book has already made clear, the concept of Rape Crisis is a loose collection of ideas, not a franchised operation replicated over a number of locations. Chapter 1 has explained that at the beginning of the British movement many groups were based on a model created by London RCC and borrowed from the American precursor. Since then there have been various developments in services and this discussion looks more closely at that initial model for Rape Crisis services, drawing on the first edition of the LRCC book. It goes on to compare this to trends in service provision today, using our interviews and questionnaire responses. What emerges here is that there have indeed been new services developed over the years, but that the core LRCC model is still visible today.

Much of the ethos of early Rape Crisis work, already outlined briefly in Chapter 1 of this volume, is implicit in the writing of the first edition of the LRCC book *Sexual Violence: The Reality for Women*. For example, the second chapter, on 'reactions to rape and sexual assault' opens thus:

> *There is no right or wrong way to react to sexual violence. You may wonder if you should or should not be feeling a certain way, how long you should feel it for or whether you shouldn't be 'over it' by now. Whatever you **do** feel is valid and right for you; each woman responds in her own way.*
> (LRCC, 1984: 8, emphasis in original)

Today, Rape Crisis continues to refuse to allow that there is a single model for surviving rape or for reacting to rape. This can be seen in resistance to suggestions for reforming rules of evidence in court to allow evidence of the medical model of 'Rape Trauma Syndrome' (see Glossary). One key aspect of Rape Crisis work remains this attempt to validate the caller's experience of her own reaction, rather than looking for a pattern that she 'should' be following. In addition, the LRCC book made it clear that the task of the Rape Crisis worker is to challenge the caller's own adherence to rape myths (ibid.: 123) at the same time as trying to create a supportive environment through which to transform fear into 'anger which is strengthening' (ibid.: 124).

At the time of the 1984 book, LRCC was running a 24-hour helpline with three full-time and two part-time workers taking the line from '10 am to 6 pm Monday to Friday' and volunteers taking over 'after 6pm and at the weekends' (ibid.: 122). Clearly this was a massive undertaking, even on the part of the 30 or so unpaid workers in the group, and no group today appears to offer an equivalent service. The LRCC book goes on to list the services they provided as:

- **'Counselling** – by phone and face-to-face'. All of this was self-referred as the group did not take 'third party referrals' (ibid.: 123). They did, however, 'offer support and information to family and friends', when required. In describing their services LRCC point out that telephone work has advantages as a woman can 'hang up or end the call at any time' (ibid.: 123) giving some power back to her in the process. They also comment that women were increasingly using the telephone line 'on an ongoing basis and/or requesting face-to-face contact'. Already then the idea of support over a period of time was evident. It is also interesting to note London using the term 'counselling' in a relaxed manner here, though sometimes offering other terms, such as 'contact' to describe their longer-term work.
- **'Referrals and accompanying'**. Finding doctors, lawyers or other specialised advice or help for women and going with them to appointments, to the police and so on.
(LRCC, 1984)

Analysis of the questionnaires shown in Table 3.1 confirms that today, most Rape Crisis centres continue to provide equivalent services, typically free of charge, with or without time constraints, to women who may be in crisis or in need of support for past experiences. In addition, most Rape Crisis centres will only accept self-referrals, seeing the approach by the woman as a crucial first step in regaining her control over her own life. Although some other centres do accept referrals from the police, social services and other associated agencies, it is on the proviso that this is the woman's choice and not a move that she is being pressurised into taking. In some areas Rape Crisis centres have very good relationships with the local police and health providers while others do not. In some areas there is a SARC where rape examinations are conducted and the Rape Crisis centre works with that team to provide services while in other areas this is not the case, as discussed in Chapter 2. From a Rape Crisis perspective, the philosophy influencing this form of partnership is that rape survivors who are listened to and treated with respect are more likely to feel a sense of justice even when the perpetrator is not convicted. It is the process of being taken seriously and listened to that is important.

The key services provided by Rape Crisis centres today remain:

- **Telephone helpline.** Most centres have trained volunteers and paid workers who staff a phoneline, usually open a few times a week for two or three hours per session, to provide information and support.
- **Face-to-face work.** Counselling or support work with survivors (and sometimes their family members) addresses the sexual violence they have experienced and this work is undertaken today variously by employed professionals, volunteer workers (often those with more experience) and in some centres by counselling students. The nature and type of approach taken within such appointments varies and ranges from individual to group sessions. These usually aim to help survivors understand their experiences as something outside of their responsibility; as part of gendered inequality and the abuser's need for power and control. In other words, this work continues to draw on the same sets of ideas that the early LRCC workers were using.
- **Accompanying.** Many Rape Crisis centres provide accompaniment for women reporting to the police, attending health care (at hospitals, clinics and GP surgeries) and to court hearings and trials. This type of service provides emotional support, answers any questions the woman has, explains the procedures (and helps to ensure they are followed); it also ensures that the woman is treated with respect and dignity. This is sometimes referred to as 'advocacy' and again is a logical extension of the work LRCC undertook.

The table shows that all of the 25 Rape Crisis centres that responded to our questionnaire provided telephone helpline services and face-to-face counselling or support appointments. In addition, many provide groupwork, community education, outreach and accompanying or advocacy. A few also provide services in prison and alternative services such as email support or befriending.

Clearly then the services available today are still based on core areas of provision which were there in the original model. In recognition of the difficulties some women have in accessing centralised services various groups have tried to find ways to take their service out to women, using outreach or specific work with women in prison, for example.

In common with many other groups, RASA

Table 3.1 Services provided by Rape Crisis centres

Services	Percentage
Helpline	100
Counselling/support	100
Groupwork	68
Outreach	40
Education	48
Accompanying	36
Prison	16
Email support	8
Befriending	8

still maintains a private address for reasons of security:

It is an anonymous address, we do not publicise the address and use a PO Box for all written correspondence. We give the address to women if they are coming for an appointment. We do not have the space or resources to provide drop-in services so we do not need to give out the address on publicity materials. We have never had any problems with 'unwanted' visitors and perhaps this is because of the confidential nature of the address. On our feedback forms, one of the questions is about the location and about the address being confidential and without fail women say it is important to them that it is confidential and 'women only' and that this adds to their sense of security and safeness.

(Merseyside)

Unfortunately, the confidentiality of the address was compromised in 2007, the consequences of which are yet to be fully realised.

One other area of work which has developed since the LRCC book is groupwork. At the beginning of the Rape Crisis movement there were some ideological misgivings about creating groups for women who had been raped which were separated off from other forms of consciousness-raising. As Chapter 1 has mentioned, back in 1987, Bernadette Manning said that the London group had considered starting this up 'about two million times during the ten years I was there and decided not to every time' (Bowen et al., 1987: 52). There was a range of reasons for rejecting that model of support, including not wanting 'to see women who had been raped separated off into these bounded groups'. At that point then, the notion of the group seemed too therapeutic for LRCC. As part of their understanding of rape they considered that 'all women are survivors of male violence' (ibid.) but they saw survivors' groups as problematic, as they would automatically identify those women in terms of the abuse they had experienced.

Views have clearly moved on in the meantime and there are precious few consciousness-raising groups available today. Clearly, a number of Rape Crisis centres are now providing a range of work in groups, for example, Guildford have run self-help groups since 1998 and Durham also run a group for two hours each week. In part, this might be in response to the pressure to provide services to so many women, with so few resources. Certainly in the time that Kate was in Manchester Rape Crisis, groupwork was a possibility raised periodically which was perceived as a way of helping a number of women at once. There was, however, a concern that these groups might create expectations which could not be met if anyone in the group was unable to respond well to the stories of others. (There is a considerable body of scholarship on feminist groupwork which we do not explore here. Butler and Wintram, 1991 would provide some introduction for those interested.)

Listening to women and taking them seriously still lies at the heart of Rape Crisis services. While some centres have very limited opening hours and can respond to an average of four women each week, other centres are responding to calls from 100 women per week. Taking these figures overall, the average centre will respond to 27 callers each week. The women who call will have a range of topics they want to discuss as this description, taken from SERICC's website, indicates:

> SERICC provides a service to women and girls over 13 years old who have been raped, sexually assaulted, experienced child sexual abuse, sexual harassment or who have experienced any form of sexual violence or attempted sexual assault. You can ring SERICC if something is happening in your life now, or if you are having difficulties about something that has happened in the past. You can also phone if you are worried about your child, someone else in your family, or someone you know. If you ring us we can offer telephone counselling and 'one to one' counselling, emotional support and practical information, we will not tell you what to do or judge your actions.
>
> (South Essex)

SERICC also provides other types of services as required, such as: sexual violence counselling; advocacy for women with learning difficulties and for women whose hearing is impaired;

support of women raped in war and conflict; and information on court procedures and criminal injury compensation claims. Elsewhere, groups also try to work with women in institutions, including prisons and secure hospitals. Clearly then, the work of Rape Crisis centres has developed from a core which we can see documented back in 1984, by LRCC. Today there are thoughtful attempts to take services out to women and to develop work in a range of circumstances where women might struggle to access services otherwise and where they have different modes of communication.

Difficulties within the services

Having outlined what forms of work dominate Rape Crisis provision today, we now move on to explore some of the tensions within this work, in yet another aspect of the 'living dynamic' of Rape Crisis work. Lack of service provision creates pressures for workers and callers alike and this discussion tries to unpick some of these difficulties, highlighting ideas for moving forwards, where possible. However, we also bring out some aspects of the positives within these complexities: as ever, radical feminism allows Rape Crisis to create new solutions to old problems.

We saw in Chapter 2 that the three centres we profiled only opened their helplines four or five times a week, for relatively short periods of time and the figures from the questionnaire reveal that overall the centres are limited in the services they are able to provide. Meanwhile there is a national expectation that service provision in a range of diverse areas, from supermarkets through to caring services, is available for longer hours, often 24 hours a day. Within Rape Crisis however, such expectations have rarely been met, and women are often shocked to find that Rape Crisis services are limited and geographically sparse:

> I remember taking an answering machine message from a woman who had called the previous evening when there was no phoneline on. She was really angry, I mean angry at us, because there had been no-one here to take her call. I called her back, as she had requested in her message, and I was really worried about how she would react to me. At first I couldn't get a word in edgeways but when I explained that I was a volunteer and in fact everyone here was a volunteer because we got no state funding she was really apologetic. Honestly, I could have cried, because she

was so sorry to me and yet she was the one who had wanted someone to talk to, and she'd just got the bloody answering machine.

(Merseyside)

As ever, the reasons for such a curtailed service are lack of funding, of workers and of volunteers. Not surprisingly then, women often phone expecting that there will be someone there to answer their call and are frustrated and hurt that, having plucked up the courage to phone, they are simply met with an answering machine. To some extent, Rape Crisis centres are now held accountable to a social expectation of 24-hour support, which they cannot meet. Clearly then, not every woman who tries to contact Rape Crisis will find the service they hope for.

For the workers, the relatively limited opening of helplines means that difficult decisions constantly have to be made in providing a service. The Rape Crisis ethos which we have already seen operating in the 'whatever is needed' approach of our case study centres, would dictate that every woman who calls should be able to talk for as long as she needs. However, that could lead to a helpline session of just one call and clearly that can be seen as inequitable. In practice, the workers will generally try to return calls from women who have left messages at the beginning of a session:

In relation to the telephone helpline, we are supposed to limit call-backs to mobile phones. The maximum call-back should be 20 minutes to landlines and ten minutes to mobiles. I have noticed that some calls into the phoneline are taking over half an hour which, when the phoneline is open for just two hours, it is not really fair.

(Merseyside)

Some centres get around some of these problems by working one line for calls during the session and another for call-backs. Nonetheless, the allocation of scarce support is an ongoing struggle for most centres adding to the pressures of the living dynamic. Of course, centres also have some forms of provision of information which are available at any time. From the early days, centres have produced a range of information leaflets and broadsheets which can sometimes answer basic questions about services, about the law or about reactions to rape and abuse. In addition, many centres now have websites and there is a national website that provides details of services provided by local centres (www.rapecrisis.org.uk). It may be that,

in the future, electronic forms of service provision will increase, but they appear to be in their infancy at present, with most centres offering merely an information point via their website.

The Merseyside centre has a website and uses information leaflets to publicise the service but the worker there was keen to point out that simple devices are still the best in getting information where it is needed: 'Women find out by word of mouth but we also have a publicity strategy with leaflets and information packs. Stickers on the backs of toilet doors are still really effective'. They send out information packs to a wide range of organisations including local police stations, universities, doctors' surgeries, hospitals, clinics and other health centres. However they know that it is important that they send them to named people in these organisations because publicity materials can 'fall into a void unless you send them to a specific person'.

Another difficulty created by scarcity of resources is waiting times. Many centres have waiting lists, particularly for individual face-to-face appointments for support. Although centres do what they can to reduce such lists to a minimum, again the problem here is generally one of funding:

Our funders tell us what geographical areas we can take referrals from, so one of the difficult things for us to say to a woman who calls from outside our area is that we cannot see her, but we have to. Even if the woman is from the 'right' geographical area, she still faces a waiting list for counselling of seven months and that was a year until recently. If she is from outside the area and asks where else can she go, we often have to say there is nowhere else.

(South Essex)

Clearly then, there are serious gaps in provision in some areas of the country and these geographical issues are revisited in Chapter 5. The South Essex group give priority to girls under 18 years of age so that they do not go onto the waiting list, and all women are encouraged to continue to use the telephone helpline until face-to-face work can begin. But not all centres have waiting lists despite huge demands. Cornwall centre explains:

We are service-user led, so it is 'boundary work'. We wouldn't encourage more than an hour per week and because volunteers are so well-trained they are always looking to moving women on so we have no problems with that and we don't set limits. Saying that, we have users

who have been around for years. We try to limit them on
the helpline to a reasonable level. I think our work is pretty
structured and 'boundaried' and we don't have a waiting
list.

(Cornwall)

Again, in RASA, once a woman can access
face-to-face services the ethos of 'whatever is
needed' is re-employed:

There are no limits to the number of sessions offered to
women. Our 'official' line is 18 sessions but in fact some
women do not need this many, others will take a break and
resume at a later stage . . . We do pay survivors' expenses
and ask them to bring bus and train tickets if possible. It
is not a huge drain because we do not offer expenses to all
women, not all women need financial help, but we do give
it to women who need it.

(Merseyside)

It becomes clear then that there is no single
solution to the problem of parcelling out scarce
resources. There is also no simple answer to the
lack of money or volunteers to provide these
services. Questions of funding have already been
mentioned in Chapter 2 and we return to this
topic in later chapters. However, even without
money it might be possible for centres to grow,
simply by finding more willing volunteers to
provide the service. In reality though, such
women are not that commonplace and those of us
who do get involved with Rape Crisis rarely stay
involved in providing frontline services over a
lifetime. We have both, to some extent, drawn
back from doing frontline work, even though we
remain concerned for the movement and
committed to the idea of Rape Crisis. The costs of
being a Rape Crisis service provider are complex
and take a serious toll on individuals. Most
centres have a turnover of volunteers and so need
to keep on recruiting to maintain the limited
service provision they currently have.

As different women come in and out of the
groups, the centres themselves endure but may
change in character and face challenges and
conflicts. Rape Crisis workers operate in an
environment of emotional intensity. This,
combined with crises stemming from inadequate
funding, time-consuming political demands and
internal differences, can lead to workers
becoming exhausted and burned-out. Although
the work can be rewarding, the taxing
combination of political activism and working
with survivors of sexual violence is rarely
acknowledged within or outside of the

movement. Sadly, there are numbers of women
who have worked in Rape Crisis and have left
with nothing but bad feelings for their time
within the group. Equally of course there are
others, such as the two of us, who consider that
they have had some of the most wonderful and
intense times of connection to others and of
personal and political empowerment, within the
Rape Crisis movement.

Within many of the centres, over the years,
there have been conflicts over racism,
homophobia, ableism, ageism and class. Some
centres attempt to overcome this by instituting
specific subgroups where the interests of
'minority' groups can be represented and so that
power relations can be examined. Hierarchies of
power exist within patriarchal society, and they
cannot be transformed within Rape Crisis
through the simple application of sisterhood.
These conflicts have sometimes been fuelled by
ignorance or unthinking behaviour by those with
structural power, but at other times they have
been fed by a wish to gain power, and maybe
even led by those within minorities. Anyone who
wants to cause strife, from within or outside of
the groups, can always point to under-provision
of services to minority groups as an indicator of
the failings of the Rape Crisis centres to respond
properly to multiple oppressions. Within
traditional Rape Crisis collectives, Freeman (cited
in Charles, 2000: 149) has shown that 'particularly
charismatic or confident women, often supported
by friendship networks, were able to impose their
views on the rest of the group. This resulted in a
'tyranny of structurelessness' no less antithetical
to democracy and participation than the
hierarchical, bureaucratic organisations, of which
these groups were critical'. The truth is that Rape
Crisis centres struggle to provide services where
they can, in often problematic contexts. Workers
constantly feel the pressure of a failure to serve
all women:

Predominantly all workers here, paid and unpaid, general
workers and counsellors, are White, with the exception of
three Black counsellors. This is part of the local geography
but we do also have Welsh counsellors, survivors are from
various ethnicities: and the counsellors' ages range from
21 to 60+; survivors from 15 years up. We also have one
profoundly deaf woman who signs and lip-reads. We have
two other women who can sign. There is a ground floor
counselling room and there are ramps for both front and
back access to the building. I think there are some ethnic
minority women that we are not reaching but I don't know
how we can overcome this. We have tried to provide

dedicated services in the past with little success. It is my opinion that we need to sustain existing services and make them more available to all women and to continue to work with minority ethnic community groups including asylum seekers, rather than make any assumptions about what we think they need.

(Merseyside)

There are millions of women in the community that we do not reach. Because we are so busy trying to keep the services going we don't look at older women, we don't look at disabled women. We try to be proactive, we have a healthy lesbian and bi group going in the agency but we have done no proactive work around disability – we don't touch most of the community. We get involved in diversity days and we are a member of Cornwall Racial Equality Council but how many forums can you go to and how much work can you do? We send out our literature and let them know we are recruiting but in Cornwall our ethnic minority groups are so hidden, I think they make up 0.05 per cent. The racism is beyond anything you can imagine, some of the kids in this area have never spoken to anyone Black. So there are whole areas that we don't even touch. I hold my head in shame about some of this.

(Cornwall)

Clearly though, there is no need for shame. In reality these women should all be fêted as heroines, for trying to continue to provide services and for constantly thinking about how to create wider accessibility. Few mainstream service providers spend as much energy considering who is not in touch with their service, whilst holding back a sea of demand with such limited resources. In addition, there are certain ongoing issues which this movement continues to explore in ways that few other organisations have. In particular, we discuss here some of the vexed questions of race and sexuality which have presented difficulties for a number of the groups.

The comments above make it clear that there are ongoing worries about the accessibility of Rape Crisis services to Black and Asian women. Over the years a number of Rape Crisis centres have tried to create a different way in, by providing dedicated helplines for these groups. According to our questionnaire there are not currently any of these in operation amongst the 25 centres responding. However, the North Staffs group in Hanley (Women's Rape and Sexual Violence Service) does run a project dedicated to local Asian women and Bradford has another project specifically for Black and Asian women. This type of provision works to create an unusual form of women-only 'space' within which it is

safe for Black women to speak of rape by Black men, without the stress of encountering racist responses from White people. Clearly though, the existence of such a 'service within a service' can create its own problems in the groups. This is antithetical to the notion of collectivity and moves away from the original notion of woman-wide consciousness-raising. Nevertheless, it has been accepted as one possible solution to the ongoing problems of access for Black and ethnic minority women.

It is a reflection of a movement that is prepared to accept and understand the impact of different oppressions for women and find ways of ensuring access and safety for oppressed women. Living with multiple oppressions, and the impact of this, is an ongoing dialogue within women's organisations now, and that should be celebrated.

(Jude Boyles, former collective member at Cumbria Rape Crisis)

Similarly, Rape Crisis continues to examine female sexuality in times of pain and suffering, from a particular standpoint. At times it has seemed that it is easier for lesbians to work within this field than it is for heterosexual women. A woman who shares her life with a man (or who wants to do so) can find the personal burden of hearing so much detail of men's inhumanity to women particularly difficult. But within the radical feminist willingness to revisit ideas from the root has come a different possibility, both for workers and for women calling the line. Within Rape Crisis centres there has often been a willingness to view celibacy as a positive sexuality choice, in a manner which the remainder of society does not. This can create a new possibility for women who want to work in Rape Crisis, and it can certainly mean that women calling the line can view their personal reluctance for sexual intimacy as a positive choice. This is clearly a very different approach to traditional responses to rape, which has tended to try to work towards making women able to accept sex, as part of any 'healing' process and pathologising women who do not want sexual intimacy.

These are simply examples of the creative avenues to which Rape Crisis work can lead. However, whilst centres remain under-funded, under-womaned and relatively isolated it is always harder to produce such positive ideas. This was an area on which the short-lived Rape Crisis Federation tried to make progress. Within the federation, there were interest groups for lesbians and for Black women in Rape Crisis. Each of these might have helped the movement to move forward with other issues involving race and sexuality, but sadly the federation failed to survive and the next chapter of this volume documents the story of that collapse.

Whilst it did exist the Federation created a network for the centres studied within this book, and one aspect in common amongst those groups was a dedication to maintaining the woman-centredness of Rape Crisis provision. However, to some this is also perceived as a problem, and so Rape Crisis centres today often face criticism for refusing to work with or for men. Clearly for some centres this criticism is sufficiently powerful to persuade them to work with male survivors of abuse. However, for those centres which are based on the original LRCC model it is not appropriate for groups (whose knowledge of rape stems from female consciousness-raising) to claim to have the skills to work with male survivors. Rape Crisis is part of the feminist movement, and understands women's needs in a way that it cannot pretend to understand those of men. However, this is not the same thing as ignoring or shunning men. Gloucestershire Rape Crisis Centre for example offered 'support and information' to a range of 'parents and other family, partners and boyfriends and professional agency personnel such as social workers, youth workers and medical staff' at the time of our questionnaire. In Birkenhead:

> *RASA has always responded to calls from men. Quite often they will be calling about their female partners, family or friends but if they are calling for support for men then we give them the relevant information about appropriate services. I have no problem with that. But we don't counsel men. It is a decision that was taken as a fundamental part of the agency when it was first set up and it remains part of our ethos. Our feedback forms from survivors consistently tell us that this is what women want – a place free from men where they can feel safe – it is simple really.*
>
> (Merseyside)

So for some of the centres the decision to work with women only provides a real meaning to women-only space. However, few centres today would refuse to speak with men: as the RASA worker says, men call on behalf of their women friends and relations, and Rape Crisis workers provide support and information. In Cornwall the focus on women is perceived as problematic by some:

> *Down here in Cornwall I'm constantly being told that not providing services for men, and running 'for women only' services, is an equal opportunities issue. I am gob-smacked that I am challenged on equal opportunities issues for running a women-only organisation. I have to tell them that we are a women-only organisation because of equal opportunities. All the time, wherever I go to talk, whatever arena I am in, it's like 'we mustn't just talk about women'. I haven't found a quick way to counter it except taking three deep breaths. Then I say we are a needs-led organisation, and women say they want safe, women-only spaces. We are a grassroots community organisation, and that's what women want. The reason why we are successful at keeping and recruiting volunteers is because they value women-only spaces. We are very supportive in enabling men to get the specialist services they need. And let's not ignore the myth that there are lots of services for women – show me where are these well-funded, skilled services for women dealing with sexual violence? Devon has not got any Rape Crisis services at all. There is the sexual abuse line for survivors of childhood sexual violence but they do nothing on rape. It doesn't take a lot to make a massive change – Greenham proved that – look at what we have achieved. When we get together we generate energy and that can change the world even if it is slowly.*
>
> (Cornwall)

In the end then, the decision to remain women-only is still revolutionary and so it is not surprising that it faces constant attack. For Cornwall's worker this policy is again defended in terms of women-only space. However, the process of articulating this takes her back to women's activism and what needs to be done to make real change for survivors. What is unspoken here is the knowledge that creating services for male survivors is not the task of feminism. Whilst we all have compassion for anyone dealing with rape, feminist services are hard-pressed and cannot afford to stop what they are doing long enough to develop work with male survivors. Allowing for such work would also mean allowing men to join the groups and this would clearly destroy the feminist consciousness-raising element which survives within Rape Crisis centres. All of this is represented in the short-hand of 'women-only space' and all of this is not easy to articulate within public meetings, as the Cornwall worker demonstrates.

Discussions in this chapter have shown that there is still a core service which can be identified as coming out of the original model from the

1970s. Services have developed since then but face constant struggles to keep up with demand, to retain workers and find agreed paths to creating greater access for all women. In the midst of these difficulties the services are also attacked for trying to maintain a feminist ideology. Perhaps miraculously, given all of this, the workers also manage to maintain a vision of a better and increased service in the future, and our next discussions look at the ways in which service provision could be improved.

Service development or wish-lists

A number of key themes emerge within discussions about service development. Not surprisingly, conversation often turns back to the difficulty of obtaining sufficient funds to keep going:

> *Funders . . . will quite often fund a new initiative and then the funding goes after a year or two. Our biggest difficulty is in covering the core costs and keeping our existing services going. If we had secure funding, the chances are that we would have time and space to think creatively about new services but we need security first.*
> (Merseyside)

However, it is still possible to identify some key concerns, such as: keeping the line open longer; creating more service provision across a range of forms of abuse; working towards better education and training and ultimately, towards an end to rape. When asked what other services they would like to provide the RASA worker emphasised the need to provide a proper service on the phoneline:

> *There are not really any additional services we would want to mount, it is more about maintaining and extending the existing services. Without adequate funding we cannot offer a wider range of services. I'd like to see the phoneline open every day, actually I'd like to see it open 24 hours a day. If we could offer more of what we already do, that's what I'd like. We need more paid staff, and the next staff member we need is an outreach co-ordinator because it is consuming so much of the time of the existing staff. We could also do with mobile phones to be used by those workers who do outreach and home visits.*
> (Merseyside)

This relates back to the problems we have already seen in this chapter, of meeting an expectation for full-time service provision, without the means to do so. As the RASA worker continues:

> *Referring to the feedback forms that women complete, a lot of women wish we provided services 24 hours. Many people think we are a big set-up with banks of phones but our phoneline, like most Rape Crisis groups, is just one phone. We do not necessarily need to provide new services though; we need to maintain the services we currently provide.*
> (Merseyside)

Where it is possible to consider what else they might do, however, groups have some key concerns in terms of broadening service-provision and providing training to other agencies. South Essex do offer a lot of training to other agencies and organisations in the local area but this is something that Cornwall do not have the capacity to do:

> *We don't really provide training for other groups. Well I do but not usually for money. It's a difficult one. We've talked long and hard about trying to have a training arm to the organisation but we would need to fundraise for a trainer. So we do awareness-raising; on some of the DV forum work we've delivered training to housing workers and stuff like that. I was talking to a woman from Newcastle, and they do training, and I brought that back here and said we should do this.*
> (Cornwall)

These comments remind us that Cornwall also work on the issue of domestic violence. Many centres are involved in multi-agency work that focuses on domestic violence (see more on this below) because rape is a feature of many domestic violence cases but Cornwall have developed this further, creating their own services on DV. Also as discussed previously, another important strand of Rape Crisis work is working with historic child abuse:

> *A large number of women who come to RASA are adult survivors of Child Sexual Abuse. Women who have recently experienced rape do not always take up counselling straight away and I think it is because it is too raw, too soon but they tend to come back again later. For women who have experienced CSA, it is often that something has happened in their life now that has triggered them to seek help for what happened then. It could be that they have entered a relationship and so there is intimacy, or they may have had a child or their child, particularly if it is a girl, has reached the age they were when the abuse happened, or they may have to attend a smear test or any of the tests and examinations that women have to go through in their lives. All or any of these can trigger CSA memories.*
> (Merseyside)

As we have already seen, the reality of Rape Crisis work is that it crosses the continuum of violence, incorporating work with women who have been sexually harassed at work and those damaged during sex work as well as survivors of CSA and DV. All of this points towards a need to develop feminist services which can acknowledge all forms of violation.

> *The thing that would most help survivors is better resources and support. I worry sometimes – we do some incredibly difficult but productive work with survivors of childhood sexual abuse – so much of our work is with adult survivors of childhood sexual abuse, and it is really complex.*
>
> (Cornwall)

The notion of broad-ranging feminist services was one which Liz Kelly discussed, back in 1988 (Kelly, 1988: 236–8). At that time she envisaged the creation of local co-ordinating groups which could allow refuges and Rape Crisis lines to work together (in the manner which SERICC and Thurrock Women's Aid once did). Sadly, the reality today is often that these groups meet with each other only when they attend the local DV forum or similar local council-run initiative.

We saw earlier that women from RASA visited Liverpool Rape Crisis for advice, when they were first setting up their centre. Sadly the Liverpool centre closed in the early 1990s, leaving RASA with a considerable geographical area to cover:

> *We cover a big area, up the coast to Southport, down the coast to North Wales, across to Chester and although there are groups in Chester, Warrington and St Helens, they tend to be up and down in their active status. In fact one of the workers from Chester used to be a volunteer here, and wanted us to take over the Chester premises, but we do not have the resources to do that. We do conduct outreach in Liverpool, and the demand for this is high, but it all comes down to resources. The Centre is well-placed for women to access, the Liverpool outreach is also a useful resource but we are generally well-placed for women coming from across the region.*
>
> (Merseyside)

This problem was touched upon earlier, with regards to SERICC's service provision and in Chapter 2 we saw that these difficulties influenced the name chosen by the RASA centre, to allow them to continue to cover such a broad segment of the country. For Cornwall their provision in a deeply rural part of the country faces other problems:

> *I guess one of the key challenges to being in a rural area is accessibility. If you are living in the wilds of North Cornwall and there is no transport infrastructure how do women access the services? If you want to outreach them, where do you see them? So venue is important. We use doctors surgeries, community centres, youth centres, all that sort of thing but women don't always want to meet there and so it's about risk assessment and home visits, are the kids around and all that. Rural outreach is really difficult. Down in Cornwall, there is also culture – and I don't mean Cornish culture but the idea of a rural idyll. In my funding bids I always call it, 'the persistence of traditional values'. It is all about the idea of the woman's role in the family, and sometimes it feels like we are stuck in the 1950s, the tea has got to be on the table and that whole thing. That's one thing. The other is that I've never seen poverty like rural poverty. I've worked in Nuneaton and Coventry but poverty there was a different thing. The isolation of women through poverty is tremendous. Men sometimes move down to Cornwall specifically to isolate their partners, knowing they'll be better able to control the women's lives. We give travel expenses to women volunteers but it's a big drain on our resources. Expenses for volunteers – 37p per mile.*
>
> (Cornwall)

All of this takes us back to the question of training and education as methods of service provision. As the worker from Cornwall indicates, they need to take the service out to women, in different settings, to create accessibility. Rape Crisis workers more broadly also argue that it is community education and awareness raising that primarily needs funding because it is the ground on which all other services are premised. If there is no awareness in the local area and the community has no knowledge or trust in the services provided then they cannot reach women in the community. We saw in Chapter 2 that RASA had undertaken work in schools. Today however the funding for that worker has long since gone:

> *We need more education in schools, Rape Crisis needs to make the same ground as DV has. Schools are still really reluctant to deal with such difficult issues. Schools are not well-equipped to even ask the questions, never mind provide the answers. Many schools now do plays around DV but research shows that the views held by young people on violence against women really need effective challenges. Don't forget that young people are surrounded by the sexualisation of women in society.*
>
> (Merseyside)

This also links back into service provision across the continuum. Consciousness-raising allowed women to see the links between all the forms of violence against women and children. These limitations on education demonstrate that keeping 'rape' in one box and 'DV' in another does not serve the needs of feminism. One way in which feminism can create real change is to allow the connections between apparently disparate crimes of violence to become visible via education work. Talking informally at the 2007 Rape Crisis annual meeting one worker commented:

> *Funding is based on crisis intervention and rarely on the other services we provide. This tells me that our funders are less interested in prevention – you know, stopping rape and protecting women – than they are in treatment. I'd rather work to stop rape.*

Perhaps this is the true vision for the future of Rape Crisis work, to move back towards campaigning and public education work which aims to create a society free of rape. In the meantime, the reality is that it only gets harder to provide a basic service in the face of rising costs:

> *Our phone costs have risen enormously as more and more people have mobile phones and we call back using these numbers. We have policies in place that try to limit this but it is not always possible. We get quite a few enquiries by email but we do not provide email counselling. I'm not sure I even believe in email counselling but women can be supported by this medium. If we can, we would encourage women to ring in and use the phoneline. As I said before though, we never turn women away and so, if they want email support, we give it. It isn't a big part of what we do, it is hard enough to effectively communicate with a woman by phone, what with the lack of non-verbal cues and this is even more limited by email, but we do what we can.*
> (Merseyside)

Working in Rape Crisis

> *Working in a Rape Crisis Centre, we are confronted by the reality of rape all the time through its effects on individual women. These effects are devastating. We also have to deal with these effects on ourselves of this constant reminder of male violence.*
> (Rachel Adams, in Rhodes and McNeill, 1985: 31)

Thus far this chapter has brought our discussion of service provision up to date and it now turns its attention to those who provide the services, considering the process of joining Rape Crisis and working in Rape Crisis. This takes us back to a discussion of the purposes of Rape Crisis work

and of the costs it brings to the women working in the movement. We have already alluded to these costs within this chapter and here we outline some of the ways that this can affect the work of the centre and how the centres try to cope with these costs.

Chapter 1 has discussed how early anti-rape activism came from consciousness-raising and other activities which gave women the opportunity to speak out about their own experiences, and this created spaces in which to discover anger. Instead of being forced by silence to feel shame at being raped, women were beginning to be able to find their rage at this violation. The anti-rape movement created a discourse which channelled women's anger and legitimated this as strength rather than weakness. The pain of rape is thus transformed to fury, and this re-conceptualisation of emotional response has played a key part in producing intense connections between women who work in Rape Crisis centres. As we have already seen, in examining the LRCC model, Rape Crisis has always known that anger can be strengthening. Rape Crisis work has also cultivated new understandings of rape which run counter to mainstream criminal justice and health discourses.

Chapter 1 outlined some core values of Rape Crisis work, and key amongst these is belief in what women have to say about their own violation. Rape Crisis workers support women in defining the assault they have experienced. If a woman defines her experience as rape, regardless of whether it conforms to the prevailing legal definition (which is not static) the Rape Crisis worker will endorse her definition. The issue of whether it is defined as rape in law is only of interest to the legal system. Rape Crisis workers accept the truthfulness of survivors whatever the circumstances of the rape. This belief means Rape Crisis workers can support and assist women to regain control of their own lives. Ideally, within Rape Crisis centres, the same generosity of belief can be offered to other workers:

> *When we started this organisation we were convinced that the agency would be based on kindness and compassion. Not very trendy words. But because I've been through Greenham and been through the revolutionary, angry, feminism I suppose what I learned along the way is that we have to be constructive with our anger. If we are destructive to each other we are lost. One of the things we try to offer here – and there's a lot of women with different*

backgrounds here – what we try to do is care, and be kind. That doesn't mean we cannot challenge each other – we do, and a lot of our training and groupwork is about that – but we can challenge opinions without destroying anyone. That is not to say that we live in a blissful community of women, because we don't, but there are ways of being with each other which are based on kindness.
(Cornwall)

Fundamentally, women who work in Rape Crisis centres care about women and care about rape. They care about rape in the lives of women and what it means to the wider society. Even when a woman stops working in a Rape Crisis centre she will continue to care about rape because working in a Rape Crisis centre is often a transforming process and shapes one's sense of self in relation to the wider world. Women who work and who have worked in Rape Crisis centres hold a wealth of information which can be used as a resource to direct and mobilise the movement, but only if this knowledge is acknowledged and documented. One aspect of this is the knowledge that women in Rape Crisis are likely to be doing their best. As the Cornwall worker acknowledges, women within the movement can lose sight of this and misdirect their anger towards other women. If we can have the belief that the women working in the group are doing the best they can, despite difficult circumstances, then perhaps women's groups within and outside of Rape Crisis can try to find a way towards the kindness and compassion spoken of above.

There is sometimes an assumption that women who work in Rape Crisis centres must have experienced sexual violence in their own lives. This can come from women using the service, and from the public more generally. As mentioned earlier in this chapter in the context of groupwork, the original feminist vision of Rape Crisis acknowledged that all women are affected by the fear of sexual violence, whether or not they have experienced violence first hand. That model also tended to view as misguided the suggestion that only survivors could work in the service. It rests on a false assumption that a survivor can best understand another woman's experience, without acknowledging the enormous range of ages, times, relationships and places involved in sexual violence. These come together to make every woman's experience unique, at the same time as she can often gain much insight and support from the experiences of others. In reality, some of the hardest times for many of us who

have worked in the movement have been the moments when the caller on the line is talking about something that happened to her, but where she could be describing your own experiences to you with uncanny accuracy. At those times it can be quite difficult to stay focused on what she wants to discuss, no matter how clear you are that you have come to terms with your own past experiences. The traditional approach of Rape Crisis then is that all women have some experience of sexual violence and can work within the movement, if they so wish.

In practice, this does mean that collectives or more modern hierarchical groups will, at various times, contain women with a range of personal experiences which may affect their ability to deal with aspects of the work. And this is where the politics of kindness can be most powerful, in finding the willingness, within a service which lacks money and workers, to allow each other the space to take a break when we need it. Alternatively, what a woman needs might be to simply take time out, because some aspect of the work is too difficult right now. Neither the hierarchy nor the collective is built to allow this easily and so what can happen is that women simply leave, as the centre becomes too complicated and demanding for them.

Workers within Rape Crisis do not generally have to declare their own history of violation but can a woman using the service become a volunteer or paid worker? The answer is that this varies from centre to centre and over time:

Previous service users rarely become volunteers but that is not because they are not allowed to. I think there is a public belief held by some that you have to have been raped at some point in your past before you can work in a Rape Crisis centre and this is clearly nonsense. I think we do such a good job of moving women on that they do not feel that they have to give something back by volunteering. Saying that, there are a lot of women involved in RASA who have experienced sexual violence and domestic violence in their lives, just as there are in the wider society. They bring valuable insights to draw on in their work here but it is not a prerequisite for working at RASA.
(Merseyside)

By comparison, in Cornwall many of the paid workers were once volunteers, and survivors have become volunteers. 'In 2005 we had two women going on to Access courses and three going on to university degrees. Women who go on to work in the community retain their links with us so that's good too'.

Whatever the reasons for becoming involved in Rape Crisis, there is always some training to go through at the beginning of one's membership of the group: in fact training for volunteers tends to be 'both extensive and ongoing' (Lupton and Gillespie, 1994: 20). When it works well, Rape Crisis training is a form of facilitated consciousness-raising. It draws on the knowledge that the anti-rape movement has gained from women's experiences allowing facilitators to raise the awareness of the trainees. At the same time, the training can allow women to develop skills they already possess, in listening to others, in reflecting back what they hear and in challenging what is being said, where that is appropriate. Clearly then, this form of training should be active and participatory. One key issue in the sessions is finding ways to think about power and how women can be helped to regain the capacity to make their own choices and construct their own definitions of what has happened to them.

Another part of the living dynamic of Rape Crisis work then is taking part in creating training programmes for new workers, paid and unpaid. Most centres hold induction training which can range from a small number of separate sessions in a relatively short period to training over a number of weeks, and this may be followed by ongoing training throughout the year. There has been a trend towards shortening these training courses. We saw in Chapter 2 that RASA initially ran 10-session courses. Nowadays this is curtailed:

> Initial training is held over the course of one weekend. I'm disappointed that this is just one weekend, as it used to be longer, but we do appreciate that women lead very busy lives. We do have follow-up and ongoing training. This includes phoneline training, Freedom Programme training, training on police and court procedures. Sahir House (HIV Support and Information Centre in Merseyside) provide training for us and we also have visits from: the local drug centre; solicitors; academics; and organisations raising awareness on self-injury, hearing and sight impairment. All this takes a lot of time to co-ordinate and deliver but it is also to do with maintaining contact with outside agencies.
>
> (Merseyside, see glossary for Freedom Programme)

In 2007 the initial RASA volunteer training resumed a four-day pattern over two weekends, whilst retaining the ongoing development training. In Cornwall they have managed to hold on to their 12-week training programme.

However, both the RASA worker and the Cornwall worker would like to have more possibilities for training:

> We do ongoing refresher training and further development for staff and volunteers but I'd love to do more in-depth training and give women more skills. I'd like to take time to develop myself too. The stability of funding would really help. We do whole sessions, in training, on active listening. We have a model of support, and we look at all the different models of support, and still use the women's movement model which is about self-help.
>
> (Cornwall)

Yet again, money and time are the constraints which limit the availability of further developments here. Clearly though, it might be possible to keep women involved with Rape Crisis centres over the longer term if they felt they were gaining more in terms of training but also that they were becoming more able to continue to do the work as a result of this.

One challenge experienced by new workers is in dealing with myths embedded in society and within their own ideas. Confronting one's own assumptions can be quite difficult, when the challenge comes in the course of a phoneline call. This aspect of the work tends to reappear at different times in a worker's involvement with direct work, and one example of this can be in reacting to the 'calm call'. There is a common notion that women are always distraught and hysterical after rape. When the woman who calls is calm, and yet has recently been raped, it can challenge a worker's own ideas about rape. One worker who had been on the helpline one Sunday afternoon described such a call:

> I had just spoken with one of our more regular callers about how she was getting on and the call had ended. I was hoping I'd get a chance for a cup of tea but the phone rang as soon as I'd put it down. On the line was a woman who was very calm but telling me about being raped that morning. She was very calm, not cold and detached, just sort of peaceful about it and said she just wanted to tell someone and get some advice about local health clinics because she didn't want to go to her GP. My first thoughts were that she must have been phoning for a friend or that maybe she was a student doing some sort of research on how Rape Crisis responds to calls from women who report a rape. I really couldn't believe that anyone could be so together after what she had described.
>
> (Merseyside)

Of course the caller might well have been someone calling for a friend, or a student conducting research, but this worker used the ethos of believing what women say and that enabled her to focus on providing the woman with the advice she asked for, with empathy, rather than acting in what could have been an inappropriate manner. A number of informal interviews on the issue of the emotional impact of the work were conducted at the national Rape Crisis conference in 2007. One worker pointed out 'It is hard to empathise with someone who is saying "I'm fine, it's not the end of the world, I just need some information"'. When your experience has been in talking with women in shock, in despair or in anger, dealing with someone who presents as perfectly calm can be unnerving. Another worker added:

I had been used to seeing my role as enabling women regain control but in this case I felt quite unneeded. Even though we use the word survivor to describe women who use our services, we understand that most women who have been sexually violated will express the victimisation of the event through tears, or silence, or anger before they move through the process of regaining control. Being confronted by a woman who does not have the 'expected' emotional response can be very difficult for workers and often that will challenge their belief in her.
(Counsellor)

This is only one of the ways that helpline work can create a sense of powerlessness in the women working the line. Although the calm call might be disconcerting, the experience of speaking with a number of distressed women in one session is also very draining. Whilst all centres have systems for supervision, to allow for support from others within the centre, these are rarely available right at the end of a session.

I'd go home in my car, after a two hour stint on the line, and I'd be in my car driving and just screaming, just screaming, you know, with rage and frustration. No-one could hear me on the motorway, so I was safe, otherwise people would think I was crackers but it had to come out. I'd done two hours of being calm for other women but I needed to rage.
(Volunteer)

Over time, women tend to find it harder to continue to experience this level of anger on an ongoing basis. This aspect of the work has been acknowledged by other researchers: 'There is a cost to caring. Professionals who listen to clients' stories of fear, pain, and suffering may feel similar fear, pain, and suffering because they

care' (Figley, 1995: 1). Rape Crisis workers have to manage their own emotional response to the work of listening to women talk about rape:

It doesn't matter if the woman is talking about something that happened yesterday, or thirty years ago, and I've heard both, because she is in that moment and you are there with her. I've heard things that I can never forget; things you can hardly believe that one human being would do to another. I wish my brain had an emotional disk drive that I could download this stuff to and leave it all behind at the end of the day. But it is impossible. Some of it comes back to you when you least want to think about it.
(Volunteer)

I carry around with me the words and images of hatred, and hurt, and loss, and destruction. Sometimes it is too hard.
(Counsellor)

The gradually increasing costs of doing direct work have been referred to elsewhere as a 'cumulative, transformative effect . . . of working with survivors of traumatic life events' (Pearlman and Saakvitne, 1995: 31). Over the years, many workers have found ways to express their feelings about the relentless nature of the day-to-day work and the hatred they feel towards abusive men. One worker talked of how she faces the feelings of violence provoked in her:

I have had to face the fact that I am capable of hatred towards another human being. It is not a productive emotion because it takes away energy that I don't really have [laughs]. The insight this has given me though is that although I feel anger, I am not violent. They are different things to me. The anger I feel towards violent men can be used positively because it gives me the motivation to carry on.
(Counsellor)

Rape Crisis work can be emotionally exhausting but as this worker acknowledges, the anger can be harnessed to fuel a commitment to the work. Rape Crisis workers see their anger as justified whilst acknowledging that it needs to be channelled if it is to be a positive part of the work they do:

In society, this society, women are not allowed to be angry. When was the last time you got angry in a meeting, in front of a man? Were you told not to get 'upset'? Our anger is diminished because we are supposed not to get angry. We are society's carers. But it is liberating to express anger, and I suppose it feels powerful to say 'I'm as angry as hell about these bastards'. So long as I don't

go out there and bop an innocent guy walking down the
road, so long as I use the energy it gives me for good, then
I'm happy being an angry woman.

(Volunteer)

As mentioned earlier, Rape Crisis workers
discuss the ways they deal with problematic
issues when they attend their own individual or
group support sessions. These sessions are a
traditional feature of Rape Crisis work, and
acknowledge the emotional expense of rape work
on women. However, this model of 'internal
supervision' is challenged where the Rape Crisis
workers also define themselves as professional
counsellors. In the original model, confidentiality
is upheld but the workers can off-load about their
own concerns, doubts and anxieties of working in
a Rape Crisis centre. Sharing the 'calm call' with
others helps to break the myth of the hysterical
rape victim:

> *We talk about rape as a society more now than ever before,*
> *but images and stories still use the stereotype of the victim,*
> *and fuel our own assumptions about what it means to be*
> *a raped woman. In reality a woman can have any response*
> *to rape. Maintaining the myth of the 'out of control'*
> *victim perpetuates the power of abusive men to hurt*
> *women. Yes, of course many women need help and support*
> *to survive rape but one of the biggest secrets is that many*
> *women get on with their lives quite well thank you. They*
> *may be glad that Rape Crisis exists as a source of*
> *information but they don't necessarily need further servi-*
> *ces. Other women will cope fine but want to talk with us*
> *a year or ten years later whereas other women need us*
> *immediately or on a long term basis. We need to talk more*
> *about the diversity of women's responses to break the*
> *shame of sexual violence.*

(Volunteer)

Multi-agency working

In discussing the origins and services of Rape
Crisis we have seen that the centres began from a
fairly isolated position in relation to other
agencies. Over time this has changed, as groups
have received funding from local authorities and
other agencies and as public policy models have
moved towards 'partnership' models of working.
This discussion looks at the meaning of
partnership or multi-agency work and at the
reasons for its current popularity. We go on to
discuss the Rape Crisis centres' involvement in
multi-agency forums and consider whether these
are effective as a way of improving service
provision or of widening public education efforts.

It is worth acknowledging that this consideration
of multi-agency working could have been placed
in Chapter 2, as one of the challenges faced by
modern Rape Crisis centres. Instead we have
chosen to discuss it here, as an aspect of service
provision.

Multi-agency partnerships have been described
as 'a collection of agencies whose mutual hatred
is subsumed by a collective desire for funding'
(James-Hanman, 2000: 269). A variety of forces,
including repeated investigations into cases of
child deaths (from the 1970s onwards) have
driven the moves towards more collaborative
styles of work amongst local health, social
service, police, CPS and voluntary agencies.
These groups send representatives to meet in
multi-agency forums creating a possibility for
discourse across a range of organisations
including Women's Aid and Rape Crisis.
However, such groupings are still resisted by
some Rape Crisis centres, which see them as
forces of co-option, pulling centres away from
their political roots. Harwin et al. (1999: 4) chart
the development of multi-agency work in the
area of violence against women through the early
to mid 1990s which gave 'rise to a substantial
number of inter-agency forums', culminating in
the circular *Inter-Agency Co-ordination to Tackle
Domestic Violence*. This was part of the work
conducted by a Ministerial Sub-committee
(Harwin and Barron, 2000) and outlined the
government's approach to the problem of
domestic violence. It also highlighted the roles
and responsibilities of statutory and
non-statutory bodies.

By 1995, there were over 100 inter-agency
projects on domestic violence (Hague et al., 1995:
10). At the Home Office, the Women's Unit
developed cross-departmental policy, while the
Crime and Disorder Act 1998 placed a statutory
duty on local authorities and the police to
develop local partnerships. Originally Rape Crisis
centres were often not involved in these local
groupings. However, from 1 April 1999, the
definition of domestic violence for the purpose of
statistical returns to Her Majesty's Inspector of
Constabulary was as follows:

> *The term 'domestic violence' shall be understood to mean*
> *any violence between current or former partners in an*
> *intimate relationship, wherever and whenever the violence*
> *occurs. The violence may include physical, sexual, emo-*
> *tional or financial abuse.*

(Hansard, 10 February 2000)

Working within this definition it might be expected that Rape Crisis membership of the partnership would be triggered. However many multi-agency groups continued to focus primarily on physical violence. This was exemplified in the *Living Without Fear* document (Cabinet Office, 1999) discussed in Chapter 2 where domestic violence was consistently prioritised, marginalising other forms of violence against women (Jones, 1999; Kelly and Regan, 2001). Rape Crisis centres were caught in a position where many multi-agency domestic violence forums did not acknowledge the groups as valid members. Yet, given the extent of sexual violence in the home, their presence should be welcomed:

I believe most DV is sexual abuse. It's still a big taboo but I do a whole presentation on how pornography is a massive part of woman abuse. If you don't understand that then you can have as many multi-agency meetings as you like but you won't move things on.

(Cornwall)

Multi-agency forums have been conceptualised as taking either a 'benevolent' or 'conspiracy' approach (Sampson et al., 1988). The benevolent approach assumes an unproblematic consensus and so multi-agency partnerships are seen positively. However, Kelly (1999: 87) cautions feminists to be wary of the term 'partnership':

The violence women suffer arises within, and out of, particular forms of partnership . . . The implied equality of status in the term 'partnership' should, for feminists at least, be treated with considerable caution.

The hidden power relationships within partnership and multi-agency working may act to 'dilute feminist or women-centred ideas' (Hague, 1998: 446) and attempts to equalise power relations are fraught with difficulties. In reality, the Rape Crisis centres and Women's Aid groups who take part are often beholden to the other 'partners' for funding. Clearly then, this cannot truly create a level playing field for discussion, development and critique of service delivery. In reality there are power differences which mere rhetoric cannot negate. Hague (ibid.) raises concerns about such imbalances between participating agencies, particularly 'that difficulties can be experienced in trying to evolve a working multi-agency response with the police'. Nonetheless, taking part in multi-agency partnership work now constitutes a large area of

work for some Rape Crisis centres and despite the inherent problems with such collaboration, centres have fought for their voice in the 'partnership':

We were consistently ignored when we'd turn up to DV forum meetings but we carried on going and now we are accepted as a central member of the group.

(Merseyside)

Some of the multi-agency groups identified in *Living Without Fear* did not exclude sexual violence from their framework, but took on a broader remit. A pioneering example of this was the Leeds Inter-Agency Project (Women and Violence) a well established group which exemplified the most innovative and effective form of multi-agency working on the subject of male violence against women. The key to their broad remit was contained within a feminist philosophy. This recognised power differences as the cause of male violence against women and identified empowerment of women as the solution (Tara-Chand, 1999). As Mullender (1996: 254) argues 'The climate in which the Project was able to take root and flourish was one where the Women's Movement was already strong and active'. In other areas, Rape Crisis centres have been instrumental in transforming their local multi-agency groups:

In 2001 SERICC with members of voluntary and statutory agencies in Thurrock, established a Violence Against Women Alliance (VAWA) to replace Thurrock Domestic Violence Panel. This move was made in line with the UK government agenda on violence against women which was informed by the UN Declaration on the Elimination of Violence Against Women.

(South Essex)

Sometimes working together with other agencies can result in valuable services. Cornwall gives an example of this:

On 17 April 2006 we launched a 24 hour helpline service for women at the point that they report to the police. So if a woman reports at 2am at a police station, only the police will have the helpline number (statistically there were 482 rapes and serious sexual offences last year – including men). So we are piloting this to see if it works because what women tell us is that when they find us, two months on, it would have helped them to find us earlier. It's a great idea – we have no money to do this – the police have been fantastic. We want to continue to raise the police aware- ness that we are there. No matter how many times we engage with police officers, and they have our leaflets to give to women, it just wasn't happening. Instead women get referred to Victim Support. So we want to be able to contact women at the point that they report.

(Cornwall)

More often however, what happens is that a lot of time is spent in discussions which amount to little in terms of service delivery. Hague and Malos (1993: 181) have expressed concern about 'the 'lowest common denominator' effect, in which activity is limited by the views of the agencies who know the least. James-Hanman (2000: 272) has made the point that multi-agency partnerships should not be used to mask the need for improvements within individual agencies:

*In many instances, inter-agency fora are trying to effectively co-ordinate a system of which the individual component parts are inadequate and unhelpful ... what is actually needed are changes **internal** to each organisation rather than changes **between** each organisation.*

(Emphasis in original)

James-Hanman goes on to discuss the issue of membership of such forums and argues that whilst some essential agencies, such as health, social services and education, are frequently missing, other individuals and groups attend simply because they are interested in the issue. Multi-agency working is therefore dependent on the individual people involved representing organisations and on their positions within those agencies. Additionally, there are clear differences between multi-agency partnerships that emerge from existing women's groups or community networks and those which are police initiated, necessitating Rape Crisis centres to 'struggle to negotiate working relationships with local police in the context of police antipathy towards them' (Lupton and Gillespie, 1994: 25). As one of the key 'insider' groups, the police have attracted much criticism, either because of their reluctance to intervene or due to inappropriate responses (Mullender, 1996; Siddiqui, 1996).

The local police and courts services here are not at all imaginative. The local police don't really have much to do with us. Of course we support women on visits to the police or courts but we have never been involved in any local initiatives apart from initial talks about a possible SARC at some point in the future. We have more to do with the dedicated DV officers rather than anyone who has any claimed expertise or even just experience in dealing with rape cases. It is depressing and I do think that Wirral

is even worse than Liverpool. Even though we are on their doorstep we are ignored.

(Merseyside)

The CPS drives us insane. We have had a lot of contact with the CPS because they kick women's cases out all the time. We have quite a good relationship with the head of the local CPS and he is one of our champions but our job is to challenge decisions which we feel are unjust.

(Cornwall)

An additional problem here has been alluded to in earlier discussion, which is that the statutory agencies can send representatives to these meetings without it having a significant impact on service provision. (One less police officer in the station cannot be missed in the way that the sole Rape Crisis co-ordinator is.) The same is not true of under-resourced feminist Rape Crisis centres. Hague and Malos (1993: 181) were the first to raise concerns about the issue of membership of multi-agency partnerships, acknowledging the potential 'conflict of interests and approaches between member agencies'. They suggest that where services are under-resourced there is a danger that 'funding will be diverted away from essential refuge provision and emergency services towards the cheaper but perhaps more fashionable option of inter-agency work' (ibid.). They also warn that frontline services and survivors may feel marginalised and overlooked by partnership initiatives. Resource issues are paramount, as is the political will to work with women's services and survivors. So, multi-agency work is demanding and resource consuming.

This unpaid extra work has been undertaken based on the knowledge that long-term social change depends on balancing the provision of immediate services with education. In order to achieve the kind of widespread social education that Rape Crisis strives for, there is a real need to establish relationships of communication with mainstream institutions. For Rape Crisis then, the motivations for involvement in multi-agency working are a complicated mix of pragmatism and idealism. Speaking from a Women's Aid perspective, Harwin et al. (1999: 27) suggest that multi-agency partnerships should be 'both welcomed and critically evaluated'; and the women's voluntary sector has begun to ask what benefits there are in participating in multi-agency partnerships which seem to limit their efforts to make real changes. If the Rape Crisis movement is to remain within partnerships, the reason why they are participating and the impact of their participation needs to be analysed further. In addition, there should be recognition that these groups need to be funded to take part in partnership work. In order to secure women's rights to freedom from violence, it has been argued that multi-agency work needs to include a challenge to male privilege (Dobash and Dobash, 1992; Cosgrove, 1996). Such privilege includes that of the police, councils, health, social services and other male dominated institutions in taking the lead in multi-agency work (Sampson et al., 1988). As a body, multi-agency groups assign responsibility and authority, and there is a danger that lead agencies (often the police) abuse their power to dominate and influence multi-agency groups, reducing the potential to develop truly collaborative relationships. Hague and Malos (1993) ask whether the multi-agency model is anything more than a political smokescreen.

Within multi-agency partnerships it seems that every time women try to enter the domain of men, the rules change:

> Women are told they'll be safe if they play by the rules but there are two snags to this. Firstly, the rules aren't written down so women can't check them and secondly, men are constantly changing the rules.
>
> (Volunteer)

The experience of the Rape Crisis centre workers interviewed for this book provides evidence of feelings of marginalisation on the one hand, whilst simultaneously being overwhelmed within a process over which individual centres have little influence.

Conclusion

This chapter has shown how hard it is for Rape Crisis centres to keep providing services with few resources. The 'living dynamic' of Rape Crisis involves coping with internal and external strife and with the toll the work has on individual women. It includes the need to train new workers every year, by taking them through the wonderful but demanding process of feminist consciousness-raising. Despite all of these problems a number of centres do manage to 'keep on keeping on' and to dream of future service

provision and of wider public education. As part of this they may now choose to engage with mainstream agencies in 'partnership' working.

In this chapter we have also touched upon the need for a politics of generosity towards those with whom we work; on possibilities for service development through electronic forums; and on the notion of sexual violence work across the continuum, rather than focusing specifically on rape, or child abuse or domestic violence. None of these are new ideas and each deserves further discussion in the future.

Feminist activism is a social activity based on the optimistic beliefs that change is both necessary and possible. Rape Crisis work is a particular form of this activism and it faces many challenges. One of these is 'to avoid having others define the appropriate responses to sexual assault and rape prevention. For example, mental health agencies may view sexual assault as an individual psychological trauma requiring professional counselling. Criminal justice agencies may expect victim services to encourage reporting and lead to successful prosecutions' (O'Sullivan and Carlton, 2001: 345). One way of beginning to take on this challenge is to have involvement with other agencies. The early movement defined itself in opposition to mainstream institutions and that political space allowed groups to create new organisational forms. The feminist Rape Crisis centres still model their service provision along the original lines but many have abandoned the isolationist stance. They take the view that feminist engagement with mainstream institutions is vital for long-term social change. Working through the conflicts of interest that such involvement brings is complex and often frustrating. Closer engagement with the mainstream has risks in terms of co-option and potential loss of the original political vision. However, it can also bring benefits which include funding, access to policymakers and, ultimately, opportunities for greater political activism. One way to make engagement with the mainstream easier and safer is to have a national voice which helps to clarify the definition and 'brand' of Rape Crisis. This is one area in which the former Rape Crisis Federation sadly failed. Chapter 4 picks up the story of that organisation.

The Rape Crisis Federation

Introduction

So far in this book we have focused on the autonomous Rape Crisis centres but Chapter 1 has made reference to the lack of a network and Chapter 3 has mentioned some of the work of the short-lived Rape Crisis Federation. Here, we revisit the reasons for delay in forming a network and examine what happened when, in the middle of the 1990s, the Rape Crisis Federation of Wales and England (RCF) was formed. Clearly then, this chapter focuses on work in England and Wales and we consider the networks in Scotland and Ireland in the next chapter.

The RCF had a short career as a co-ordinating body for the movement in England and Wales, as it closed in the early years of the new century, having lost its central funding. These discussions chart the existence of the Federation and analyse its legacy. Some aspects of the work of the RCF are now being renewed under the auspices of a successor organisation, 'Rape Crisis (England and Wales)' and we outline the position with regards to this new group, at the end of this chapter.

Susan Brownmiller has provided insights into the movement in the US and claimed that 'heroic volunteers, [are] never sufficiently honoured and seldom financially rewarded' (1999: 328). What we seek to do here is to honour the work involved in creating the RCF and examine its achievements, but also to investigate why the organisation closed and what can be learnt from these experiences. The story begins in the early 1990s when a number of Rape Crisis centres came together to discuss the possibility of forming a national organisation which could provide a co-ordinating focus for the English and Welsh movement. This chapter draws on personal experience, archive material and interviews with former RCF trustees and consultants, to attempt to shine some light on the structures and development of the organisation. It is fair to acknowledge that both Helen and Kate had some level of involvement in the Federation. Kate was present at some early meetings and was commissioned to write and deliver a training package for the organisation in the early days.

Helen first became involved in the late 1990s when she joined the Board of Trustees. What follows then is our attempt to reconstruct the story of the Federation, from archive documents, from our own knowledge and contributions from some of the women involved in the processes.

The discussions here show that a national body has much to offer to member groups but that it is vital that the priorities and structures of that national organisation are properly thought through from the outset. Without a clear philosophy, coming from the grass-roots centres, there is a risk of co-option at a national level, which cannot serve the member groups well.

LRCC and the original stance on federation

As Chapter 1 has outlined, London RCC was not the only Rape Crisis centre to emerge in the 1970s. Kent was formed in 1977, Tyneside was founded in 1978, Birmingham opened in 1979 and both Sheffield and Manchester had formed some years before opening their helplines, also in 1979. During this time, new centres made visits to established groups and, as more centres opened, emerging networks began to form, meeting informally and often with little supporting funding. At this point there was no national co-ordinating body, although at the Bristol Anti-Rape Conference in 1978 there was a discussion about forming a federation similar to the Women's Aid Federation England (WAFE). However, not all centres supported this idea:

> We [LRCC] wanted to stay autonomous because we thought that way we would have more of a chance of developing in ways that met the needs of the women calling us . . . Why would we have done that – that's about male power building? We would have ended up sitting in endless meetings.
>
> (Bowen et al., 1987: 56)

Nonetheless it is clear that some level of co-ordination of aspects of the work went on for a while after this, as women from five Rape Crisis centres organised a conference in Leeds two years later (Rhodes and McNeill, 1985: 11). In the meantime, women from Rape Crisis had also been meeting under the name of FAST (Feminists Against Sexual Terrorism) to discuss 'the problems they are having' (ibid.). There was concern at this time that Rape Crisis was becoming separated from the rest of the Women's Movement and that there was a need to refocus on activism around rape and other forms of violence against women. Two years later another conference was held in Manchester. This focused on sexual abuse of girls and was organised by Manchester Rape Crisis. This time, though it is not clear that other groups were involved in the organising, they undoubtedly attended and continued networking in that way (ibid.: 135). In between these two events, the first national WAVAW conference also took place, in London (ibid.).

Clearly then, it is somewhat simplistic to see the early groups as isolated. Women from a range of centres were involved in these conferences, in the planning meetings, in WAVAW groups and in FAST. As Chapter 1 attempts to outline, feminism in the late 1970s and into the 1980s was dynamic and lively. It involved newsletters and a plethora of publishing houses, activist networks and other organisations. Over time though, the idea of setting up a formal federation for Rape Crisis faded and so, throughout the 1980s, 'each group was set up separately and each remains autonomous' (London Rape Crisis Centre, 1984: ix). The reality of isolation for Rape Crisis centres truly set in as the other activities of Women's Liberation slowed down and RCCs were left holding back the tide of pain that their services continued to uncover (Lovenduski and Randall, 1993).

In the 1990s, discussions about creating a formal network re-emerged. By then there was a real danger that, without some formal grouping, Rape Crisis centres would become politically and socially isolated and it was therefore timely that the suggestion of a federation be reconsidered.

Before we look at what happened next, we want to analyse the pros and cons of federating. Here we unpick the reasons for the group that emerged but also the potential costs of joining together in this fashion.

To federate or not to federate: that was the question

Some of the early arguments against a federation can be seen in London's comments above. Putting a federation together was perceived as a process of 'endless meetings' and, in the context of the demands already placed on Rape Crisis workers' time, we can see that this would not be an attractive move. Given the levels of work revealed in foregoing chapters it is not unreasonable to suggest that, without funding, a network looked unachievable. It would require so much time and energy to create this network that the project could detract too much from existing service provision. Against this can be set the potential for time-saving (particularly if training could be delivered centrally) instead of being another burden on local women's time. Similarly, if media enquiries were responded to from a network office, that might also free up women's time within the local centres.

However, a network or federation was also perceived as being less flexible, less able to change to meet women's needs. Indeed, we have seen that, in the early days of Rape Crisis, the work was developing fast to encompass more and more forms of abuse and to cope with the increasing demands being placed on the service. However, the discussion above also shows that there is another side to this question of flexibility. In the early days women from Rape Crisis were meeting, fairly often, to discuss the work and to create activism outside of the service provision. Without doubt the flexibility of the individual centres was actually being supported by the possibility for networking with other workers. We also saw this in Chapter 2 when SERICC were able to consult with Manchester regarding ritual abuse survivors. Again, this is only one incident of the informal networking which went on and which still takes place today (for example, Chester Rape Crisis sent women to RASA volunteer training in 2007). In addition, the strength of the women doing direct work was being supported by the possibilities for activism in putting together conferences and taking part in WAVAW groups. So, the lack of flexibility argument is clearly worthy of further investigation. Nonetheless there was a real fear that centralisation would create a model of Rape Crisis which would then become too formal and too unchanging. This might be characterised as one of a group of 'cons' which stemmed from a fear of creating another patriarchal-modelled institution.

Another 'con' can be seen in the comment from London RCC that a network would be 'about male power building'. Clearly if a network or federation was formed then this would be antithetical to collective working. Once a body was created which had some form of authority over other groups, or some form of co-ordinating role, then a hierarchy would come into being. The feminist wish to challenge power differentials in human relationships was such that, originally, this was considered not appropriate for Rape Crisis. Ceding power to a central body would create the possibility of power imbalances and that would then be open to 'male power building', or misuse. There are many examples which show how this does happen within wider society. Every time a company director, a securities trader or trade union boss is caught taking money from the till they demonstrate that assigned authority is open to misuse. They take the trust of those they work for or represent and use it in inappropriate ways. Similarly, when a Minister of State has to resign their post as some scandal has shown that their department has acted outside of government policy, then again, they have misused the power given to them on trust. As Chapter 2 has shown, within feminism there was a will to create organisations where democracy operated in an open way. In these collectives, that responsibility was shared, and these types of misuse were rendered (at least theoretically) impossible.

In fact though, there is the possibility of a different type of objection to a federation hidden within this comment from London RCC. As the original UK group they actually held a considerable amount of power within the movement and so, whilst expressed in perfectly formed feminist idealism, it is possible that this argument hides a wish to hold onto the power that London then had, as originator and model for other centres. Certainly the reality of the movement has always been that some groups have had more authority than others. Often these have been the groups sited within major conurbations, such as London, Manchester and Birmingham. However, these sites of power are shifting and have changed over the years as new centres have joined and old ones have closed.

Another argument against a network was a fear of creating divisiveness, where there were differences in political approach or ethics. By the early 1990s, when the topic of a network reappeared, there were a range of centres in existence and, as we have previously mentioned, not all of these shared the same originating pattern. The model of Rape Crisis which came from the women's movement remained the most dominant but there were also other versions in existence. In addition, there were centres which operated a form of feminism but where the workers were perhaps unaware of the early history of the movement and so there was not the same connection to certain ideas, such as collective working. It was clear then that forming a network could emphasise these differences and that fear was voiced at early discussions.

Having said all of this, there were many reasons for creating a network and these were sufficiently powerful to eventually outweigh the concerns already canvassed. Perhaps the most obvious group of advantages are those relating to the creation of a national voice. Given that Rape Crisis has always hoped to change the world, it was clear by the 1990s that some form of authoritative voice could make a real impact on public views. The Rape Crisis movement had succeeded in creating public awareness of the problem of rape but rape myths still persisted. From the perspective of the Rape Crisis centres, national discussion was seen as often naïve. Whilst some local centres were contacted by the media for comment on particular issues, they were not always able to feel they had done justice to the media discussion, simply because they were always balancing so many competing needs at once. In addition, it is fair to say that the collective structure could work against responding to spontaneous media enquiries, as women might not always feel at liberty to reply without first calling a collective discussion of the topic in question.

It was seen as possible then that a national network could create a voice which would respond to media enquiries with a feminist anti-rape politics and which could also contribute to government discussions and in lobbying for change more generally. In addition there was a hope that a national body might create representatives to speak of the collective knowledge of the experience of surviving rape. This would be a challenge to the media's constant desire for 'a victim' to talk to, in relation to any story concerning rape. All of this would, however, depend upon finding funding for full-time workers to undertake duties such as these.

It was also possible that a national body might be able to co-ordinate funding bids and even find money for a national helpline. As we have seen, finance has been a constant problem for Rape Crisis centres and there was always awareness that this was somewhat different for refuge groups. Though few Women's Aid groups appeared wealthy, they did not seem to have the same hand-to-mouth struggle that Rape Crisis continues to face. WAFE did provide a national voice on topics concerning domestic violence and, there was a view that perhaps it might have helped the individual groups with funding problems. In fact, most refuge groups survived because of the welfare benefits they received on behalf of the women they housed and so their funding problems were always different from those of Rape Crisis centres. Nevertheless, there was a perception that a national body might help Rape Crisis to break out of the endless cycle of poverty it had inhabited since its inception.

This came with a counter-balancing concern though, that the national body could become a competitor for funding, perhaps applying to the major funding bodies (such as the National Lottery and Comic Relief) and reducing the likelihood of local centres receiving grants from these sources. As ever then, the question of a national group was caught in the balance between competing concerns. Other perceived advantages of a national federation were the possibility of enhanced networking and skills sharing as already mentioned above. A more formal possibility for enhanced or coordinated training was also envisaged and again this was a lesson from the Women's Aid Federation, which had long run centralised courses on a range of topics.

All of these arguments have implications for any national network and needed to be considered before such a group was set up, to ensure success. Clearly fears about 'endless meetings' could be met by establishing a framework for co-ordination and considering the counter-balancing advantages of networking, in terms of time saved in writing training packages or in dealing with the media. Similarly, concerns about the potential for a lack of flexibility in the new network could be addressed via the style of organisation set up. Where a network creates an extra tier in a hierarchy and then delegates to its member groups it is not likely to be responsive to the lessons the grass roots are learning from women's testimony. Alternatively however, a network which acts as a conduit for knowledge and communication between member groups could, in fact, act as a means of ensuring greater flexibility within the network as a whole.

Fears about the patriarchal nature of hierarchies and the potential for divisiveness within the movement could be addressed by creating a clear philosophy and appropriate structure for the fledgling network, from the outset. The original WAFE model was one of collectivity within the offices of the Federation, which referred back to a national conference for a renewed remit, each year. This also meant that responsibility for WAFE was shared collectively by the groups, not delegated to a few individual women willing to join a Board. There was, then, a model available for consideration of a feminist approach to centralisation. Finally, the worries over competition for funding could again be dealt with within the policies and philosophies of the network. In the event, as we show below, there was a lack of detailed consultation at the inception of the Federation and the steps made along the way to involve member groups do not always appear to have been well followed through. If we consider what we already know about the situation facing the groups who set up this federation, the levels of work they were facing and their lack of resources, then it is not surprising that the network which was set up progressed in a far less co-ordinated manner, at least in the early months. Nevertheless, and with the glorious benefit of hindsight, it is easy to see that this lack of strategy may well have contributed to the eventual failure of the project.

In the remainder of this chapter we draw on the arguments for and against federating, set out in this discussion, and Table 4.1, below, provides a summary of the major points, adding in some notes on the implications of these for the national network. The table is intended to be read left-to-right, with each of the disadvantages set against a counter-argument which presents a possible advantage and potential implications to consider in setting up a network.

By the late 1980s, many feminist-based Rape Crisis centres were still meeting with each other informally to provide help and assistance in keeping services afloat. From these regional meetings of Rape Crisis centres the idea of a federation re-emerged and led on to a conference in 1992, organised by Nottingham Rape Crisis Centre (Jones, 2004). Although there were mixed feelings about developing something on a

Table 4.1 Arguments for and against a network

Against	For	Implications
Endless meetings	Provision of training and response to media	Awareness of the potential drain on member groups in running the network
Inflexibility in responding to women's needs	Sharing of knowledge and activism through the network	Style of centre, needing to be part of a network rather than under a head office
Patriarchal power-building within hierarchies	Potential to create a network which equalises access to knowledge and hence reduces power divisions	Careful consideration of structure, model for collective structure available within original WAFE structure
Potential for divisiveness where the member groups were not identical in structure or policy	Opportunity to re-establish a clear philosophy	Need to define the nature of the network clearly from the outset
Lack of ownership if national statements not reflective of local view	National voice for media responses and lobbying	Again, need for clarity of politics and approach
Threat to local funding	Possibility for national funding	Need for a strategy for fundraising

national basis which might compete for funding, the decision was made to 'go for it' (SERICC).

A small working party of eight women from Rape Crisis centres across the country formed the Rape Crisis Federating Reference Group (RCFRG) in 1993 to bring the idea of a national organisation into a reality. Their key tasks were to:

- Consult with the Rape Crisis movement.
- Establish an organisational structure.
- Develop policies and guidelines.
- Fundraise.
- Find staff and premises.

Immediately the problems of federating become apparent in this brief list. The eight women were taking on an enormous set of tasks and with no resources except a decision to 'go for it'. The needs we have already identified, to consult groups and to establish a structure and policies, were acknowledged in this workload but it was not clear how these could be achieved. The Federating Group decided to start with a name for this future organisation and there remain some notes from these early discussions within the Rape Crisis Federation archive. In a memo to the Federating Group, one member considered the question of names:

It will be necessary to make sure we have an impact as a Federation, and that the name is instantly recognisable. I have been playing with a few acronyms and suggest you might like to do the same. I came up with:

- *Federation of Rape Centres – F O R C E*
- *Federation of Incest, Rape and Sexual Trauma Lines – F I R S T-Lines*
- *Coalition of Rape Agencies – CO-RAGE*

We need to become known once the Federation exists. This means we need to be heard and to be seen to be in the public eye. An instantly recognisable name then helps to fix the organisation in the minds of public and potential funders.
(Archive material)

After some debate the decision was made to name the new organisation 'The Rape Crisis Federation of Wales and England' to be known in short form as 'RCF' and so the group moved on to tackle the tasks on their list.

Setting up the RCF

It must have been clear to the Federating Group that for real progress to be made someone needed to be found to work on this project full-time. That meant that some money was needed and so the group looked for funders willing to support the formation of the RCF. It is apparent however that there was a lack of strategic planning here, what emerges is more in the traditional style of voluntary groups – taking money from the pots available, rather than deciding what is required and then looking for appropriate finance. Early grants came from the Allen Lane Foundation, which initially funded a one-year project to survey the training needs of the Rape Crisis movement. Here the agenda was training focused and this was set by the interests of the funder, rather than by the needs of the movement itself. The Allen Lane Foundation later agreed a further two-year grant (£20,000 pa) to fund the Training Co-ordinator's post and so, in October 1995, a worker was employed. This led to a focus on training from the RCF, and that in turn produced some useful training packs, which we discuss in due course. However, the Allen Lane funding also brought with it an emphasis on professionalism within training, which was arguably at odds with the participative, consciousness-raising approach to training that the movement had developed hitherto.

In March 1995, some start-up funding came from Calouste Gulbenkian (£10,000, followed by a further £10,000 in 1996) to aid the overall development of a federation. The Barrow Cadbury Trust pledged £20,000 from June 1995 for 12 months to fund a Development Worker who would canvass the views and needs of Rape Crisis centres across the country (a further two-year grant was later received to continue the post) . Here then was a worker who could liaise properly with the groups and begin to establish a centre-led agenda for the new federation.

The fledgling organisation also tried to get government support. The Voluntary Services Unit of the Home Office was contacted in December 1995 to enquire about the likelihood of central government funding but there was no response. A reminder in June 1996 produced a response, but this was not encouraging as the Home Office merely referred the group to the Department of Health. The Federating Group also considered applying to the Charities Board of the National Lotteries and although a draft plan for an application was drawn up, the decision was taken that, in order to give the new organisation the best chance of success, they would wait until after the launch to apply. This outline gives a flavour of the lack of focus of these initial fundraising efforts. However, it is worth stressing that all of this work was being undertaken by a small group of women, spread around the country, in the days before internet communication and with no back-office resources.

As a result of these fundraising efforts, a worker was employed by the Federating Group from mid-1995 who was able to develop the idea of the RCF. The early fundraising lacked strategy but did not represent a threat to local centres since the Federating Group was only receiving seed-corn money and the funds from Calouste Gulbenkian, Barrow Cadbury and Allen Lane were for tasks specific to the creation of a network, not to running a Rape Crisis service.

Development work

Referring back to the remit of the Federating Group above, we can see that they had found money and staff, but had yet to consult, to choose a structure or to write policies for the new organisation. At this point then, there was a clear need to develop a centres-led mission for this new federation, by consulting with the groups to build the policies and structures of the new group.

Once the development worker was in post, she did begin to work on some of these tasks. Straight away though, some problems began to emerge caused by the differences between individual Rape Crisis centres and in particular with regards to the question of women-only service provision. From the earliest days of the Federation then there was an element of divisiveness and the archive materials make it clear that there was no over-arching political vision, even amongst the women working towards the new Federation. This discussion examines some of the difficulties the workers encountered in trying to continue this development with a diverse and (effectively) absent management group, drawn from centres around the country.

During 1995, the development worker canvassed the views of the Rape Crisis centres via a questionnaire which contained guidelines for membership, drawn up by the RCFRG. These included the requirement that groups within the Federation would be women-only and would provide services to female survivors of male violence. The aim of the questionnaire was to gauge support for the Federation and help develop a set of policies and guidelines. Working alone, with a federating group that met infrequently, the worker met some opposition to the new guidelines in the questionnaire. In feedback to the federating group in November 1995 the worker reported:

I have now received 30 returned questionnaires, and a couple of phone calls from other groups who are waiting to fill theirs in. The response is generally welcoming, some with reservations. There are groups who have problems with some of the draft guidelines and a few have asked if there will be affiliate membership, rather than full, if they cannot meet all the criteria.

(Archive material)

A number of centres that responded to the questionnaires either worked with men on their management boards or were providing services to men. From the archive it is apparent that the development worker took the view that the federation should try to accommodate all types of Rape Crisis group. Not surprisingly, the Federating Group's view was that only women-only services could be eligible for membership of the federation. Clearly, it was unfortunate that the group had employed a development worker who did not support this core value of Rape Crisis and this points to the importance of clarity as to the politics and philosophy of the organisation.

At the same time, decisions had to be made over the structure of the new federation. The development worker canvassed legal advice and the decision taken was to opt for formal incorporation:

Incorporation seems to offer the best option, providing a set procedure for settling disputes should they arise. As the Federation hopes to involve a membership, and a growing one as time passes, the scope for dispute is apparent (as it is now). The Federation will need to have some way of settling any major disputes and incorporation offers laid down procedures. If the Federation does grow, then the sums of money being handled will also increase. Although it is planned to have strict accounting procedures, the impact of any mis-handling of finance could be substantial for individual trustees. Incorporation would mean liability limited to a nominal sum. In terms of seeking grant and other finances, incorporated status gives a more profes-sional image which enhances credibility. I would therefore suggest that incorporation is the more suitable option. It is likely that if the Federation does become established and grow, then at some point in the future incorporation would become necessary, it therefore seems sensible to start out with it in place, rather than incur extra expense and problems later.

(Archive material)

This is not a balanced view as it does not take into account any of the drawbacks of a formal corporate management structure, in terms of moving further away from the original vision of Rape Crisis, or creating tiers of management within management in the national network as a whole. This also takes as a given the notion of finding women willing to coordinate the organisation and sit on its Board of Trustees. In the event, over the next few years a stable Board was not established and this further weakened management which was already problematic, given that all the women were drawn from those active within member groups.

The development worker also had the practical task of setting up an office base and in 1996, the Lankelly Foundation agreed to fund co-ordinator and administrative posts once an office base in Manchester was organised. Premises were identified and the launch of the Federation was then planned for October. An extract from the development worker's report dated January 1996 captures the emotion at the beginning of this busy year:

I am now just over halfway through the 12 month contract, and starting to believe that it will all happen. I know some of you are probably as nervous as me about taking the final steps to make it real. It still does feel very nebulous in some ways, and in part that is to do with the isolation in the way the group works. Once there is a central base for the Federation, then hopefully that will make life a lot easier for both staff and management members. Having more than one person under the same roof will help – assuming we get the finance to allow for that . . . Waiting for responses from the trusts, waiting for decisions – and waiting for the spring! I feel that my steam has run down, if not out.

(Archive material)

The archive also contains another document entitled *The Federating Process* in which the development worker discusses some of her frustrations at working with a disparate and absent Federating Group. In this document she discusses the process week by week, from setting up a base to work from, through to the launch of the new organisation. In week two she records a visit from a member of the Federating Group: 'although in one sense this seemed a bit early, it also meant I felt like I belonged to something!' By the following week however, she writes: 'isolation of post becoming obvious. Easy to go off at tangent and focus on what feels easier or more accessible. Need to have clear idea of priorities set by RCFRG (with flexibility)'. Although this sense of isolation abates, by week seven there is evidence of further concerns: 'frustration with length of time from requesting cheques to actually receiving them – caused by distances involved and busy-ness of RCFRG members . . . Actually believe that probably just no one else feels this gap as much as me and therefore not thought about it'. Although she appreciates that members of the Federating Group are busy, in week 12 she is quite explicit about her 'sense of frustration, I want to sit down with someone and discuss all this, and get to grips with what the group wants'.

It can be argued that these issues, of absentee management and isolation for the workers were never satisfactorily addressed by the organisation and were to contribute to its eventual closure. Close to the launch, problems with regards to the philosophy of women-only provision were still evident. Letters from Basingstoke, Southampton, Northampton, Luton and Warrington Rape Crisis centres were received in August 1996. These centres believed Rape Crisis should provide services for men and that the new organisation should accept groups which provided these services as full members. A formal response was sent, acknowledging these arguments but reserving the right of the federation to progress as a women-only organisation.

The launch

On the 2 October 1996, over 100 women met to celebrate the official launch of the Federation. Representatives from 35 Rape Crisis Centres in Wales and England journeyed to Manchester to be part of this momentous occasion.
(RCF newsletter, 1996 Archive materials)

At the launch, speakers included Professor Sue Lees, an academic and vociferous advocate of the Rape Crisis movement; Lynn James, from Women's Aid Federation England; and two speakers from the London-based 'Women and Girls Network', Kim Thomas and Ruth Whitfield. In correspondence with the newly-formed organisation just prior to the launch, Sue Lees had identified what she saw as the key issues:

The contradiction between the need for funding, collective leadership and confidentiality; the problems of challenging male violence and organising politically at the same time as providing adequate counselling services . . . the time has come for a degree of central co-ordination and planning, which should not detract from organising politically or allowing some autonomy to local groups.
(Letter dated 9 September 1996, Archive material)

From this we can see that Sue Lees was aware of some of the key issues facing the new federation, although 'collective leadership' is at best a curious phrase. The Federating Group put forward some objectives for the launch event:

- *To provide the opportunity for members of the Federation to meet with each other.*
- *To provide the opportunity for members of the Federation to skill share and to learn from each other.*
- *To celebrate the beginning of something very exciting and essential to all Rape Crisis Groups and women living in Wales and England.*
- *To provide the forum for Black members to meet and develop the Black Workers Network.*
(Launch Pack, 1996: 3)

Straight away then, one of the interest groups mentioned in Chapter 3 was at the forefront of the agenda. The proposal for a lesbian workers group also came out of these early discussions, as we see below.

At the Launch, the members of the Rape Crisis Federating Reference Group ceded to the Rape Crisis Federation Management Group (although some women from the initial group continued with this Management Group). The new body produced a newsletter, and the first edition, which reported on the launch, also carried adverts for two job vacancies, the first for a part-time co-ordinator (30 hours per week) for the newly formed federation and the second for a part-time administration worker (17.5 hours per week). Two networks were also announced: the Black Women's Network and the Lesbian and Bi Women's Group, with details of future meetings and membership.

The development worker appears to have moved on by the launch and so the Federation started with just one part-time worker, a training co-ordinator. She was joined by an administrator, for a ten-week period to assist with the launch (Launch Pack, 1996: 6). The Federation went on to recruit two new workers who took up their posts in February 1997 (RCF newsletter, 1997: 3). By mid-1997 the Federation was well established with 45 affiliated member groups (see Appendix 2) and the informal regional meetings which had brought the Federation into being ceased. The original office base was in the St Thomas Centre in Manchester but a successful NLCB bid in 1998 resulted in the establishment of a new office base in Nottingham.

The key task for the co-ordinator in these early months was to contact and visit Rape Crisis centres to determine what was wanted from the Federation. It is interesting to note that earlier consultation was not considered sufficient and this worker was, therefore, engaged in an activity which had theoretically been a key part of the Development Worker post. According to women from SERICC, who recall this process, four key issues were identified:

1. A national voice for the Rape Crisis movement.
2. Campaigning and lobbying.
3. Funding for Rape Crisis centres (along similar lines to Victim Support).
4. Training.

Comparing these issues to our original table of advantages of federating, we can see that there is considerable overlap here. Around the end of 1997 then, the organisation was launched and established with workers and an office base. It had some priorities from the groups and a management structure in place.

Following the launch the Federation continued to grow and began to work on some of the key priorities. Eventually, in the face of a funding crisis, the organisation closed in 2003, and we return to the story of that closure shortly. Before that though, it is appropriate to examine some of the key achievements of the federation.

Achievements

For around six years the English and Welsh Rape Crisis centres had a national body in the form of the RCF. The groups had identified four key issues which they wanted that organisation to work on and this discussion attempts to evaluate the successes of the RCF in responding to these needs.

National voice

The first stated aim was to create a national voice for the movement. It is perhaps worth repeating briefly that this 'national' voice was only ever representative of England and Wales. The Scottish and Irish networks were established separately and we return to examine these in Chapter 5. We also suggest there that the interests of all of the centres might be best served by forging closer links between these separate national bodies.

During the second half of 1997 however, the newly formed RCF saw great success in bringing English and Welsh groups together under one network as a further five centres became affiliated to the Federation (Colchester, Hounslow, Lancaster, Nottingham and York) bringing the total membership to 50 groups. Within this network, RCF was able to establish a number of sub-groups, providing forums for exploring good practice, equality of opportunity and access to services for all women. Specialist groups were set up around sexuality and race, as we have already mentioned, creating space for discussions about multiple oppressions.

As time went on, the Federation was also able to undertake other work which would build towards that 'national voice' for Rape Crisis. One example here is the database work which was mentioned in the last chapter. Collecting data from the centres would clearly facilitate the provision of good information to funders and others, but could also feed into responses to the media, covering stories about rape. Initially the media 'phoneline' consisted of two mobile phones, carried by unpaid Board of Trustee members and answered whenever media enquiries were made. This resulted in Board members being called at any time of the day or night, while at their own paid employment or even out shopping. Later, funding was obtained from the government and women experienced in media work were employed to take on the work. One of the workers later identified key strategies used by RCF in its media work:

- *Whatever the issue raised by the media, using this as an opportunity to promote our own agenda.*
- *Using the latest research and statistics to back up our response.*
- *Developing consistent 'sound-bite' responses.*
- *Ensuring we were available to do key high profile TV or radio interviews, or debates whenever possible.*
- *Supporting survivors who wanted to highlight injustices or other significant issues from their own experiences, in the media.*
- *Agreeing to joint campaigns with certain women's magazines/newspapers.*

(Harne, 2004)

Training

Another key issue for groups was the development of training, and we have already commented that this was a focus for the

Federation from the earliest days, following the involvement of the Allen Lane Foundation. An early initiative was the development of a 'Minimum Training Standards' pack which member groups were asked to endorse. Looking back, it is perhaps not clear that this was the most urgent training need felt by the member groups, and so it may be that the drive for this did come from external, professionalising influences, such as the funders themselves. However, the new Federation was also quickly able to develop some training packs in areas which were considered of concern to member groups. These related to fundraising, with a pack entitled *Tips for Better Fundraising*; there was also a media pack *Making the Media Work for You* written by Julie Bindel and a pack on negotiating service-level agreements which Kate wrote. In retrospect one wonders why further packs were not developed, since the ones listed were reportedly valued by the member groups. Certainly there is room here for further development work in the future, to help Rape Crisis groups to learn from the 30-year process of consciousness-raising and pass that knowledge on to future generations.

Campaigning and lobbying

The remaining aims prioritised by the member groups were lobbying and campaigning, and obtaining funding for members. This last aim was never achieved, but the federation did make considerable progress in the area of lobbying and campaigning. The first aspect of this was Federation involvement in organising with Justice for Women (JFW) a conference entitled, *Rape and the Criminal Justice System*, which launched the new Campaign to End Rape (CER). The conference made three key demands:

- *A full investigation by the Home Office into the attrition rate.*
- *A shift in the burden of proof in consent defences in line with Victoria, Australia, so that the defendant has to prove he sought and got consent, and within this the removal of the right to defence counsel to use previous sexual history evidence.*
- *Special prosecutors for cases of sexual violence against women and children.*
  (Julie Bindel, RCF newsletter, 1997: 7. Archive material)

These demands coincided with the initial lobbying points of the fledgling campaign and all

delegates were asked to sign up in support of CER. The emergence of this campaign as an important lobby group on rape is discussed in more detail in Chapter 6 and the RCF continued to support CER throughout its existence.

Sometime later, and in response to the lobbying by RCF and CER, the Federation was invited to take part in the consultancy panel for the Home Office *Sex Offences Review* (Home Office, 2000; Jones and Barnard, 2001). Conducted over a two year period, it was described by then Home Secretary Jack Straw as developing 'a new code of sex offences to take us into the new century . . . only the beginning of a debate on the way forward' (Home Office, 2000: i). Helen was part of the RCF Board of Trustees by this time and represented the Federation on that review panel. The 'willingness of government to canvass and to listen to the views of RCF was seen as a first step in representing and responding to the views of women' (Jones, 2004: 62) and the RCF felt that they had finally arrived on the national stage.

This was confirmed when, in recognition of its expertise in the field of sexual violence, the RCF secured core operational funding from the Home Office in April 2001. The confidence brought by this funding cannot be under-estimated, as it 'secured the RCF's place at many governmental fora, facilitating a level of networking – nationally and internationally – which would have been impossible without the funding' (Jones, 2004: 62). However, despite this optimism, it became clear that, whilst access to national consultation was important for the lobbying agenda of the Federation, it was also 'labour intensive' work.

The Home Office review panel was just the start of a long list of consultations which RCF took part in, including 'the Crown Prosecution Service (CPS) Consultation on the Handling of Rape Cases, the Home Affairs Committee on the Sexual Offences Bill, the Sentencing Advisory Panel on Sentencing Guidelines on Rape, the Metropolitan Police on Drug Assisted Sexual Assault and the Joint Review by the CPS and Constabulary Inspectorates' (Jones, 2004: 62). The focus on national issues arguably took the RCF away from the grassroots concerns of its member groups and certainly whilst the Federation itself secured government funding there was no real progress in finding any financial security for member groups.

Funding

Indeed the centres were facing funding crises and RCF research found that 'All member groups report facing drastic cuts to funding . . . The net effect will be that waiting lists will inevitably increase and in worst-case scenarios the services may cease in that locality' (Archive materials). Although the government had stated a commitment to joined-up thinking on supporting the voluntary sector, particularly in relation to victims of sexual offences, there was no evidence of joined-up resources (Jones, 1999). When RCF was first launched there were 'around 60 localised Rape Crisis centres, in 2004 there are only 43' (Jones, 2004: 64) and Chapter 5 reports on further closures since then. Yet, the funding that RCF received from central government was not allowed to be distributed to local groups to save them from closure.

It can be argued that it suits the needs of government to make use of feminist energies, without giving real access to appropriate levels of resources. Former Chair and Board of Trustees' member Shahidah Janjua expressed the concerns held at the time:

In my view the Home Office set the agenda in a variety of different ways. Yes, they used RCF to do their work for them thereby setting the agenda at all levels, including political and operational.

So the RCF did achieve a national voice and lobbying position, and government funding. However it may have done this at the expense of gaining ground on other key concerns of member groups. Again this could point to weaknesses in the strategic planning within the organisation. From the archive it is apparent that the task of running this organisation was proving taxing. At many of the annual meetings there was a high turnover of women resigning from the Board. Board members were drawn from volunteers working within local groups and many found the task of running the Federation too great to maintain over time. We have also referred earlier to the stresses encountered by workers relating to absentee management and it is apparent now that this was rarely a happy experience for either group of women, and all of this doubtless contributed to problems with creating and delivering strategic plans for future work.

Other achievements

These were complicated times, however, and with the biggest reform of sexual offences in 50 years going through parliament, clearly the RCF had important national work to attend to. A lobbyist was employed to ensure that key provisions fought for during the Sex Offences Review were continued into the Bill that came before parliament in the summer of 2003. This can be claimed as one of the major achievements of the short-lived Federation. Although not perfect, the legislation includes many gains on what went before, although fine laws are nothing without attitudinal change (Cook, 2003; Jones, 2003).

Sadly, one aspect of a lack of strategic planning was a lack of a diverse funding base. Once it received government funding, the RCF over-relied on the generous grant from the Home Office. This was combined with increasing workloads dictated by one government-level consultation after another. Ideologically the RCF had wandered far from the feminist principles of the movement it represented. When an employment dispute resulted in the dismissal of two staff members the Board called an Emergency General Meeting of the member groups in February 2003 to explore the extent of the problems and to refocus the work of the national group back to the needs of its membership (Jones, 2004).

The wider women's movement endorsed the work of the RCF by awarding the Chair the Emma Humphreys Memorial Award in October 2003 (Jones, 2004). Just days later, the Home Office withdrew funding from the RCF. In a letter from the Home Office, on behalf of Baroness Scotland, the decision was explained as being due to concerns that the Home Office had about the solvency of the Rape Crisis Federation (Archive materials). Yet it was withdrawal of Home Office funding that secured the demise of the RCF. Alternative funding streams had not been obtained and when the Home Office withdrew its support, regardless of the wishes of the wider Rape Crisis movement, there was no alternative but to close.

The closure of RCF was the culmination of a period where its principles, traditions and structures of governance were sorely tested. It is remarkable timing that just as the Sexual Offences Bill was due to be enacted, just as an Inter-Ministerial group on sexual violence was formed and just as the Government was due to report to the United Nations on action taken to eliminate discrimination against women (as required under CEDAW) the Home Office chose to withdraw their financial support of this national group that defended women's rights to live their lives free from the fear of male sexual violence.

(Jones and Westmarland, 2004)

I have learnt some valuable lessons through working with the state. It takes our knowledge and expertise and uses it against us. It asks us to do endless research on issues we, in the movement, have had years of experience of, through our work with women and our own experiences, but it doesn't hear our voices, or when it does it misuses the information, in the same way that it misuses the research findings, which only tells it the same things we have told it countless times before. We need to think again, about how we go forward from here, women's lives, our lives, depend on it.

(Shahidah Janjua, former Chair and Board of Trustees member of the RCF)

When the Federation closed, in November 2003, a letter was sent to the Home Office on behalf of 15 Rape Crisis centres. This letter is useful to us now as it listed the achievements of the Federation, from the perspective of those 15 member groups. The letter expressed 'shock and deep disappointment' at the withdrawal of funding from RCF and highlighted the hard work of the women on the Board, the workers and the consultants to resolve the difficulties. Finally, the letter noted that the closure meant there would now be:

- No national contact point for women urgently seeking the support of local Rape Crisis groups.
- No new developments such as a national rape and sexual abuse helpline.
- No national lobbying/raising awareness work around women's experiences of rape and sexual abuse (local groups do not have time and resources to do this work hence the need for the RCF).
- No national voice for Rape Crisis centres and women survivors therefore the loss of a valuable source of 'user' input.
- No specialist media workers to work with the national and local press to challenge common myths about women's experiences of rape and sexual abuse.
- No national database for detailed statistics on women survivors and perpetrators.
- No national networks or support groups for Rape Crisis workers leading to greater isolation, and no opportunity to share good

practice (particularly on meeting the needs of minority and disadvantaged groups such as refugee and black women).
- No national Directory of Rape Crisis groups leading to reduced co-ordination and communication between centres.
- No national website for public use.

Despite our reservations about the lack of a clear politics and strategy, it is apparent that the work of the RCF was valued by the women in the centres themselves.

Happily though, a new group emerged from the closure of the RCF. The Rape Crisis Co-ordinating Group met for the first time in December 2003 and has managed to maintain some aspects of the work of the old RCF. In particular the website continued as a publicly accessible information point. After a gap of two years, the Rape Crisis Co-ordinating Group secured a small grant from the Home Office in 2005 to bring existing Rape Crisis groups together to find a way forward for future work. This group has now been renamed as 'Rape Crisis (England and Wales)', formalised its structure, gained charitable status and has employed its first paid staff. It is almost as though the movement were back at the beginning of the 1990s, with exploratory funding to bring groups together. However, and very sadly, that is not the case. The number of Rape Crisis groups has continued to fall so that there are now around 43 listed on the Rape Crisis website (eight of these groups provide services for men and so only 35 groups can be said to be part of the feminist model). London Rape Crisis, Sandwell Rape Crisis and Leeds Rape Crisis closed in 2003. Milton Keynes, Grimsby and Scunthorpe closed in 2004 and South Wales (Cardiff) and Hounslow Women's Counselling Service closed in 2005. In 2007 York Rape Crisis and Cambridge Rape Crisis closed, although there is hope that the Cambridge group may re-open. Other centres continue to be perilously close to closure due to funding crises and we return to review the current picture of the groups in the next chapter.

Conclusion

London Rape Crisis Centre never did join the Federation: perhaps their prediction about it being too time-consuming was right. The RCF had many successes in its short history and these highlight a clear need for a national voice, which we can hope that the newly formed national Rape Crisis group will grow to become. However, the Federation was caught between the twin pressures of serving the needs of its member groups and serving the needs of its political masters who ultimately held the purse strings. Sue Lees had stated some of the key problems very clearly in her letter of 1996 (quoted earlier). The conflict between the attempt to obtain formal funding for a national body and for member groups was never satisfactorily resolved. A clear hierarchy existed with the RCF obtaining (albeit brief) power at a national level. At the same time the member groups were closing due to their own powerless state. Finally however, the lack of strategic planning within RCF created a situation where the loss of funding could destroy the organisation and thus damage the now depleted movement further.

It is clear that strategic planning and feminist ideals are needed now, within the Rape Crisis movement, as the numbers of groups in England and Wales continues to decline. Chapter 5 updates the picture, looking at which groups are succeeding and at the spread of services. The legacy of the RCF is that we can learn how to create a more effective national grouping, if we unpick its history and look critically at the advantages and disadvantages of networks, and at how to maximise the positive and minimise the negative. We hope that this chapter has contributed to that process.

CHAPTER 5

Rape Crisis Now: Surviving or Thriving?

Introduction

This chapter tries to provide a snapshot of the current state of feminist Rape Crisis service provision across the UK, with a particular interest in the financial resources available to the groups and in the geographic spread of services. It is difficult to come to a definitive conclusion as to how many Rape Crisis groups exist and how they are constituted. We are writing this chapter on a specific day in 2007 and the total number of Rape Crisis groups on this day will differ from the number next year, the year after that or whenever you are reading this chapter. What we can do is give you the information you need to check out the number of groups for yourself, and then give you an overview of what that picture looked like at the time we conducted our research.

Our aim is to identify how many Rape Crisis services are still providing a service and to compare these with other forms of provision. Overall we aim to establish whether there is enough provision of support to survivors of all forms of rape. It should be easy to find out how many Rape Crisis services exist. Most groups who see themselves as fitting this label are listed on the Rape Crisis website (http://www.rapecrisis.org.uk/members.htm last accessed 20.07.07) which provides details on local groups in England and Wales and the networks in Scotland and Ireland. Caution must be exercised however because, as we have shown, not all services for survivors of sexual violence now describe themselves as Rape Crisis groups. Their names have changed, and in some cases their services have grown away from their original model too. In addition, there may be other groups which do not fit within the Rape Crisis model at all but who work with survivors of sexual violence.

This chapter concentrates once more on the groups most closely identified as part of the Rape Crisis movement whilst also acknowledging services outside of that umbrella, in an attempt to provide a more thorough picture of services that exist to meet the needs of survivors of sexual violence. Chapter 2 began to unpick the relationship between Rape Crisis and the dominant form of statutory sector provision for survivors of sexual violence, the Sexual Assault Referral Centres (SARCs). This chapter returns to consider the role of the SARCs, offering a critical examination of the work of these groups with some reference to the newer initiative of the ISVAs (Independent Sexual Violence Advisors). Our aim here is to concentrate as far as possible on the services for rape survivors that have sought charitable status and to compare them and their resources with services within the statutory sector which most closely mirror them.

Chapters 2 and 3 provided detail about the feminist Rape Crisis movement in England and Wales using information from questionnaires completed by most of the groups listed on the Rape Crisis website as well as providing case studies of groups who participated in interviews. This chapter reviews the services in existence in the UK and concludes that, whilst Rape Crisis is still the dominant model for service provision, it is horribly under-resourced, and the network in England and Wales is currently in crisis. This takes us back to the vexed question of providing support to men who have been raped. In fact, Ryan-Flood (1998: 70) suggests that there is little scope for 'services for male survivors to develop in the same way as services for women, without the support of a social movement'. As we have established earlier, there remain good reasons for the Rape Crisis model to concentrate on work with women. It will be for others to develop work with male survivors more completely.

We are aware here of the danger of speaking about 'the Rape Crisis movement' in the UK with barely a reference to the networks of groups in Wales, Scotland or Ireland. In fact, as we will see, there is now little provision in existence in Wales, giving a stark example of the problems of group closure and patchy service provision. We have mentioned both Scotland and Ireland in Chapter 1 and used the Irish experience of state funding as a case study in Chapter 2. However, these networks deserve further consideration and we begin this chapter by providing a little more on their development.

Scotland and Ireland

Rape Crisis groups in Britain and Ireland share many of the same hopes and challenges but it is important to recognise the differences too. As Chapter 1 indicated, the initial groups in Ireland and Scotland opened in the late 1970s, around the same time as centres began to emerge around England and Wales. Writing about the Scottish network, Christianson and Greenan discuss how the early 1990s saw the start of discussions 'on the theme of federating or constituting our links more formally, and in 1994 a statement of common policy was adopted by seven centres' (in Breitenbach and Mackay, 2001: 74). In comparison, the Rape Crisis Network Ireland (RCNI) was set up much earlier (in 1985) consisting of six Rape Crisis centres.

In Scotland the first two groups opened in Glasgow in 1976 and in Edinburgh in 1978 with an organisational structure 'inspired by the American and then London model of collective working' (ibid.). These groups were also founded on feminist principles, recognising rape as a violent, not a sexual, crime in the same manner as those in England and Wales. Challenges to the legal system (which is independent and distinct from the system in England and Wales) included a private prosecution for rape in 1982. The appeal court ruled that a retrial could take place, following an earlier trial collapse. This resulted in a high-profile resignation of the then Solicitor General for Scotland, Nicholas Fairbairn (the case is discussed in an obituary of the Appeal Court judge, http://www.guardian.co.uk/obituaries/story/0,3604,853210,00.html last accessed 20.07.07).

Another landmark on the road to challenging public opinion and legislation, again in 1982, was when a 'rape in marriage' prosecution established the principle of marital rape in Scotland. Although it took until 1989 to secure a conviction for marital rape in Scotland, this preceded legislation in England and Wales (discussed in Chapter 6). In Scotland, just as elsewhere, blaming the victim had been a useful strategy in diminishing men's responsibility for violence. In both Scotland and Ireland it can be argued that there is a cultural stereotype of the strong, capable matriarchal figure. In marital rape, then, the myths are that she is either 'too weak' to suffer the ordeal of the court or 'too strong' to have been assaulted by her husband. Smyth (1996: 56) has highlighted the 'paradoxical construction of women as simultaneously

'victims' *and* as responsible for their own fate: *She brought it on herself* (italics in original). Each identity position acts to cast doubt on the credibility of the woman. Within such a discourse it is difficult to conceive of the woman as having been victimised, and because of this it is important that victim-blaming is understood within a context of cultural, gendered social roles and normalised behaviour. Christianson and Greenan make the point strongly: 'Attitudes to women in society have always affected the way juries came to their verdicts, making the incidence of 'guilty' verdicts much lower in rape cases than in cases of violence not including sexual assault' (in Breitenbach and Mackay, 2001: 72).

The Rape Crisis Scotland website shows that the groups in Scotland developed their work to include adult survivors of child sexual abuse, in the same ways that we have already seen in relation to English and Welsh centres. In addition, there are the same concerns over language ('survivor' and 'support' being preferred to 'victim' and 'counselling'), and a lack of secure funding. The national office opened in Scotland in 2002 and receives funding from the Scottish Executive. There are currently nine group members of the network: Aberdeen, Dundee, Edinburgh, Glasgow, Kilmarnock, Hamilton, Dunoon, Stornoway and Perth.

Writing about the role of women in politics in Ireland, Galligan (1998) suggests that the emergence of concern about male violence against women followed a similar route in Ireland as that of other countries. She discusses how the women's movement mobilised from around 1968, and that throughout the 1970s there was a growing 'politicisation of women's status in Ireland' (ibid.: 113). Fiona Neary, the co-ordinator of the Irish network, endorses this, arguing that until the 1970s and the re-emergence of feminism: 'Women were silenced by fear and shame, and the silence of women gave license to every form of sexual and domestic exploitation' (Neary, 2000: 1). A report *Rape in Ireland*, was submitted to the Ministry for Justice in October 1978 (Council for the Status of Women, 1978) and following this a number of women's groups emerged to lobby for legislative change and to ensure a space for debate within public and political arenas:

On 13 October 1979, a night time protest march in Dublin attracted an attendance of 5,000 women, including many in public life.

(Galligan, 1998: 114)

It was at this time that the *Campaign Against Rape* group recognised a need for a counselling service and decided to establish a Rape Crisis group. This became known as the Dublin Rape Crisis Centre (DRCC). As we have seen, a network was then formed and from 1985 the Rape Crisis Network Ireland (RCNI) aimed to work towards:

- *Gaining recognition and respect for the work of the regional centres.*
- *Obtaining a secure and acceptable level of statutory funding.*
- *Assisting and supporting new RCCs to set up.*
- *Bringing about major reforms in the area of rape legislation.*
- *Promoting good working relations with statutory bodies such as the Gardai and Health boards.*
     (Rape Crisis Network Ireland website, 2007a)

It is worth noting that these aims were in existence some years before the RCF was formed and so the English model could have looked to Ireland for a clear and concise set of aims. It does not appear that this was considered however, and as Chapter 4 has shown, the RCF worked to a much looser set of objectives.

After many years of lobbying on these issues the RCNI received funding from the Department of Health and Children in 1999. A recent report conducted by the RCNI revealed that when a survivor of sexual violence discloses 'the first person is likely to be a close friend or family member . . . Only 12 per cent of survivors contact a counselling or support agency' (RCNI website). This knowledge helps the network to focus their work on local level awareness and they continue to serve their membership (see Appendix 3) through a 'five goal' plan that includes campaigning and education:

1. *Supporting RCCs.*
2. *Supporting the network.*
3. *Lobbying for change.*
4. *Supporting survivor services.*
5. *Education and awareness.*
     (Rape Crisis Network Ireland website, 2007b)

Still working to a clear set of aims then, the Irish Network has grown beyond its original scope, to cover more of the country. We have already seen that this is in stark contrast to the English and Welsh experience of ever shrinking numbers.

Both the Irish and Scottish networks currently have what appears to be fairly stable funding (certainly in comparison with England and Wales). This allows them to continue with their work. However, we have already commented that the network in Ireland appears to be constrained by the government funding they receive, and it also emerges that there is still a widespread inadequacy in state responses to rape evident across Britain and Ireland. We have already referred to the low conviction rate in England and Wales, and this pattern is replicated across the UK and Ireland.

O'Malley (1996: 376) claims that between 1980 and 1993, the maximum number of convictions for rape in Ireland in any one-year period was 12. This poor level of response continued, as Figure 5.1 shows: in 1996, there were 180 rapes reported to the police, 67 prosecutions and two convictions (Bacik et al., 1998: 264). Research has shown that Ireland has the highest attrition rate in Europe for rape (Bacik et al., 1998; Kelly and Regan, 2001). In 2004, 15 Rape Crisis groups in Ireland received 45,000 calls and saw over 2,200 people face-to-face for support and ongoing counselling (RCNI website). However, DRCC estimated that only 29 per cent of rape victims report the crime to police and that only 17 per cent of those go to trial. Nationally the picture is even bleaker as the RCNI suggest fewer than one in ten complainants in cases concerning sexual violence engage with the criminal justice process at all (RCNI website). Under-reporting and attrition within the system are clearly very serious problems in Ireland.

Figure 5.2 shows the position in Scotland, where roughly one in 20 rapes are reported to the police and conviction levels remain poor. 'In 2000 a total of 562 rapes were recorded by the police. There were proceedings against 50 suspects where rape was the main offence involved, with 27 convictions' (Rape Crisis Scotland website). Such under-reporting of sexual violence is well-known across Europe (Kelly and Regan, 2001) but Ireland, compared to 20 other European countries, experiences the highest number of cases 'falling out of the system' (RCNI website).

All these networks have a common background in radical feminism. They also share issues such as under-reporting and a lack of appropriate response from their respective criminal justice systems. In England and Wales there remains a core of feminist Rape Crisis groups, though the political approach within these shows some signs of diversity, as previous chapters have indicated. In Scotland the network is small but appears to have held fairly closely to

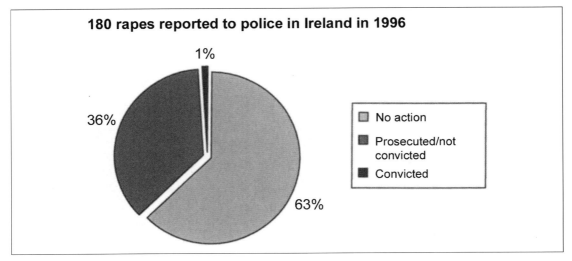

Figure 5.1 Rapes reported in Ireland in 1996

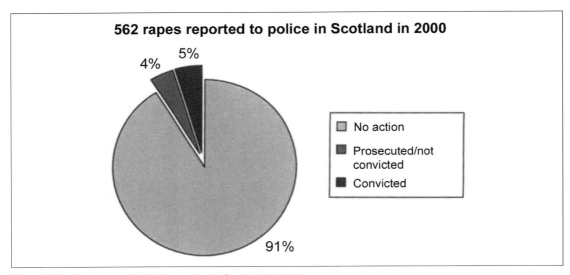

Figure 5.2 Rapes reported to the police in Scotland in 2000

the original Rape Crisis ethos. This may be due, in part, to the existence of other strong feminist agencies in Scotland, such as the influential Women's Support Project, Glasgow (http://www.womenssupportproject.co.uk) and the public education group Zero Tolerance, based in Edinburgh (http://www.zerotolerance.org.uk). However, women in Scotland report pressures we have also seen in relation to the groups in England and Wales. Scottish feminists comment on the 'expectation amongst women who contacted Rape Crisis centres that they would be helped by trained

'counsellors', as well as an assumption on the part of women volunteering for work with Rape Crisis centres that this is what they would become' (Christianson and Greenan, in Breitenbach and Mackay, 2001: 73).

In Ireland, meanwhile, the longest established network is the one with the most secure funding but it has also moved furthest away from its feminist roots. It is argued that one manifestation of this is a tendency for rape to be treated as an individual, medical problem, wherein 'sick' women are 'healed' (Ryan-Larraghy, 1997). Where this happens the original feminist understanding of rape has ceded back to the dominant story of rape as a problem for women and not a problem for society. Clearly this de-politicising of rape results in less effective services. Gillespie (1996) has warned that the provision of services for men should not be at the expense of women, and has further cautioned that the inclusion of men, as staff or service users, renders the gendered nature of rape invisible. Additionally, and as we have already seen, DRCC is an example of a group which has adopted a mainstream professional approach to offering services and sometimes charging money. It is no longer a women-only service, as it offers support for men, and also employs men as counsellors.

This is similar to the position of some groups in England and Wales. Even where a woman-only service has been retained it has been noted that 'the focus was on developing our role as service providers, in contrast with earlier joint work which had been very much focused on campaigning for legal and social change' (Christianson and Greenan, in Breitenbach and Mackay, 2001: 74). We return to the topic of campaigning work in Chapter 6. However, merely because some groups have moved away from their feminist beginnings, this should not be taken to indicate the demise of radical feminism. It does mean that we have to think more carefully about the diversity of services provided and one way of doing that is to look at those that are officially registered, in relation to charity status.

Charitable status

This discussion begins to try to find out how many Rape Crisis centres there are in existence. A good place to start in this quest to establish the range of services is the main registers for charities, the Charity Commission in England and Wales (http://www.charity-commission.gov.uk/registeredcharities/first.asp), the Office of the Charity Regulator in Scotland (http://www.oscr.org.uk), the Voluntary Activity Unit in Northern Ireland (http://www.dsdni.gov.uk/index/voluntary_and_community.htm) and the Irish Revenue Service (http://www.revenue.ie/pdf/sn45.pdf). Comparing data from these different sources uncovers some services that are not listed under the various Rape Crisis websites yet still provide services to survivors of sexual violence.

New legislation has brought the Scottish and English charity legislation into greater alignment. A result of this is a greater restriction on which groups can become charities. Registered charities face a heavier burden of regulation than other 'not-for-profit' organisations but they acquire tax advantages in return. The Charity Commission in England and Wales has a register that can be searched on-line. A simple search using the keyword 'rape' gave 63 results comprising of 35 groups that are listed on the Rape Crisis (England and Wales) website and also some that are not (this search was completed on 15 April 2007 so an update is quite likely to produce different numbers, as discussed above). The current Rape Crisis website is in many ways an historical legacy from the former Rape Crisis Federation which had excluded from its membership any groups working with men (see Chapter 4). For this chapter we were interested in the difference between the list of Rape Crisis groups held on the website and those groups listed on the Charity Commission database. Examination of the stated aims of the groups listed on the Charity Commission database show that only three (Chorley and South Ribble Rape and Sexual Abuse Helpline; Luton and Districts Rape Crisis Centre; Waveney Rape and Abuse Centre) of the 63 groups specifically include men in their *charity objects*. Other listed groups may not actually be in operation, for example the group called 'Safer' (in Sunderland) has never submitted an annual return and probably no longer exists. London Rape Crisis is also listed and is known to have closed some years ago. In other cases, some entries appear to relate to the same group, so that the number of active groups represented here is considerably less than 63. An accurate number is probably around 45, as at 15 April 2007.

If a similar search is run on the Charity Commission database to *include* groups that have been removed from the register (usually because of closure, amalgamation or name change) 93 results are given. These former groups range from the Avon Sexual Abuse Centre, which closed in 1994, to the Rape Crisis Federation which was removed from the register in April 2005 after its closure in 2003. The group in Avon reminds us that not all services for survivors of sexual violence have the word 'rape' in their title. When we amended the search field to the *charity objects* rather than the *title* (still using the key word 'rape') this produced 42 groups. Whilst acknowledging that other charitable organisations provide related services (for example *Survivors UK*, whose charitable objects state that the purpose is to promote the 'benefit of men who have experienced sexual abuse'), the aim of this investigation was to identify services which have a stated focus on 'rape'.

In Scotland there is a similar register of (active) charities. The database of the Office of the Scottish Charity Regulator differs from that of its counterpart in England and Wales insofar as it cannot be searched against the *charity objects* of the group but only keywords in its *title, charity number or address*. Conducting a *title* search on this database, using the keyword 'rape' yielded 16 results; however this included drapers and therapeutic organisations (as the key word 'rape' is contained within words in their title). The 12 groups clearly identified on the register include those on the Rape Crisis Scotland website.

In contrast, there is no concept of a registered charity in Ireland. While the *Voluntary Activity Unit in Northern Ireland* oversees charitable groups in the north, there is no register, and throughout Ireland there is no requirement that charities register: indeed there is no mechanism for registration as a charity. Some organisations include what they describe as their registered charity number on their notepaper but this is merely the charity number allocated by the Revenue Commissioners which recognises the organisation for the purposes of tax laws. A list of such organisations is available on the Revenue's website (The Irish Revenue Commissioners, 2007) and this contains details of most of the groups identified on the Rape Crisis Network Ireland (RCNI) website.

This comparison of the various registers within the Rape Crisis networks that exist in each country shows that most services for survivors of sexual violence that are listed with the Rape Crisis networks in each country are also listed with the state in some way. Importantly, what this analysis shows is that within the voluntary, charitable sector, most support provision is conducted by groups that are part of the Rape Crisis movement. The searches do not reveal a wealth of organisations outside of these networks providing the same services. The sustained histories of these Rape Crisis groups not only speak of the ability of women-centred organisations to survive but also to thrive within an uncertain funding climate. Not all groups make it: the England and Wales Charity

Commission's database of closed groups is testament to that. For many groups survival has been a struggle but one that was worth facing. They have survived because to close would mean a cessation of the only service women had available to them. The next section considers what provision is available from the state and how this differs from that of the voluntary sector.

Mainstream provision

As we have outlined, there is a now 30 year history of Rape Crisis in the UK. The work of the movement has not gone unacknowledged by the state and the government is well aware of lack of funding, patchy police response, low conviction rates and has recently responded to the crisis in sexual violence in investing in Sexual Assault Referral Centres (SARCs) and by funding Independent Sexual Violence Advisors (ISVAs). This discussion attempts to evaluate these alternative models for supporting survivors, with an interest in how they compare to the Rape Crisis model.

As Chapter 2 has discussed, the first SARC opened in Manchester in 1986, and a SARC is in essence an attempt to provide a one-stop legal and health service for someone who has been raped which, as we have already shown, differs from the Rape Crisis model in a number of important ways. In Ireland the equivalent service is known as a Sexual Assault Treatment Unit (SATU) and has been described as 'professional, it's immediate, it's sensitive' (manager Sheila Vereker, cited in the *Irish Examiner*, 30 August 2005). The Sexual Assault Treatment Unit at the Rotunda Hospital Dublin was the first such unit to open in the whole of Europe, in 1984. It operates in close liaison with An Garda Siochana (police) and Dublin Rape Crisis Centre. Despite its long history of service provision only 58 victims of sexual violence were helped in 2001. Whilst this service may be valuable in serving some survivors, it does not reach the majority of those who are raped. A similar argument has already been raised in Chapter 2, with regards to the English SARCs. From the information we have to date we can conclude that Rape Crisis and the SARCs or SATUs do not always work with the same survivors. However, in the UK the Home Office states that SARCs are widely recognised as presenting the way forward for provision of services to victims of rape and sexual assault. In reality though, this sweeping conclusion is not justified. As Chapter 2 has shown, SARC service provision is centred on reporting to the police. Yet, there is insufficient evidence to indicate whether SARCs promote any increase in reporting. It is reasonable to hope that SARCs might improve complainant satisfaction and hence, complainant ability to testify (see below). However SARCs have also been described as a 'more expensive and extensive form of provision than that developed in most areas in the late 1980s and early 1990s' (Lovett, Regan and Kelly, 2004: viii). The Rape Crisis model is capable of serving a far wider cross-section of survivors and provides much better value for money.

SARCs and SATUs also aim to enhance the investigation and prosecution of cases by gathering evidence within a rapid timeframe. Health services such as GUM (Genito-Urinary Medicine) clinics, AandE, and GP surgeries, already deal with the health needs of survivors of sexual assault but offer a varying quality of service. SARCs and SATUs claim to offer consistent standards of care, and research points to high levels of complainant satisfaction (Lovett, Regan and Kelly, 2004). Importantly SARCs and SATUs can offer various services in one location. As Chapter 2 has outlined, services are for men as well as women and there is no legal requirement that there is a formal report to the police (though there generally is). Forensic evidence can however be stored should the survivor decide to make a report to the police in the weeks following the attack.

Some SARCs and SATUs employ a crisis worker or alternatively liaise with the local Rape Crisis group who can provide support throughout the reporting process. Staff are trained to deal with the immediate trauma of sexual violence and this immediate medical care may reduce the likelihood of longer-term support needs and counselling. They typically offer a forensic examination, other medical care such as infection screening and post-coital contraception, therapeutic counselling and the opportunity to make an official statement to the police. At the time of writing there are four SATUs (see Appendix 4). However a recent report suggested that three of these are at risk of closure, due to a lack of state funding (http://www.irishhealth.com/?level=4andid=8978) and the Rotunda Hospital's Sexual Assault Treatment Unit is no longer a 24-hour service

since a decision was taken to close it at weekends in 2006 (http://www.sinnfein.ie/news/detail/16867). There are 15 SARCs (see Appendix 4 for full list) although three of these are in London and there are none in Wales or Scotland. Counselling at SARCs is usually time-limited 'thus service users needing long-term counselling may be referred to other local organisations including Rape Crisis' (Lovett, Regan and Kelly, 2004: 70). There is anecdotal evidence to suggest that in areas where SARCs are established, the number of referrals to Rape Crisis rises, often putting an over-stretched organisation under further strain. Clearly then, as Rape Crisis groups deal with a wider range of cases, they are a useful resource for SARCs where counselling sessions for rape survivors have been exhausted or where survivors of historic abuse approach the SARC and find there is not a service available to them.

It seems then that both models are useful, and adequate need can be demonstrated for both a SARC/SATU and a RCC within any town or city. Research on SARCs has highlighted the importance of having a female doctor (or specialist nurse), the benefit to women of being seen in a non-institutional setting, being respected, and having control over the process (Skinner, 2000): these are features which have been learned from the Rape Crisis model.

Outside of SARC areas women may receive excellent treatment from local police and hospitals: they may also receive awful treatment. Rape Crisis groups get to hear about the good and the bad practice that exists within the statutory system. Women interviewed within Rape Crisis centres provide further evidence:

> *I was contacted by this man from Victim Support. He said he could offer me a shoulder to cry on. I was really shocked. Why did they get a man to contact me? I thought it was really insensitive.*

> *The staff at the SARC were really wonderful but they couldn't keep on giving me counselling sessions.*

> *I went private and paid for counselling recommended through my GP but I wasn't comfortable with the therapist.*

Figure 5.3 shows data from Lovett, Regan and Kelly's research into three SARCs. Many women received the 'best support' from their friends or relatives (St Mary's 53 per cent, REACH 39 per cent, STAR 47 per cent) while only one area rated the SARC as best (St Mary's 18 per cent, REACH

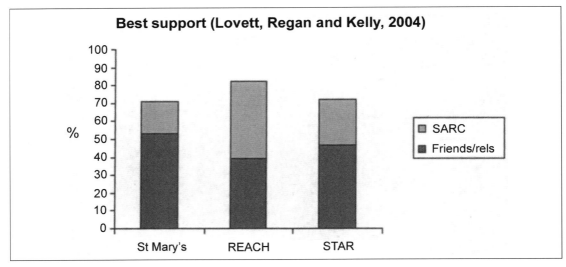

Figure 5.3   Support received from SARCs, friends and relatives

43 per cent, STAR 25 per cent) (2004: 66). This confirms previous research on women's support systems identified by Wilcox (2000: 36) who suggests that while resources should not be taken away from current work on male violence against women and that 'agency support remains crucial', attention to informal networks is also of significance. This was also noted in Ireland where it was found that if a survivor discloses, 'the first person is likely to be a close friend or family member' (RCNI website). Clearly however, Rape Crisis remains important in these instances as Rape Crisis has always offered support to community supporters such as family members. SATUs and SARCs do not replicate this provision.

In all then, SATU and SARC coverage remains geographically patchy and service provision is limited. It rests on a position which assumes that Rape Crisis will pick up cases where SARC resources are exhausted; where the abuse is historic or where the person needing support is a family member or friend. Further critical evaluation of the role of these groups is required as the Home Office sponsored research claims the 'professional group that benefits most directly from a SARC are the police' (Lovett, Regan and Kelly, 2004: 67). Government policy which assumes that SARCs (or SATUs) alone are sufficient service provision is creating further problems for the future and the Rape Crisis lobby needs to be clear and assertive about the plain need for their services.

It is interesting to note, however, that more recently the Home Office has begun to fund another form of support (Independent Sexual Violence Advisors, or ISVAs), perhaps already aware that the SARC model cannot really meet the requirements of survivors. From October 2006, 38 ISVA posts have been funded by the Home Office, with the intention that these workers will be based within SARCs or other specialist agencies and will link in to statutory organisations, helping women to access a range of services (http://press.homeoffice.gov.uk/ press-releases/support-victims-of-sexual-abuse, accessed 10 October 2007). At present it appears that a number of these posts are based within Rape Crisis groups and so this is operating as a roundabout way of validating the work of those organisations. Clearly though, 38 posts, to cover the whole of England and Wales, can only make limited impact.

In conclusion so far then, we can say that Rape Crisis clearly is very important in service provision and appears from our earlier investigations to remain under-resourced at present. We now go on to look at the funding that these groups do attract.

Government funding of Rape Crisis centres

This discussion reviews what we know about government funding of the Rape Crisis model, for the whole of the UK. Chapter 4 discussed the withdrawal of government funding from the Rape Crisis Federation (RCF) in 2003. In England then the only national funding at present is the small grant to the newer group, Rape Crisis (England and Wales). This group covers Wales but as the next section shows, provision in Wales has almost disappeared.

We have already seen that a number of Rape Crisis centres have now gone and that the Federation closed following a withdrawal of government funding. This lack of care for Rape Crisis services was replicated in the North of Ireland when, in 2002, Belfast Rape Crisis Centre also faced funding withdrawal by the state. The Minister from the Department of Health, Social Services and Public Safety, Bairbre de Brún, explained that, 'The Belfast Rape Crisis Centre has only today, made an application to my Department for funding for the current financial year, some eleven months after the period to receive applications opened' (Press Release 30 September 2002). The Department had not received a strategic plan from the centre and so had decided to withhold funding. Fortunately, Belfast Rape Crisis was able to stay afloat for long enough to meet these demands from government. It is naturally disappointing that government departments cannot ask why there are problems with these requirements, rather than simply withdrawing funding from over-stretched services. We view government failures of this kind as particularly problematic, when coupled with the many other disadvantages that women experiencing rape are dealt by a troubled criminal justice system, and in terms of the lack of provision we are uncovering here.

In the south of Ireland funding has also been an issue. Although the government provides some money, this is not considered to be adequate. Speaking to the *Irish Times* in 2004, Fiona Neary, co-ordinator of the RCNI said: 'We know that, under current funding levels, we are not reaching the people we need to reach. Yet year on year we see an increase in people contacting our services. It's an impossible situation'. She added that some centres were not advertising their services because they knew they would not be able to cope with the subsequent increase in demand.

In 2005 a public plea was made by Sinn Féin spokesperson on Justice, Equality and Human Rights, Aengus Snodaigh TD, for the Irish Government to provide additional resources to Rape Crisis services. Pointing out that their clients had to wait between one and six months for counselling, an additional €1 million was called for to allow them to extend their services (Sinn Fein website, 2005). This followed a period where funding had been restricted and indeed, Galway Rape Crisis Centre (GRCC) had been threatened with closure in April 2002, due to a funding crisis. The centre, which conducts over 50 appointments every week, had not had a funding increase from the Western Health Board in three years. The centre's co-ordinator Agnes Warren explained: 'We have a shortfall every month . . . It is a constant battle' (IrishHealth.com, 2003). The position was improved a little when the Rape Crisis Network in Ireland was allocated €50,000 by the new Commission for the Support of Victims of Crime in mid 2005.

In Scotland in January 2004, the Scottish Executive announced funding of £1.76m for Rape Crisis services. Speaking in response to the announced funding Sandy Brindley, Scottish Network co-ordinator, said: 'The Aberdeen Centre only receives around £5,500 core funding a year and has to rely on donations, which gives some idea of the problems our centres face'. Meanwhile, in England and Wales the Home Secretary announced £4 million funding in April 2004 to develop services for victims of sexual assault. A substantial proportion of this has been used to support and increase the number of Sexual Assault Referral Centres (SARCs) including the development of three new SARCs and the extension of services in five existing SARCs. In Wales in 2007, £150,000 was identified from Welsh Assembly Government funding to develop SARCs which may involve partnership with Rape Crisis services. Although some Rape Crisis groups may receive funding from entering into partnership with SARCs, not all groups have benefited from the generosity of the state, with inequalities in services still evident throughout the country, despite assurances from politicians: 'It is vital that the contribution of the sexual violence voluntary sector, and the pressure they relieve from statutory services is recognised on a national and local level' (Paul Goggins, MP, cited in WRC, 2006: 1).

The Victims Fund

The Victims Fund was established in 2004 to provide monies to the voluntary sector and is now overseen by the Ministry of Justice. The

Victims Surcharge, which came into effect on 1 April 2007, is an additional charge payable on top of fines levied by the courts and, it is estimated, will generate up to £16 million a year to maintain the Victims Fund:

> *The Victims Fund supports the development of community based services for victims of sexual offending. The Government has placed £1.25m for the 2007/08 financial year into the Victims Fund to continue developing the capacity and stability of existing voluntary and community sector (VCS) support services for victims of sexual violence and abuse. The grant scheme is open to all existing VCS organisations in England and Wales with experience and expertise in working with victims of sexual violence and abuse*
>
> (Rape Crisis website)

Part of the crisis of funding for Rape Crisis centres emerged in the mid-1990s in 'the context of competition with groups seeking to duplicate RCC work' (Lupton and Gillespie, 1994: 23). This has been exacerbated in 2007 by the allocation of monies from the Victims Fund as defined above (also see Appendix 5). Rape Crisis workers are justified in feeling aggrieved that organisations, who they feel lack the extensive experience that they have gained through years of working with women, are being funded through this money. The funding is given for one year at a time which contravenes the government's own 'Compact' guidelines on funding the voluntary sector and it has been suggested that 'much of the money has gone to set up Sexual Assault Referral Centres (SARCs), and a disproportionately low amount has gone to the frontline women's services' (WRC, 2006: 2). There have been suggestions that Ministry of Justice decisions on which applicants to fund are favouring those organisations who also provide services to men. As we have seen here, the majority of Rape Crisis centres continue to provide services exclusively for women and girls and even those groups that do specifically provide services for men tend to see themselves primarily providing for the needs of women. Yet for over 30 years, Rape Crisis has been the only specialist service providing men with referral services. In a macho world, men have feared the stigma of turning to statutory services and have frequently called Rape Crisis services. This poor level of public funding across the women's voluntary sector is not confined to the UK and Ireland. Smith (2001) has pointed out that in the USA the women's voluntary sector faces the greatest challenge, and that those agencies that provide services for abused women are the most marginalised:

> *In the area of domestic violence services, nonprofit agencies had been operating without federal support, and many without state or local support, for most of their histories ... Shelters were typically funded by a combination of support from foundations, local government grants, private donations, and user fees.*
>
> (Smith, 2001: 434)

Just as funding for services within the women's voluntary sector in general, and the Rape Crisis movement specifically, is under threat, so demand for Rape Crisis services is increasing. In total, few services across England, Wales, Scotland and Ireland receive adequate state funding. In 2007 less than £50,000 was allocated to Wales (see Appendix 5). This was less than any of the geographical regions of England. Those centres that do receive funding are under pressure to conform to non-feminist standards to keep this. Furthermore, the groups which do receive funding have sometimes seen sudden withdrawal of that support, making continued service provision even less secure. On this unhappy note, we turn to examine the network of services that currently exist in England and Wales, and attempt a review of relative wealth and service spread.

A geographical lottery of service

We have now seen that SARC and SATU service provision is incomplete and patchy. We have also indicated that there are considerable variations in Rape Crisis provision across the UK, including the gaps in government funding identified above. This discussion tries to sketch a picture of the current spread of provision of Rape Crisis across England and Wales and at the relative funding for that provision. This exercise is undertaken using the information on the Charity Commission database and completes the picture of Rape Crisis provision today, revealing a geographical lottery of service.

We already know that basic health care provision is not standard across the country. If you live in the South-East of England you apparently have some of the worst-performing services in the country according to 2005 health league tables. Anna Walker, the chief executive of NHS watchdog the Healthcare Commission, was quoted in *The Guardian* as saying the poor performance in the South-east was 'quite striking' (27 July 2005). Similarly, there is also a geographical factor at play determining what sort of response a victim of sexual violence might receive from the police. Even within London a review has revealed geographical differences of approach. In 2005 the Metropolitan Police set up a review into how it conducts rape investigations, after a high-profile case revealed differences in treatment of cases between boroughs. This inquiry was demanded by Judge Martin Reynolds, after a case in May 2005 which:

> ... left a pimp free to repeatedly rape and beat a teenage girl and force her to work as a prostitute. Agrol Xhabri, 22, was jailed for 12 years after abducting the 17-year-old Latvian girl from her father's house in East London last year in broad daylight. Over two months he beat her, threatened to cut her 'into little pieces', raped her around 30 times, strangled her and kept her prisoner in a room, allowing her out only to force her to have sex with other men.
>
> (*The Guardian*, 25 May 2005)

Under the 2002 police Rape Action Plan all forces are required to review their facilities for examining victims of sexual violence. The plan calls for investigating officers dealing with sexual assault cases to be experienced officers. However, in May 2005 a daring piece of investigative journalism by *The Observer* newspaper found that police trainee detectives were being put in charge of complex rape investigations in the Metropolitan Police Sapphire Unit. Launched in 2001, London's 32 Sapphire Units are to investigation what SARCs are to forensic evidence gathering, and have been heralded as the police flagship rape investigation units.

The truth then is that police provision, health care provision and SARCs are all geographically varied. Rape Crisis provision is no different, except in that the well-funded groups are rare and that all groups do strive to provide clear and strong services to any woman who contacts them despite problems with funding.

As one indicator of this we provide here a map of England and Wales, showing the Rape Crisis centres in existence as at 2004, with some idea of their annual expenditure, as an indication of wealth. Figure 5.4 provides this 'at a glance' overview of where groups were geographically at that time, and at their expenditure levels for 2004 as an indication of wealth. This information is drawn from what is available publicly, via the

Charity Commission and shows an acute lack of services in Wales. On this map there are two Rape Crisis centres shown within Wales, but one of these groups has since closed (see below). There is also a lack of provision in the South-West of England, across Devon and Cornwall. Two of the most financially robust groups, Southampton and Portsmouth are in very close proximity to each other but there are few groups to the south-west of these. It is also noticeable that 11 of the 50 groups shown, over 20 per cent, were providing services on less than £10,000 per year.

Returning to the Charity Commission database, some further assessment of the relative affluence of Rape Crisis groups within England and Wales can be conducted, again using the annual expenditure figures and bringing this investigation up to date in 2007. Once more, the first information from this source concerns closures. Table 5.1 shows that seven groups showed partial financial information or no financial history, up to 2007. For groups such as Create, South Wales, Milton Keynes, London and Brighton this is because they have closed and no longer provide a service. The only remaining groups in Wales are a group in Caernarfon and another in South Wales (New Pathways, see Table 5.3) which provides services to men and women. Clearly provision is pathetically stretched. There has been some funding from the Victims Fund but this amounts to less than £50,000 in 2007 for the whole country. In addition there have been moves to provide some more limited funding by the Welsh Assembly. Clearly a real effort needs to be made to create appropriate services for Wales and in total, it is now clear that there are fewer Rape Crisis centres in existence today in England and Wales than there have been at any time since the mid-1980s.

Based on the information reported, 11 groups operated services on an annual expenditure in 2006 of less than £15,000. Clearly such groups are unlikely to be able to afford to employ staff or provide a helpline for more than a few hours per week. Working under such a financial constraint makes it profoundly difficult to provide the level of face-to-face counselling, advocacy and support work to meet demand. Nonetheless, we know well that a number of the groups here have continued to provide services despite these pressures.

Aylesbury runs a helpline, answering around 20 calls per week, offers email support, escort to appointments, befriending, and outreach, and

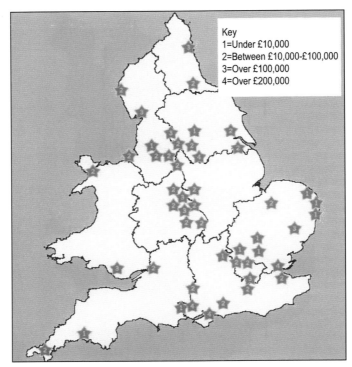

Figure 5.4 Expenditure of Rape Crisis centres 2004

Table 5.1 Expenditure of charities: groups with limited or no financial history (Charity Commission website 4 June 2007)

Name	2003	2004	2007
Create Freedom From Sexual Violence (Tees Valley)	No financial history	No financial history	Removed from register (2006)
Halton Rape Crisis Counselling And Research Group	No financial history	No financial history	No financial history
Milton Keynes Rape Crisis	£6,553	£4,118*	Removed from register (2006)
Rape and Sexual Abuse Line South Wales Limited	£2,905	No financial history	No financial history
Rape Counselling And Research Project (London Rape Crisis Centre)	£18,989	No financial history	No financial history
Safer	No financial history	No financial history	No financial history
The Brighton Rape Crisis Project Limited	No financial history	No financial history	Removed from register (2007)

*Return is for 2005

Table 5.2   Expenditure of charities: groups with less than £15,000 per annum expenditure (Charity Commission website 4 June 2007)

Name	2003 (£)	2004 (£)	2006 (£)
Aylesbury Vale Rape Crisis	7,886	9,845	10,046
Cambridge Rape Crisis Centre	5,454	5,489	5,719
Chelmsford Rape and Sexual Abuse Counselling Centre	5,129	5,390	No financial history
Chorley and South Ribble Rape and Sexual Abuse Helpline	3,443	6,076	No financial history
Dorset Rape Crisis Line	2,949	3,312	3,585
Herts Area Rape Crisis and Sexual Abuse Centre	9,644	8,946	9,312
Norwich Rape Crisis Resource Centre	10,530	9,055	12,263
Plymouth Rape Crisis Line	7,800	8,709	14,252
Suffolk Rape Crisis	781	663	No financial history
Waveney Rape and Abuse Centre	6,300	6,119	5,411
York Rape Crisis Centre	4,960	5,215	No financial history

conducts around ten face-to-face sessions with women each week. The group also replies to consultation documents, participates in multi-agency work and gives talks to local organisations. The group in Herts also runs a helpline once a week for two hours, sees three to five women per week and offers additional support and information on other agencies for family and friends of survivors. Plymouth, which covers a vast geographical area, also offers a helpline and face-to-face services. Their helpline runs three times each week, and in addition they offer facilitated self-help group work.

At the other end of the scale, of the 60 groups identified on the Charity Commission site (see earlier) 12 had expenditure over £100,000 in 2004 and of these, only six had an expenditure of over £200,000 in 2006.

Eight of these 12 groups were successful in their bids to the Victims Fund in 2007, which perhaps suggests that they are better able to jump through the application hoops set by the government. All but one of the groups with an income of over £200,000 were funded by the Victims Fund in 2007 which may indicate that the government feels more secure in their investment into these groups than in the less wealthy groups.

From our case study groups, it is now apparent that Cornwall and Merseyside fall with the majority of the groups, into the middle category of those with expenditure of between £10,000 and £100,000 p.a. It is interesting to note, however, that across England the small number of more wealthy groups is reasonably well spread. It seems possible that the newly constructed national Rape Crisis group could draw on the expertise of these groups to put together some funding tips for all the groups to draw upon.

Plowden (2003: 416) argues that 'Government and voluntary organisations had become indispensable partners for each other in the context of public services. The largest voluntary organisations were large professional entities with thousands of paid staff, and assets and turnover measured in hundreds of millions of pounds ... [and there were other] much smaller groups'. The 'large professional entities' are represented in the UK by big name charities such as Oxfam (2006 expenditure £282.7 million) or Barnardo's (2006 expenditure £165.4 million) which employ thousands of people. In the UK Victim Support is illustrative of a large charity providing support services to its users. Its annual return for the year ending March 2006 showed an

Table 5.3 Expenditure of charities: groups with more than £100,000 per annum expenditure (Charity Commission website 4 June 2007)

Name	2003 (£)	2004 (£)	2006 (£)
Bradford Rape Crisis and Sexual Abuse Survivors Service	104,968	134,206	144,006
Colchester Rape Crisis Line	65,348	106,554	82,974
Coventry Rape and Sexual Abuse Centre	135,595	153,435	170,224
Doncaster Rape and Sexual Abuse Counselling Centre	146,900	200,665	201,681
Derbyshire Rape Crisis	78,520	106,126	212,069
New Pathways (Merthyr Tydfil)	115,567	182,086	286,121
Portsmouth Area Rape Crisis Service	216,681	225,376	193,189
Rape and Sexual Abuse Support Centre Croydon	100,024	161,238	234,734
South Cumbria Rape and Abuse Service	78,640	141,289	113,385
South Essex Rape and Incest Crisis Centre	300,170	258,504	318,676
Southampton Rape Crisis and Sexual Abuse Counselling Service	186,003	203,995	282,702
Tyneside Rape Crisis Centre (Sexual Assault Counselling and Information Service)	140,298	123,903	124,228

expenditure of £31.35 million and most of this income comes directly from government grants. By comparison the total income of even the most affluent Rape Crisis group is minimal. For Victim Support and the government, provision and funding are inter-linked, in the way that Plowden suggests. For Rape Crisis networks in Ireland and Scotland, government has become an important funder. However, as we have discussed this has presented some difficulties in terms of the type of service provision offered, in Ireland. For centre-level funding in England and Wales the government represent a drain on resources as so much is demanded back in responding to consultations, attending multi-agency meetings and liaising with police and other statutory bodies. Chapter 4 has shown that loss of government funding by the RCF proved fatal, so there is clearly a value in retaining independent funding. However, this does tend to mean that poverty has prevailed within Rape Crisis and this has also led to a patchy network of provision, with no centre in London, little provision in Wales and little in the South-West.

Two examples are illustrative. The first is of SERICC, as we have already seen, one of the largest and most well-established Rape Crisis groups in the country. Table 5.3 shows its total

expenditure for the year ending March 2006 as £318,676. SERICC provides a wide range of services (detailed earlier see Chapter 2) and are effective campaigners but they also expend much time and energy, with great success, on fundraising. The second, Milton Keynes Rape Crisis had a total income of £11,102 in the year ending March 2003. A volunteer commented at the RCF annual meeting in 2003 'we are constantly trying to submit funding bids but when they [the funding body] don't even reply, it feels like, well why do we bother?' Milton Keynes Rape Crisis closed in August 2004 due to lack of funding. It could be argued that this is part of a larger trend in cuts in local government funding across the voluntary sector. Under New Labour, local government has been put under greater pressure to constrain funding against targets. The number of Rape Crisis services that have closed since 1999 with York Rape Crisis and Cambridge Rape Crisis being the most recent to close in 2007.

While some Rape Crisis groups continue to provide ever more services to ever more women on what can only be described as shoestring budgets, some groups do not survive. As we have now made clear, a number of Rape Crisis groups have closed in recent years, and the primary reason given is lack of funding. In Ireland, Smyth (1996: 69) writes with concern about the danger of 'being subsumed into and co-opted by the very system feminists set out to challenge and change in the first place'. The same can be said of England and Wales where it has been argued that 'Our knowledge is harvested by the statutory sector . . . and our opinions are used to develop practices and protocols, which we don't get any recognition or funding for' (Maddy Coy, cited in WRC, 2006: 2). While Rape Crisis services in Ireland do receive some financial support from the state, funding levels are inadequate and there is concern that funding comes with strings attached. In Scotland the picture looks healthier, but even there some groups remain seriously impoverished.

Conclusion

This chapter has shown that most services for female survivors of sexual violence come from within the Rape Crisis movement. While state funded SARCs and SATUs exist to serve a criminal justice, evidence-gathering, function and a medicalised first response to physical and health needs, these services are incomplete and patchy. They can only struggle to meet most of the needs of any woman, within such limiting perspectives, and they fail to meet all of the needs of most women. Treating rape simply as a crime or a health issue ignores that what women most need is to be believed and to be heard. These simple needs came first, not from professionals, but from women themselves and this knowledge built the Rape Crisis model. Today, Rape Crisis groups differ in their size, wealth and location but

the skills and expertise of feminist Rape Crisis support and its potential to empower women should not be under-estimated.

The lessons of 30 years in Ireland and Britain show that social change does not come easily, and that it is only when women speak out that such change can be achieved. Today, even women's mainstream magazines are speaking out about the lack of justice available to women. In 2005 *Glamour* magazine organised a petition calling for justice for rape victims. The campaign was prompted by the low conviction rate for rape in England and Wales and by the concern that attacks against women were not investigated. Their survey found that two thirds of women survivors of rape were dissatisfied with the way they were treated after the attack and only half were happy with the way the case was investigated. It is a challenge for Rape Crisis groups to retain their campaigning role as they tackle the endless demand for their services and are threatened by the push to 'compromise their distinctive service philosophy in order to gain wider credibility and financial security' (Lupton and Gillespie, 1994: 8). This chapter has given a flavour of some of the central problems now faced in terms of funding and service security. We have seen that similar challenges face the movements across the UK and Ireland, but that it is the centres in England and Wales that appear to be doing worst, at the present time.

We return to the beginning of the Rape Crisis movement next, in examining the development of campaigning since the early days of the struggle. However, we also consider ways to develop the Rape Crisis network and aim to ensure activism and provision across the UK continues well into the twenty-first century.

CHAPTER 6

Stop All the Raping! Ongoing Campaigns

Introduction

This book began with a review of the foundations of the Rape Crisis movement, and that analysis showed that the idea of Rape Crisis came out of the campaigns and discussions of feminists in the late 1960s and early 1970s, in America. Anti-rape feminism was founded on a wish to change the world, and so the Rape Crisis movement has never used a simple sticking plaster approach to the issue of rape. This chapter brings our consideration of Rape Crisis to a close by taking our discussions back to the campaigning roots of the anti-rape feminists. Here, we consider how the British Rape Crisis movement has worked with groups as diverse as 'Fawcett', 'YWCA', 'Amnesty', and 'Zero Tolerance'. However, we also discuss campaigns which have come directly out of the Rape Crisis movement itself, namely the 'Campaign to End Rape' and the 'Truth About Rape' campaign. Inevitably there will be groups that are not mentioned in this chapter as it is not our aim to document every aspect of each campaign. Instead, we try to give a flavour of the types of campaigning and the ways that the work has developed and changed, since its beginnings in the 1970s.

In this chapter we develop a working model for identifying factors common to anti-rape feminist activism. We are interested in activism in its broadest sense, not only in campaigning in the streets, and so our discussion takes us back once more to the tension between independent campaigning, lobbying work and partnership meetings.

We then examine the emergence of the Campaign to End Rape and test its method of working against our model for feminist campaigning. We then turn our attention to the Zero Tolerance advertising campaigns and assess these as a product of anti-rape feminism. Finally, we look at the newer trend to campaigning using electronic resources online and we use the Truth About Rape campaign as an example of work coming from Rape Crisis which has tried to use some of these newer tools. All of this serves to stress the possibilities for feminist activism but also the importance of that work to the effort to support women who have experienced rape.

We reach the end of our book in this chapter and we conclude by reviewing some of the points coming out of our survey of Rape Crisis provision in the UK and Ireland. The attempt here is to develop some analysis of the kinds of steps that could be taken now, to enable Rape Crisis to continue to provide its valuable services to women, whilst also retaining the radical politics of anti-rape, which help to inform the work but also to sustain the women involved in the movement. First of all though, we begin by looking again at the relationship between the ideas of feminism and the campaigning of Rape Crisis centres.

Framing the issues

Although many groups have been involved in campaigning against rape during the last 30 years, little has been written about their strategies and successes. As Chapter 1 has shown, we do know that the anti-rape movement was created through women's testimony and that 'the huge amount of theory on violence . . . was produced out of practice' (Setch, 2003: 60). The consciousness-raising sessions of the 1970s developed feminist knowledge rooted in the reality of women's lives and this led to activism. Yet, there is little to draw on to establish:

- How the campaigns that followed were run.
- What was paid for and what was done for free.
- Where the money came from.
- Who took which roles.
- Which strategies worked, and which failed, and so on.

Sadly this chapter can only begin to unravel some of these areas, though there is certainly scope for further work in documenting these valuable experiences.

The great mobilisation of women began with a vision, supported by action: 'The vision was of a world transformed' (Dobash and Dobash, 1992: 15).

In the UK, this 'mobilisation' resulted in 'a plethora of activities including legal groups such as Rights of Women (ROW) day nurseries, Rape Crisis centres, battered women's shelters and pro-abortion groups '(Gelb, 1986: 108–9). The Rape Crisis movement set up services, developed policies and practices, formed action groups and, more recently, worked within a multi-agency structure whilst struggling against state authority and male dominance. The political action in all of this and the campaigning strategies within Rape Crisis have been sustained by:

- Radical feminism, as outlined here in earlier chapters.
- Feminist activism, which feeds and sustains the direct work with survivors.
- Connections to and with women's groups working in related areas. Just one example here has been the feminist coalitions set up repeatedly to respond to deportation threats against individual women.
- Critical events, such as the change in the law on rape in marriage, or the war in former Yugoslavia and knowledge of mass rape there.
- External threats, such as funding crises or the appearance of other 'professional' service providers, such as SARCs.
- Criticism and competition from counter-movements, such as the men's movement or the victims' movement.
- Connections to national level organisations, including the short-lived RCF.

Some of the threats here have acted as catalysts for dedicated campaigns (such as the work undertaken by the Manchester group and other groups against funding cuts, discussed in Chapter 2). Some have meant that women have left Rape Crisis, either permanently or temporarily, to undertake different work (for example, women went to former Yugoslavian countries to work with survivors of the rapes there and to work within the international court system, to try to achieve redress for those survivors). What is clear, however, is that a strong political analysis has always aided Rape Crisis work, and the campaigning activities of the groups have always fed and nurtured that analytical framework. The departure of women to work in former Yugoslavia also resulted in more knowledge accrual, when the lessons from those women's experience were fed back into the UK movement.

Rape Crisis grew out of activism, and needs activism to continue to grow. However, the theory behind this activity is also vital. Knowing one's own position and having something to criticise are essential to any form of campaigning, and this framework, together with support (from new activists and national level organisations), has fostered the Rape Crisis movement since centres first began to open in the 1970s. Without a philosophical basis, without goals to be achieved and the feeling that you are making a difference in the world, the best-funded of groups might wither. The twin aims of the movement were to change society and support women. Campaigns were central to the politics of meaning-making for the anti-rape movement. The consciousness-raising sessions of the 1970s had given rise to bundles of narratives which developed a collective identity through shared understandings but it was campaigning that consolidated shared identity and which cemented the commitment to change.

The nature of campaigning has, however, changed over the years. Early Second Wave Feminists identified themselves quite differently from the traditional women's groups that had survived the political gender doldrums of the 1940s and 1950s (Gelb, 1986). Women's organisations such as the Women's Institute, the Fawcett Society, National Council of Women and the YWCA (see Glossary) were seen as having little in common with the Women's Liberation Movement of the 1970s and 1980s. These older groups worked for women, but within traditional female roles. Women's liberation is about changing the meaning of what it is to be a woman. Nevertheless, links were forged, as the 1990s saw the political climate move towards a rights agenda and a more feminism-slanted understanding of male violence against women was accepted by mainstream society. Whilst this mainstream was still likely to resist the idea that 'any man is a potential rapist' (per Brownmiller, and discussed in Chapter 1) there was a baseline shift towards an understanding of rape as a misuse of power. Feminist journals such as *Trouble and Strife, Eve's Back, off our backs* (still produced, see http://www.offourbacks.org/, and see the Glossary for more on these publications) and *Spare Rib* stimulated this shift in analysis together with anti-rape group newsletters and academic texts.

What this has resulted in is a much more disparate range of campaigning styles and approaches than we originally saw in the 1970s. When 'Rights of Women' and others were fighting for laws on rape in marriage, the style and the philosophy was clear-cut. The coalition that was the 'Rape in Marriage' campaign was clearly rooted in anti-rape feminism. Campaigning against rape now spans a wide range of areas, initiatives, and perspectives which strive for social change.

Identifying the feminist model

Bearing this in mind it is perhaps worth spending a little energy in trying to outline the original feminist version of anti-rape campaigning, in order to evaluate the shifts that have occurred since and to allow us to identify the modern campaigns which still draw on these, now traditional, models of work.

As Chapter 1 shows, early campaigns called attention to the issues and to poor provision and protection offered by the state by holding conferences and speak-outs, publishing leaflets, holding street demonstrations and vigils or by writing to newspapers and MPs. Other forms of activism were also directed towards creating change. London Rape Crisis produced their book as one form of activism, and gave the clear message that 'rape is the responsibility of men . . . We cannot take responsibility for prevention' (London Rape Crisis Centre, 1984: 115) thus raising awareness of the anti-rape movement's philosophy in the process. Much of this early work was small scale and somewhat ad hoc. WAVAW groups (Women Against Violence Against Women) were independent and carried out campaigns of direct action, against shops selling pornography, through pickets, demonstrations, sit-ins and other strategies. All of these campaigning activities allowed women to learn that they had a voice and could use it and it would be wonderful to find ways to keep this sense of possibility within the Rape Crisis movement. With this in mind, we now try to identify some common factors of campaigning which makes the effort feminist.

It can be argued that successful campaign strategies share similar characteristics and objectives:

1. Personal or group interests intersect with political imperatives to conceive the need for a campaign.

2. The campaign message (and available resources) determines and frames the manner of transmission of information.
3. If successful, the campaign captures public and political attention and provokes a response.
4. Public or political opinion is influenced. Legal, policy or societal change follows.

We might use the Rape in Marriage campaign as an example here. The personal and group interests of women within the movement came together with the imperatives of growing public and legal awareness of a potential problem in the law. The problem identified was the age-old exception to rape law which said that no man could rape his wife. The need to transmit this message to a wide audience, including lawyers and politicians, helped to determine the types of strategy which the group used to highlight their message (see: Radford, 1990, 1991, on this campaign). Public attention was captured by an exception which seemed very out of step with the society of the late 1980s. Women who saw themselves as equals within society were shocked to learn of the ongoing existence of this formal male privilege. Responses came from many quarters, including a Law Commission Report (discussed by Radford, ibid.) and subsequent legal journal coverage which named 'our warrior feminists' as the group responsible for this debate (Glanville-Williams, 1991: 205). Eventually and rather grudgingly the courts began to move on this issue, finally allowing that the exemption was out of date, in a House of Lords case in 1991 (*R v R* [1991] 3 WLR 767). This decision was (unsuccessfully) challenged as an infringement of the man's human rights (*CR v UK* 48/1994/495/577) showing that the campaign does not always end when change appears to be achieved. Finally the law was formally re-worded by parliament (in the Criminal Justice and Public Order Act 1994) although research demonstrates that even this successful campaign did not bring all the results we need in practice. Sadly, it is still true that cases of 'relationship rape' are generally harder to prosecute than many other types of cases (Harris and Grace, 1999) despite the knowledge that rape in marriage *is* now a crime (rape in marriage within Scotland has been discussed separately, in Chapter 5).

This example does show the four signifiers of successful campaigns above, but this model can also be applied to many non-feminist campaign strategies (try it out in relation to drink-drive public awareness, for example). Taylor has used a different threefold model to understand the particular strategies of social activism: 'shifting political opportunities and constraints, the forms of organisation used by groups seeking to mobilise, and variations in the ways that challenging groups frame and interpret their grievances and identities' (Taylor, 1999: 12). By understanding these aspects we may be able to unpick and identify the common facets of feminist anti-rape activism, as opposed to broader campaigning strategies.

The importance of Taylor's 'shifting political opportunities and constraints' can be seen in a move away from a mass-movement optimism of the 1970s anti-rape movement towards the more isolated and pessimistic approach of some of the work in the 1990s, outlined above. Feminist anti-rape activism has always been at its most creative and influential when it has been drafted by women closely involved in direct work (such as the LRCC book) and when it has struggled to find an outlet, despite scarce resources ('Reclaim the Night' marches or early feminist conferences are strong examples here, discussed briefly in Chapters 1 and 4). If we want to identify the factors influencing this finest version of feminist anti-rape work then the signifiers might be links to women's testimony and a determination to succeed despite a lack of resources.

Forms of organisation are identified by Taylor as another key facet and these have always been crucial to anti-rape feminism. As this book has shown, the collective is a part of the activism of feminism. It is not a mere organisational choice but an attempt to live in the type of society which feminism aims to create. By working in a non-hierarchical manner, feminism has sought to create mini-societies without power differentials. Clearly then, campaigning work within feminism can be expected to be modelled on consensus working, and on knowledge and power-sharing. Finally, Taylor tells us to look at the ways in which campaigns frame their 'grievances and identities' for commonalities. Naturally, anti-rape feminism should name itself as women-centred and political. It should use the language of the anti-rape movement and not that of therapy. 'Women' should be 'fighting' for 'change', rather than 'victims' 'asking' for 'help'.

Commonalities of the activism at the root of the Rape Crisis movement can now be suggested as:

- Drawing from women's lived-experiences and creating activism despite a lack of resources.
- Based on collectivity.
- Expressly feminist, political and conscious of the use of language.

We return to this model in the following discussion, but turn next to look in a little more detail at the ways in which campaigning has developed over time.

Out of our ghetto and into the world

As Rape Crisis centres became more embedded within the towns and cities of the UK, so they became more able to provide a base for activism and develop a campaigning strategy. When a town has a Rape Crisis centre the local media can consult with it to add weight to media reports, while the local health and social services, the SARC and probation service will see it as a valuable (and usually free) resource. In the 1970s and 1980s the vested interests of a Rape Crisis centre intersected with political injustices, leading to campaigns based on raising awareness (utilising demonstrations, speak-outs, banners, placards, posters and leaflets) to catch the eye of the local media and lead to further public and political response.

Feminist political commentators have charted the shift in feminist activism during the 1980s where 'women's movement activists were becoming much more inclined to deal with state organisations' (Lovenduski, 1995: 125). This should not be seen as an over-arching transition from one style of campaigning to another. Feminist debate throughout the 1980s to the current day continues to see tussles over the question of what is appropriate campaigning. The 1980s and 1990s saw Rape Crisis becoming a more mainstream part of the social world of many communities where 'groups have had to perform a delicate balancing act between maintaining a commitment to feminist theory and practice, while working closely with the more traditional mainstream agencies' (Lupton and Gillespie, 1994: 5; also see Chapters 2 and 3). The move towards multi-agency partnership for example, meant that anti-rape activists could move from standing outside and shouting, to sitting indoors and talking. It was suggested that feminist campaigning could be less public but more influential as negotiation techniques were learned to make the message more palatable to government, locally and nationally and as the political structure changed (Heidensohn, 2000; Gregory and Lees, 1999). From banners and placards, campaigning moved to also include consultation papers and advisory committees. Randall has discussed the 'tendency for feminists to achieve positions of influence within government' in some places, but cautions that their impact might be 'severely circumscribed by the over-riding priorities and perspectives of the extremely male-dominated party-state hierarchy' (Randall, 1998: 202).

Susan Faludi takes this analysis further in her influential work, *Backlash: The Undeclared War Against Women*. She charts the achievements of feminist activism but also the 'counter assault on feminism' (Faludi, 1992: 70). Focusing initially on the US but later extending her analysis to include Britain, she outlines how 'increasing political leverage of feminist interests and the infiltration of a "feminist network" into government agencies' resulted in a myriad of counter measures against the Women's Liberation Movement (ibid.: 265). She attacks the myth of feminist influence in the political arena by showing that, at that time:

> ... in the UK, more than nine out of ten appointments made by the Ministry of Defence, the Department of Energy and the Inland Revenue were men. And even though, in the law profession, there are, according to Helena Kennedy QC, 'very able, bright women who could be made judges tomorrow, such QCs as Barbara Mills, Head of the Serious Fraud Office [since appointed Director of Public Prosecutions] Mary Arden in Family Law, criminal lawyers Ann Curnow and Ann Mallalieu, and civil lawyer Barbara Dohmann', none has at the time of writing been appointed to the bench. There are only two female High Court judges out of 83, and only 19 female Circuit Court judges out of 426.
>
> (ibid.: 399)

Speaking to the Association of Women Solicitors in March 2007, Mrs Justice Dobbs reviewed the evidence and research, and quoted an Equal Opportunities Report which concluded that at the current rate of appointments to the High Court 'it will take about 40 years for women to reach an equal number to that of men on the bench' (Dobbs, J. (120307)).

This imbalance in government positions and judicial appointments is the reality against which any feminist gains needs to be set. It is also the backdrop to closer involvement with mainstream

politics. With this context a 'backlash against women's rights succeeds to the degree that it appears not to be political, that it appears not to be a struggle at all' (Faludi, 1992: 16). From the early days of activism, feminists have been aware of the dangers of co-option into the mainstream. Sitting indoors and talking carries risks in terms of the watering down of feminist political demands for change. Charles (2000: 148) confirms this and warns that the 'muting of the feminist challenge is achieved in capitalist societies by the transformation of feminist organisations into bureaucracies, and that is brought about through engaging with the state'.

The anti-rape movement now works much more closely with government and state agencies than in the past. This engagement, and the concomitant requirement to be accountable, poses threats to non-hierarchical ways of organising and to women-only services. Many Rape Crisis centres are now partners within multi-agency groups at a local level and this is important so that the voices of those who are most affected by male violence can be heard. However, while energies are expended on partnership working, evidence from our questionnaire suggests that very few Rape Crisis centres are involved in other forms of campaigning work. It is essential that the 'community and voluntary sector must find a balance between participating in social partnership, campaigning, advocacy and protest' (Broaderick, 2002: 107). A danger exists in the impact of campaigning being seen, not as an outcome of an effective message skilfully delivered, but as 'dependent on external factors such as political environment and resources available' (Gelb, 1986: 103). As women are co-opted into the mainstream through the application of 'partnership' so we become more aware of the competing pressures faced by statutory agencies, and so we may be less strident in our claims for change and for resources. All of this demonstrates that it is vital to retain clarity about the reasons for engagement with the mainstream of central or local government. To retain feminist independence is to remain true to the women using the Rape Crisis service. It appears that this requires an independent campaigning agenda.

A central concern is whether involvement in multi-agency partnerships opens the door to participation for women's groups, or whether the demands of multi-agency working constrain the actions and silence the voices of women's groups.

Keeping women's groups on board has at times been a concern of ideological necessity. Where the women's voluntary sector has been involved, state agencies have taken the moral high ground, claiming consultation through the inclusion of the sector. A good example of this occurred in the Government White Paper which preceded the Sexual Offences Act 2003. This document boasted about taking the views of Rape Crisis on board at the same time as the government withdrew funding from the Rape Crisis Federation. Charles (2000: 155) suggests that incorporation can act to 'redefine the issue of male violence against women . . . presenting it in gender neutral terms and robbing the issue of its capacity to challenge oppressive gender relations'. But more than this, perhaps, the women's voluntary sector has been kept involved because keeping it actively involved in the multi-agency partnership diminishes the resources available to it to mount alternative strategies and challenge the state. If Rape Crisis becomes a 'partner' it can be tamed, and Faludi's articulation of the quiet nature of 'backlash' is demonstrated successfully. The Rape Crisis movement came of age when Tony Blair became Prime Minister but its maturity was ignored by many in its dealings with multi-agency partnerships in the 1990s. Whilst not dismissing the evident benefits that a multi-agency approach can bring to the issue of male violence against women, we are in need of a critique. From a purely statistical point of view, partnership working does not appear to be reducing male violence against women. It may be that it is enough that women's groups are being included in partnership working, that a start has been made. But women's roles within partnerships have traditionally been of secondary status in the private sphere, and we should not be surprised if that is how they are perceived within the public sphere. From being powerless and excluded, caution is required to ensure that inclusion within partnerships does not result in exhaustion or assimilation and even less power. We have already demonstrated that these 'partnerships' are not relationships of equality but are complex mechanisms. The Rape Crisis movement is beginning to question whether it has the energies and resources to continue to participate in multi-agency partnerships. Involvement in partnerships requires time and effort, and these are scant resources within the movement. It is a costly business for the Rape Crisis movement to maintain representation on multi-agency partnerships and government consultancy panels in addition to maintaining service provision.

This helps to show that there is a stark set of choices to be made by any Rape Crisis group. Each has to choose, on a decision-by-decision basis, whether it is better to be inside and talking, or outside and shouting. These choices are always accompanied by balancing considerations of energy and woman-power against constraints of funding and perceived effects on that funding of co-operation or non-co-operation. It is in this complex climate that campaigning has tended to ebb within Rape Crisis centres. In the following discussions we give other examples of forms of campaigning and coalition working, sometimes with agencies with a liberal rather than radical feminist approach. We begin this further discussion by examining the formation and development of two campaigns, which came directly from the Rape Crisis movement and which have been variously influential in raising awareness and in affecting government policy and legal change.

Campaign to End Rape

Campaign to End Rape (CER), a radical feminist group, was formed following the Brighton conference on violence against women (see Glossary) in 1997 (the conference which launched CER has already been mentioned briefly in Chapter 4). The idea for the campaign came from a workshop Kate facilitated with other women at Brighton (according to the abstracts from Brighton this was due to be Liz Kelly and Jan Jordan but Kate thinks that Linda Regan might have stood in for Jan on the day). This workshop was fabulously attended, by women from the UK and many other countries. As a result, a network was set up, which for a short time tried to keep in touch with all of these women. Sadly, in the days before email was commonplace, this did not survive. However, the UK-based section of this mailing list did become the founding members of the Campaign to End Rape and the surviving address lists and other early correspondence demonstrate that many Rape Crisis centres were represented amongst these founding women (archive currently held by Kate). Other Rape Crisis centres came on board in the following months and much of the early speaking work of CER was undertaken at Rape Crisis centres across the country, generally at their AGMs. Early funding was by donation only, but at various points the RCF helped out with finance and spread the word about this fledgling campaign.

The early CER group had three main campaigning platforms, all of which concerned the law on rape but which centred on both the letter of the law and its practice. These aims came out of knowledge gained by Kate, Liz and others via Manchester Rape Crisis, of the problems with the law on rape in practice. They therefore met the first of the criteria above, stemming closely from women's lived experience. The work was undertaken with no formal funding, though the launch conference was paid for by the RCF and Justice for Women, rather than directly by CER (which had no money at that time). The group began as a collective and continues to this day to operate without any formal hierarchy. In the early days of the campaign great efforts were made to ensure that women from around the UK had a voice in the aims and direction of the work and women were encouraged to set up local CER groups. In the event these groups did not come into being in any number and the campaign continued with a core group of women facilitating the work and issuing a newsletter to keep the campaigning group as broad as possible. The third signifier we identified above was to be expressly feminist and careful in use of language, and CER has always been clear about its radical politics and has spoken about women, rather than victims (Cook, 1997, describes the foundations of this campaign).

Here then is a 1990s campaign, which tried to provide an outlet for the campaigning drive of Rape Crisis group members who could not always find the time to organise initiatives independently. The group was lobbying on issues which concerned the law. CER was immediately involved in work at a national level and the messages it wanted to send had to be addressed broadly. This meant that the group was open to forming coalitions, and when the YWCA signed up as members they also showed they wanted to become actively involved by offering to fund an advertisement in the national press. This aimed at improving the lot of women who were taking cases through the criminal justice system. The advert was supported by a huge range of women's groups, including CER, the RCF, Zero Tolerance, Fawcett, Southall Black Sisters and many others. Its strap line read 'Is this what rape victims really deserve?' (archive materials).

Immediately then, working with a wider range of women's groups resulted in a watering down of one of the identifying features of feminist anti-rape campaigning, when the language of the advert abandoned the traditional feminist avoidance of the term 'victim'.

Nevertheless, the working relationship with the YWCA flourished for a time and was particularly helpful to the fledgling CER in creating the possibility for national lobbying during the passage of the Youth Justice and Criminal Evidence Act 1999, which aimed to provide more protections to 'vulnerable' witnesses in court and to tighten the rules on the admissibility of sexual history evidence in sexual offence cases. Both of these aspects were high on the CER agenda and, with the mailing lists and funding of the YWCA, the new campaign began to contact all MPs and lobby widely. CER was able to ensure that the message, rooted in Rape Crisis ethos, about the importance of protecting women's testimony and about not digging in women's sexual history, was made broadly known.

CER continued to lobby and work towards changes in the law and was given a representative seat on the Sexual Offences Review (the CER member was Sandra McNeill), which meant that the existence of the campaign allowed an extra seat at the table to be taken by someone representing women's experience. We have written elsewhere in more detail about the importance of this campaign in its lobbying capacity (Cook and Jones, 2007), but the effects of this high-profile work on the constitution of the group has not previously been documented more widely.

CER survives, and continues to see its main role as being to lobby at a national level in relation to any aspect of the law on sexual offences. By 2001 women within CER were concerned that the group had slimmed down, almost to a panel of 'experts'. The topics we discussed at meetings required such a detailed knowledge of the law that women from Rape Crisis groups were often put off from becoming more directly involved. The group was operating on a consensus model, but the size of the group reaching agreement was now small indeed.

During this period the group had discussions about how to open things up again and get more women involved. There was a recognition that the legal work was difficult to invite many women into but that there was much left to be done in other areas. As a result, an open meeting was organised, for January of 2002, in London. This was advertised as widely as possible, but with the bill being paid by the RCF there was an inevitable tendency for Rape Crisis to be the core of the group that finally met. In a lively and inspiring meeting, women got together to discuss how to bring the anti-rape message to a wider audience. As a result, the Truth About Rape (TAR) campaign was launched in November of that year. At the launch in Manchester funds were raised by auctioning items donated by 'famous women', including a splendid top from Barbara Windsor, signed books and DVDs (Josephine Cox and Sarah Waters) and cartoons by Jacky Fleming. In fact TAR has been lucky to have Jacky's involvement from the beginning, which goes a long way to explaining why the visuals this group has produced have been so striking. Taking a multi-media approach TAR set up a website and began an email membership list which now spans the globe. By the time of the launch the group had developed a set of six postcards to use as public education tools, and the anti-rape campaign was once again available to be opened out to a wider membership. Later a further set of six cards were developed and at the time of writing, more are underway.

Both TAR and CER are still working now, and we return to discuss TAR further when looking at electronic communications in feminist campaigning work. Before that, however, we will look briefly at one other mass-campaign, the Zero Tolerance Charitable Trust, whose Scottish-based public awareness work began in the 1990s.

Zero tolerance

A new form of campaigning emerged when a small group of women in Scotland got together in the early 1990s to develop a feminist campaign, aimed at raising public awareness of violence against women. In a sense this was a 'truth about rape' campaign and we include it here as an example of a feminist-inspired successful campaign and as one inspiration behind the later TAR group. The Zero Tolerance (of violence against women) model was borrowed from earlier campaigning work in Canada, so this was new only to the UK and Ireland (see http://www.zerotolerance.org.uk/index.php last accessed 20.07.07).

While issue-led public education campaigning has a long history, rape and sexual violence have not been amongst the topics traditionally covered by the state and were largely absent from the policy debates in the 1970s and 1980s (Harwin et al., 1999). Until the early 1990s, the only form of state-sponsored advice to women tended to depict them as victims and implied that women should limit their own activities to safeguard against attacks from violent men. Such tactics continue to be used, for example during a spate of murders of women in Ipswich in 2006, when the leader of Suffolk County Council appealed to all women in the town not to venture out alone (*Daily Telegraph*, 13 December 2006). Yet despite these messages from official sources, it has been feminists who have been the target of criticism for promoting a climate of victimisation. There have been suggestions that feminist analysis and language 'transforms perfectly stable women into hysterical, sobbing victims' (Roiphe, 1993: 112).

Roiphe's analysis is that by offering women protection, women's autonomy is compromised and women are constructed as helpless (Cook and Jones, 2007). Far from depicting women as victims, the 1990s saw public awareness campaigns that depicted women as strong and defiant: 'No longer advice-laden missives, campaign materials became eye-catching and thought provoking' (Jones, 2003).

A leading influence in this switch was the Zero Tolerance (ZT) campaign. Public awareness campaigns can have influence on individuals and society but much of the impact of a campaign depends upon how it is conceived (Burton, 1990). The images and slogans of the ZT campaign promoted the message and directly challenged the behaviour of men. The first campaign concerned prevalence (and the posters can still be seen on the Zero Tolerance website) and featured the strap-line 'No Man Has the Right', emphasising that 'violence against women and children is a crime'. Later work focused on the excuses abusers give, justice issues and respect(-ful behaviour).

As the website still evidences, Zero Tolerance came from a strong feminist background and derived its power from its clarity of approach based on three factors:

- Its grounding in a feminist understanding of male violence against women.
- Its consistency of approach.
- Its repetition of the message that no man has the right to violate women.

Launched in November 1992, the first Zero Tolerance campaign was funded by Edinburgh Council's Women's Committee. The campaign was developed following concern about a research study of students aged 12–16 years old at three local schools (Kitzinger and Hunt, 1994) in which a large percentage of the boys said they would probably use violence in their own future relationships.

> *The Zero Tolerance campaign designers recognised that if they were to move feminist ideas into mainstream thought, it was essential that the images used were not of battered, bruised and defeated women but ordinary women, women going about their everyday business. It was important to show that abused women are **people like us** to avoid the tendency to marginalise abused women that had often resulted from previous campaigns.*
>
> (Jones, 2003 emphasis in original)

By inverting the typical 'victim' imagery the ZT campaign aimed to challenge social myths and provoke public and political response. This campaign used feminist ideas and worked within a mainstream forum, gaining funding from local councils, and eventually moving on to work with government. The Zero Tolerance campaign was founded on the feminist belief that male violence against women is fundamental to the social control of women and took the position that male violence against women is a crime. From its inception, Zero Tolerance targeted the state's failure to prevent, control or punish male violence against women and its equal failure to provide for the needs of women.

> *For campaigns on social issues, a simple but focused message is often the most effective form of communication . . . Messages need to be clear, concise and relevant. It is through the use of simple images and snappy slogans that the public absorbs the message. This can open the door to public debate and help the ideas behind the slogans gain political legitimacy.*
>
> (Jones, 2003)

It is worth considering whether a major endeavour like Zero Tolerance conformed to our model of feminist campaigning. We have tested campaigns to see if they draw directly from women's experiences. This campaign was founded on feminist research into violence against women and fought hard to get the messages of that research to a wider audience. In the strictest sense then, it was one step removed from the experience of women. However, the early campaigns were also evaluated, using focus group discussions and so, in this sense, the work was based directly on lived experiences. ZT have also gone on to commission other studies and remain concerned with direct work. So, in this sense we can say that ZT comes from a feminist anti-rape campaigning model. Here though, is an example of feminist campaigning work which did have major funding, although that was never the multi-million pound funding of the mainstream charities (Oxfam, Victim Support, etc. discussed in Chapter 5). This was simply big money by the standards of feminist anti-rape work. Nevertheless, this did make the work different from other forms of campaigning in the UK movement.

In examining campaign models, we are also interested in the structure of the organisations. The Zero Tolerance Charitable Trust was set up formally in 1995 (according to the ZT website) and there was a hierarchy imposed here by the legal structure of charitable bodies (with a Board of Trustees overseeing the work of the employees). Prior to that formal step, however, the earlier work of the group was conducted along a fairly traditional feminist structure and in this respect clearly grew from the experience of women working in direct services.

Finally, we have been concerned to examine whether the group is political, and expressly so, and whether there has been an awareness of the use of language. The website belonging to ZT still makes the feminist aims of the group clear and ZT is probably a prime example of a group who found it necessary to be especially careful about the use of language. Simply because their messages were so public they were struggling from the early days to retain that feminist message and hold off the challenges of co-option, in the form of a watering-down of their images and words. In this sense then, ZT is clearly an example of anti-rape campaigning.

It can be argued that the 1990s Zero Tolerance campaigns were the finest moment which anti-rape feminist campaigning has yet seen in the UK. Of course, it has not been successful in all areas. As the campaigns grew and were taken on by different council areas, they were sometimes used as 'low cost options for some local authorities wishing to be seen to be taking some action' (Harwin et al., 1999: 37). Political expediency was forecast almost before the campaign began. Commenting on The Home Affairs Select Committee on Domestic Violence, Roz Foley argued, 'if we let non-feminist institutions co-opt this [Zero Tolerance] kind of campaign, what we will get will be the usual crap that puts the onus on women to change our behaviour, and not on men to change theirs' (Foley, 1993). Despite this, Zero Tolerance has been immensely influential in steering public awareness campaigns away from victim-blaming strategies and the use of victim imagery. Utilising the typology of campaigning described earlier, the Zero Tolerance campaign joined feminists interested with the political move towards multi-agency working, helped to challenge myths and disputed the simplifications and misleading assumptions surrounding male violence against women. The campaign asked key questions of the quality and efficiency of responses by statutory agencies and, in its use of researched data and statistics, made public the injustices experienced by women. Using public awareness campaigning to deliver its message, the Zero Tolerance campaigns have provided a portable model that has been used as far away as Australia and have also influenced other 'second-generation' campaigns such as Operation Kvinnofrid in Sweden: 'Operation Kvinnofrid deals with changing people's attitudes, which is a slow process. Kvinnofrid is not a project – it is a long-term operation' (Gunilla Sterner (Head of Equal Opportunities Division, County Administrative Board of Stockholm), Rapport, 1999: 7).

Real space meets cyberspace: campaigning by computer

In the twentieth century it was argued that 'in each nation the [feminist] movement adapted to the history, culture and politics of its own society' (Gelb, 1986: 103): increasingly though, we may be able to learn from one another in the twenty-first century age of global communication and the internet. This chapter has already shown that there is much continuity between early campaigning in the advent of Second Wave Feminism and the current day. However there are also differences in the forms of activism undertaken by feminists today. Feminist groups continue to take direct action as well as participating in partnership approaches and being involved in lobbying. There are also continuities in relation to groups who reject state funding and regulation. CER still operates on a shoestring budget to try to influence the direction

of public policy responses to rape. ZT continues to work in the public sphere, using public education tools. TAR has also moved on, since its earliest forays into public awareness campaigning, though it too continues to work without mainstream funding, in a bid to retain true independence.

It may also be time for the Rape Crisis movement in the UK to work more on electronic resources, moving on from information-giving websites to developing more interactive forms of work using electronic media. It is clear now that considerable amounts of campaigning are undertaken by many individuals around the world, without ever leaving the armchair. Groups like *Make Poverty History* have shown that mass-participation campaigning can be fed by online involvement (see www.makepovertyhistory.org/ last accessed 20.07.07). This final discussion also shows how a few feminist groups are using electronic media to campaign effectively, before we bring our book to a close by trying to draw together all of the strands for change we have canvassed within this volume.

Blogs, wikis, chatrooms, discussion (or message) boards and websites are new information streams which, unlike the magazines of yesteryear, flow back and forth between reader and contributor. Today the information consumer is just as likely to be the information producer. In the world of electronic media, the truth about rape seems increasingly complex as multiple voices tell their stories and consciousness-raising becomes global in its reach.

These forums provide new ways for women to communicate, plan action and make a difference. From the feminist inspired *Bush Telegraph* (www.bushtelegraph.uk.com) which provides a place for conversations and comments, to the *Holla Back* initiative (http:// hollabacknyc.blogspot.com/) which encourages women to take photographs of harassers and post them on the site:

> . . . Holla Back NYC empowers New Yorkers to holla back at street harassers. Whether you're commuting, lunching, partying, dancing, walking, chilling, drinking, or sunning, you have the right to feel safe, confident, and sexy, without being the object of some turd's fantasy. So stop walkin' on and holla back: send us pics of street harassers!

In some senses these are simply modern methods of re-inventing the feminist newsletter or the feminist 'Ogle-in':

A bunch of us would gather on a street corner and turn the tables on leering, lip-smacking men by giving them a taste of their own medicine . . . It was incredibly liberating to reverse the wolf whistles, animal noises, and body-part appraisals that customarily flowed in our direction.
(Brownmiller, 1999: 195–6)

Holding men accountable does, however, now have worldwide potential through the medium of the internet. In addition, the low-cost reality of internet-based activism must not be under-estimated. Perhaps the new Rape Crisis co-ordinators could look for funding for women to work as online campaigners? Or to develop online support resources? There are ideas within these reinventions of traditional feminist techniques which the Rape Crisis movement might be able to co-opt for itself.

TAR is one feminist activist group in the UK that has tried to develop a web presence which is more than merely an information point. As we have already seen, this campaign, which was launched officially in November 2002, began as a feminist activist group which wanted to work with public education messages. It drew inspiration from ZT but without looking for mainstream funding. When TAR launched, its key priorities were to establish clear campaign aims and objectives, develop a postcard campaign and construct a website. The first work from TAR was a set of six postcards which highlight the ridiculous nature of some of the commonly held beliefs surrounding rape. The tool of parody was used, to ask people to reconsider the 'truth about rape'. At the time the campaign had very few funds (for which read, no money!) and so it decided to utilise a free website service to claim an internet presence for the campaign. TAR was never in a position to pay an outside organisation to design or maintain the site but was fortunate that Helen had the skills and the time to do this. This free site received over 5,000 visits in its first six months, indicating a real interest in the issues and the value of a website as a medium of communication. The website provides examples of media reports on rape, a section on the campaign postcards, a page specifically for students and also a members-only section. After receiving some donations from supporters, the campaign was able to afford its own site in summer 2003 which really opened up the potential of the website. It now includes information on legislation, and the group has tried to make this site interactive, by encouraging

contributions from members and by launching a discussion group for survivors of rape, accessed through the TAR website. The site also showcases a second series of postcards which take the form of a 'Rape Quiz', with one question and answer on each of the six cards. The most recent phase of the campaign is to move into the global social networking world of Facebook and there is a link to this from the homepage of the website.

TAR has received messages, comments and enquiries not only from across the UK but also from Europe, Canada, New Zealand, Africa, Asia and the USA. Everyone involved is a volunteer, there is no hierarchy, and no-one makes any money from the campaign. Although the active membership remains relatively small, there is a much larger group of members who receive information from the campaign, and many Rape Crisis centres within the UK are a part of this campaign in that last sense. The campaign also works across the older (more tangible) forms of campaigning, by giving talks and handing out literature, as well as within the cyber-sphere of online activism. The website gives examples of 'armchair activism' which are easy actions with powerful effects. This is one of the new styles of campaigning facilitated by computer technology and the power of global communications.

Back in the 1970s and 1980s a favoured campaign was to place stickers on any posters or anything else found to be offensive to women. The stickers might have said: 'This is offensive to women', or 'You have just lost my custom, your product is degrading to women'. Far from being an outmoded form of protest the same strategy is alive in the twenty-first century. A campaign across London Underground stations used 'This degrades women' stickers to campaign against an Eminem album which was found to be problematic. Today's campaigners can easily print their own stickers with whatever slogan they prefer. No longer dependent on a friendly and supportive local printing firm, twenty-first century feminists are doing it for themselves. It seems to us that the new generation of feminist activists can learn from the lessons of the early Rape Crisis pioneers, but those now working in Rape Crisis can also take lessons from new technology and the manner in which it makes activism into a low-cost endeavour.

Although the government took funding away from the Rape Crisis Federation, resulting in its closure and despite the continuing struggle for local Rape Crisis groups to continue to provide services, there is a saying that only that which has been given, can be taken away. Although there may not be proper funding for the movement, there is still enough dedication and passion to make a difference. Back in 1985, Dusty Rhodes and Sandra McNeill wrote the following in the preface to their collection of papers from feminist conferences. We hope that something similar can be said for feminist campaigning generally and that this discussion makes some modest contribution to reinvigorating that work, in all its glorious forms.

> *What do we expect our conferences to achieve? At least an end to isolation – 'Am I the only woman who has this problem, thought this, been worried about that? Many of us come wanting answers and solutions now. Most of us go away with new questions. At best they give us encouragement, hope, a new awareness. These papers contribute to a new way of seeing the world as it is, and hopefully to changing it for the better.*
> (Rhodes and McNeill, 1985: 5)

We now draw our work to a close by reviewing some of the lessons learned and concentrating on the messages from women's lived experience within Rape Crisis.

Conclusion

It was clear to us when we first started writing this book that we were choosing to write about Rape Crisis at a scary moment in its history. Having completed our review, we are hopeful that the spirit of the Rape Crisis pioneers does live on in the work of the movement, even though there are now so few groups left, in England and Wales. We have tried to put these groups into context with those in Ireland and Scotland, and we hope we have not done a disservice to those networks, of which we have less personal experience. We are, however, heartened to see that the Scottish Executive does appear to be capable of recognising the importance of Rape Crisis work, even if it is still true to say that some of the Scottish groups are terribly strapped for cash. We wonder whether the Scottish experience can be imported into Westminster? Can the funding given in Scotland be used to challenge the pathetic responses of the UK government to the plight of English and Welsh Rape Crisis? Can we also include the group in Belfast within this umbrella and then – logically – we have asked ourselves, whether there is room here for the

development of a UK and Ireland network of Rape Crisis centres, to try to learn from each other and gain strength in numbers?

Having written about the state of Rape Crisis we have decided that we will donate royalties from this book to benefit Rape Crisis. So if you paid good money for this book, be assured that you are now part of the anti-rape movement. Every time an individual, group, library, university or government department buys a copy of this book they will be contributing to the Rape Crisis movement: what a glorious thought. The money will fund activities to find ways to bring the various networks closer together in the future. For that reason alone we hope we have penned a best seller.

Certainly we are of the view that strength is found within our politics. It is, as this chapter has shown, the activist drive which supports the work with women, and that activism is fed by liaison with other workers. We hope that Rape Crisis can begin to move into a phase whereby it looks for better local coalitions with other groups working on violence against women (taking us back even to suggestions about services across the continuum of violence). Stronger coalitions could bring us to a time where the statutory agencies have to follow our agenda rather the current position. In particular, it would be positive if women in Rape Crisis groups could strive to ensure that these draining 'partnership' meetings are not the only spaces in which we meet with our sisters from refuges and other agencies.

We are speaking here of 'networks' of Rape Crisis and yet we have shown that there are great gaps in the geographical spread of provision at present. In particular we have identified a need to ensure that new groups are developed in London, in the south west of England and in Wales. That said though, there are many other gaps in provision which could be mended by the development of new groups (Liverpool being just one more major city which no longer has a feminist Rape Crisis centre). A key influence in the gaps in network provision is funding. We have tried to explore the dilemma between mainstream funding and independent money in an open-minded way. We can see that a clear need for Rape Crisis services can be demonstrated. It is not true to say that SARCs provide similar services, they do not. Rape Crisis can afford to demand more from the 'partners' who gain much by co-opting feminist groups into their agencies. Rape Crisis can consider attending where funding is provided to pay for the expertise and credibility that workers lend to the processes undertaken. Rape Crisis can also consider shouting out, to the press and through the use of internet technologies, when the police and courts fail individual women, when local and central government fail to provide vital funding and when they are overwhelmed by demand for their services. In these ways Rape Crisis can be clearer about its own survival.

The experience of women in the movement shows us that money from government is always fraught with expectations about the nature of the work, and is also laden with the danger that the rug of funding can be pulled, at dramatically short notice. It seems to us then, that the best strategy for Rape Crisis is 'both/and'. This would mean striving to develop mainstream funding, by being assertive about the tremendous amount on offer in terms of Rape Crisis expertise. But at the same time, there is a need to develop independent sources of finance (legacies and donations, for example) which will ensure service provision can retain its political analysis and continue to be a force for change. Another observation we have made is that the groups which have been more successful in terms of fundraising could offer some of their expertise to others, who are struggling with ridiculously small budgets. In reality this would not be a one-way process, as it is our experience that both sides always learn from each other, whenever the wonderful women of Rape Crisis do come together.

We have referred above to keeping the politics of anti-rape feminism alive and this chapter has demonstrated how important this is, in terms of support work and of worker satisfaction. This book then, is hopefully a small step in the direction of saving the knowledge of the Rape Crisis movement, to ensure that everyone within it (and indeed, many outside of it) can learn about the roots and development of the Rape Crisis idea. This book is only a part of this effort though and we hope that other women will be able to set down the stories of their Rape Crisis centres and to investigate aspects of the work which we are bound to have moved over too quickly, and without proper attention. One lesson from the roots of Rape Crisis is that the concept of the collective is a part of anti-rape work. In striving towards a rape-free world we can explore power in relationships differently in organisations where everyone has an awareness of the problems of power imbalance. The collective helps to keep that knowledge alive and is therefore a useful tool in developing women's lives, and in developing theory and practice. It is possible to maintain collectives whilst satisfying the statutory bodies and funders who regulate charitable organisations, as our practice can remain less public and more reflective. All of this can also help Rape Crisis to be self conscious of its efforts to resist co-option. When a partnership or funder makes demands which are opposed to the needs of a non-hierarchical organisation it is always worth reflecting on the value of those demands to Rape Crisis in the long term.

We have ended here with a plea to develop electronic resources. It seems to us that some of the younger women becoming involved in activism can learn much from the lessons of the pioneers within Second Wave Feminism. However, we also see that the older movements, such as Rape Crisis, are not always making the best use of these cheap resources to campaign, to provide information and to provide support. We hope that, in the fullness of time, links can be made with some of these internet campaigners, which will allow Rape Crisis to make more use of the dynamic ferment which is the internet.

Last, but not least, we end with a plea to retain the term 'Rape Crisis'. Whatever the 'crisis' is set to mean, whether it is a rape event, a memory triggered for an individual, the systematic failure of criminal justice to protect women, or the closure of another dearly-loved centre, the crisis is real – and the name is enduringly powerful.

References

Armstrong, L. (1978) *Kiss Daddy Goodnight*. New York: Hawthorne Books.

Bacik, I., Maunsell, C. and Gogan, S. (1998) *The Legal Process and Victims of Rape: The Findings*. Dublin: The Dublin Rape Crisis Centre.

Benedict, H. (1992) *Virgin or Vamp: How the Press Covers Sex Crimes*. Oxford: Oxford University Press.

Bevacqua, M. (2001) Anti-Rape Coalitions: Radical, Liberal, Black, and White Feminists Challenging Boundaries. In Bystydzienski, J.M. and Schacht, S.P. (Eds.) *Forging Radical Alliances Across Difference: Coalition Politics For the New Millennium*. London: Rowman and Littlefield.

Blair, I. (1985) *Investigating Rape: A New Approach For Police*. London: Croom Helm/Police Foundation.

Bowen, R. et al. (1987) Writing Our Own History. *Trouble and Strife*. 10: 49–56.

Breitenbach, E. and Mackay, F. (Eds.) (2001) *Women and Contemporary Scottish Politics: An Anthology*. Edinburgh: Polygon

Broaderick, S. (2002) Community Development in Ireland: A Policy Review. *Community Development Journal*. 37: 1, 101–10.

Brownmiller, S. (1976) *Against Our Will: Men, Women and Rape*. Harmondsworth: Penguin.

Brownmiller, S. (1999) *In Our Time: Memoir of a Revolution*. New York: Dell Publishing.

Bunch, C. (1987) *Passionate Politics: Essays 1968 to 1986*. New York: St. Martin's Press.

Burton, G. (1990) *More Than Meets the Eye: An Introduction to Media Studies*. London: Edward Arnold.

Butler, S. and Wintram, C. (1991) *Feminist Groupwork*. London: Sage.

Cabinet Office/Women's Unit (1999) *Living Without Fear. An Integrated Approach to Tackling Violence Against Women*. London: The Stationery Office.

Campbell, B. (1997) *Unofficial Secrets. Child Sexual Abuse: the Cleveland Case*. London: Virago.

Campbell, R. and Martin, P.Y. (2001) Services for Sexual Assault Survivors: The Role of Rape Crisis Centers. In Renzetti, C.M., Edleson, J.L. and Bergen, R.K. (Eds.) *Sourcebook on Violence Against Women*. Thousand Oaks, CA: Sage.

Campbell, R., Baker, C.K. and Mazurek, T.L. (1998) Remaining Radical? Organizational Predictors of Rape Crisis Centers. *American Journal of Community Psychology*, 26: 3, 457–83.

Charles, N. (2000) *Feminism, the State and Social Policy*. London: Macmillan.

Christianson, A. and Greener, L. (2001) In Breitenbach, E. and Mackay, F. (Eds.) *Women and Contemporary Scottish Politics: An Anthology*. Edinburgh: Polygon.

Collins, B.G. and Whalen, M.B. (1989) The Rape Crisis Movement: Radical or Reformist? *Social Work* 34: 1, 61–3.

Cook, K. and Jones, H. (2007) Surviving Victimhood: The Impact of Feminist Campaigns. In Walklate, S. *Handbook on Victims and Victimology*. Cullompton: Willan.

Cook, K. (1997) Raging Against Rape. *Trouble and Strife*. 35: 23–9.

Cook, K. (2003) RapeLaw.Consent@Freeagreement.co.uk: An Assessment of the Legal Definition of Consent, in the Light of the Current Review of Sexual Offences Law. *Contemporary Issues in Law*, 6: 1, 7–22.

Cosgrove, K. (1996) No Man Has The Right. In Corrin, C. (Ed.) *Women in a Violent World: Feminist Analyses and Resistance Across Europe*. Edinburgh: Edinburgh University Press.

Council for the Status of Women (1978) *Submission on Rape in Ireland*. Dublin: CSW.

Coussins, A. (1998) Tipping the Scales in Her Favour: The Need to Protect Counselling Records in Sexual Assault Trials. In Easteal, P. (Ed.) *Balancing the Scales: Rape, Law Reform and Australian Culture*. Federation Press.

Crow, B. (2000) *Radical Feminism*. New York: New York University Press.

Daily Telegraph, 13 December 2006.

Department of Health (1994) *The Extent and Nature of Organised and Ritual Abuse: Research Findings*. London: The Stationery Office.

Dobash, R.E. and Dobash, R.P. (1992) *Women, Violence and Social Change*. London: Routledge.

Dobbs, J. (120307) www.judiciary.gov.uk/publications_media/speeches/2007/mrs_j_dobbs_120307.htm

DuPlessis, R.B. and Snitow, A. (1998) *The Feminist Memoir Project: Voices from Women's Liberation*. New York: Three Rivers Press.

Echols, A. (1989) *Daring to be Bad: Radical Feminism in America 1967–1975*. Minneapolis: University of Minnesota Press.

Faludi, S. (1992) *Backlash: The Undeclared War Against Women*. London: Chatto and Windus.

Figley, C.R. (1995) *Compassion Fatigue: Coping With Secondary Traumatic Stress Disorder in Those Who Treat the Traumatized*. New York: Brunner/Mazel.

Firestone, S. (1970) *The Dialectic of Sex: the Case for Feminist Revolution*. New York: Bantam Books.

Foley, R. (1993) Zero Tolerance. *Trouble and Strife*, 27.

Friedan, B. (1963) *The Feminine Mystique*. New York: W.W. Norton.

Galligan, Y. (1998) *Women and Politics in Contemporary Ireland: From the Margins to the Mainstream*. London: Pinter.

Gelb, J. (1986) Feminism in Britain: Politics Without Power? In Dahlerup, D. *The New Women's Movement: Feminism and Political Power in Europe and the USA*. London: Sage.

Gelb, J. (1995) Feminist Organization Success and the Politics of Engagement. In Ferree, M.M. and Martin, P.Y. *Feminist Organizations: Harvest of the New Womens Movement*. Philadelphia: Temple University Press.

Gillespie, T. (1996) Rape Crisis Centres and 'Male Rape': A Face of the Backlash. In Hester, M., Kelly, L. and Radford, J. (Eds.) *Women, Violence and Male Power*. Buckingham: Open University Press.

Ginsberg, E. and Lerner, S. (1989) *Sexual Violence Against Women: A Guide to the Criminal Law*. London: Rights of Women.

Glanville-Williams, P. (1991) The Problem of Domestic Rape. *New Law Journal*, 205–6.

Grant, J. (2001) *Governance, Continuity and Change in the Organised Women's Movement*. Centre for Women's Studies, University of Kent (unpublished PhD thesis).

Gregory, J. and Lees, S. (1999) *Policing Sexual Assault*. London: Routledge..

Griffin, G. (1995) *Feminist Activism in the 1990s*. London: Taylor and Francis.

Griffin, S. (1979) *Rape: The Power of Consciousness*. San Francisco: Harper and Row.

Hague, G. (1998) Inter-Agency Work and Domestic Violence in the UK. *Women's Studies International Forum*, 21: 4, 441–9.

Hague, G. and Malos, E. (1993) *Domestic Violence: Action For Change*. Cheltenham, New Clarion Press.

Hague, G., Malos, E. and Dear, W. (1995) *Against Domestic Violence: Inter-Agency Initiatives* (SAUS Working Paper 127). Bristol: The Policy Press.

Hall, R. (1985) *Ask Any Woman: A London Inquiry Into Rape and Sexual Assault*. London: Falling Wall.

Hanmer, J. and Sutton, J. (1984) The Early Days of Women's Aid. *Trouble and Strife*, 4.

Harne, L. (2004) *Using the Media to Combat Sexual Violence Against Women and Children: Media Work and the Rape Crisis Movement*. Unpublished paper.

Harris, J. and Grace, S. (1999) *A Question of Evidence? Investigating and Prosecuting Rape in the 1990s*. London: Home Office.

Hartsock, N. (1998) *The Feminist Standpoint Revisited and Other Essays*. Oxford: Westview Press.

Harwin, N. and Barron, J. (2000) Domestic Violence and Social Policy: Perspectives from Women's Aid. In Hanmer, J. and Itzin, C. (Eds.) *Home Truths About Domestic Violence: Feminist Influences on Policy and Practice*. London: Routledge.

Harwin, N., Hague, G. and Malos, E. (Eds.) (1999) *The Multi-Agency Approach to Domestic Violence: New Opportunities, Old Challenges*. London: Whiting and Birch.

Heidensohn, F. (2000) *Sexual Politics and Social Control*. Buckingham: Open University Press.

Hester, M., Kelly, L. and Radford, J. (1996) *Women, Violence and Male Power*. Buckingham: Open University Press.

Home Office (2000) *Setting the Boundaries: Reforming the Law on Sex Offences*. London: HMSO.

IrishHealth.com (2003) Rape Crisis Support. http://www.irishhealth.com/ index.html?level=4andid=4044

James-Hanman, D. (2000) Enhancing Multi-Agency Work. In Hanmer, J. and Itzin, C. (Eds.) *Home Truths About Domestic Violence: Feminist Influences on Policy and Practice*. London: Routledge.

Jenny for Choices (c1986) Choices for Young Women. *WIRES*, March–April, 169: 3.

Jones, H. (1999) Kind Words and Compromises. *Trouble and Strife*, 40.

Jones, H. (2003) People Like Us. Internet publication for *Truth About Rape* campaign. http://www.truthaboutrape.co.uk/plu.html

Jones, H. (2003) Rape, Consent and Communication: Re-setting the Boundaries? *Contemporary Issues in Law*, 6: 1, 23–36.

Jones, H. (2004) Opportunities and Obstacles: The Rape Crisis Federation. *The Journal of Inter-disciplinary Gender Studies*, 8: 1–2, 55–71.

Jones, H. and Barnard, J. (2001) Knocking at the Door: The Rape Crisis Federation. *The British Council Network Newsletter*. 23: 15.

Jones, H. and Westmarland, N. (2004) Remembering the Past But Looking to the Future. Internet publication for *Rape Crisis*. http://www.rapecrisis.org.uk/history.htm

Kelly, L. (1988) *Surviving Sexual Violence*. Minneapolis: University of Minnesota Press.

Kelly, L. and Regan, L. (2001) *Rape: The Forgotten Issue*. London: University of North London.

Kelly, L., Lovett, J. and Regan, L. (2005) *A Gap or a Chasm? Attrition in Reported Rape Cases*. Home Office Research Study 293. Home Office Research, Development and Statistics Directorate.

Kitzinger, J. and Hunt, K. (1994) *Zero Tolerance of Male Violence: A Report on Attempts to Change the Social Context of Sexual Violence Through a Public Awareness Campaign*. Edinburgh: Edinburgh DC.

Koss, M. (1993) Rape: Scope, Impact, Interventions, and Public Policy Responses. *American Psychologist*, 48: 10, 1062–8.

London Rape Crisis Centre (1984) *Sexual Violence: The Reality for Women*. London: Women's Press.

London Rape Crisis Centre (1999) *Sexual Violence: The Reality for Women*. 3rd edn. London: The Women's Press.

Lovenduski, J. (1995) An Emerging Advocate: The Equal Opportunities Commission in Great Britain. In McBride Stetson, D. and Mazur, A.G. (Eds.) *Comparative State Feminism*. London: Sage.

Lovenduski, J. and Randall, V. (1993) *Contemporary Feminist Politics*. Oxford: Oxford University Press.

Lovett, J., Regan, L. and Kelly, L. (2004) *Sexual Assault Referral Centres: Developing Good Practice and Maximising Potentials*. Research Study 285. London: Home Office.

Lupton, C. and Gillespie, T. (1994) *Working with Violence*. London: Macmillan.

MacKinnon, C. (1987) *Feminism Unmodified: Discourses on Life and Law*. Harvard University Press.

Martin, P. Y. (2005). *Rape Work: Victims, Gender, and Emotions in Organization and Community Context*. New York: Routledge.

Matthews, N. A. (1994). *Confronting Rape: The Feminist Anti-Rape Movement and the State*. London: Routledge.

Millett, K. (1970) *Sexual Politics*. New York: Doubleday.

Morgan, R. (1970) *Sisterhood is Powerful*. London: Random House.

Mullender, A. (1996) *Rethinking Domestic Violence*. London: Routledge.

Naffine, N. (1997) *Feminism and Criminology*. Cambridge: Polity Press.

Neary, F. (2000) *A Consideration of the Model of Service Provision Employed by Rape Crisis Centres in Ireland*. Galway: Network of Rape Crisis Centres Ireland.

New York Radical Women, (1968) *Notes from the First Year*. New York: NYRW.

O'Malley, T. (1996) *Sexual Offences: Law, Policy and Punishment*. Dublin: Round Hall Press.

O'Sullivan, E. and Carlton, A. (2001). Victim Services, Community Outreach, and Contemporary Rape Crisis Centers: A Comparison of Independent and Multiservice Centers. *Journal of Interpersonal Violence*. 16: 4, 343–60.

Painter, K. (1991) *Wife Rape, Marriage and Law: Survey Report, Key Findings and Recommendations*. Manchester: Manchester University.

Pearlman, L.A., and Saakvitne, K.W. (1995) *Trauma and the Therapist: Countertransference and Vicarious Traumatization in Psychotherapy with Incest Survivors*. New York: Norton.

Plowden, W. (2003) The Compact: Attempts to Regulate Relationships between Government and the Voluntary Sector in England. *Nonprofit and Voluntary Sector Quarterly*, 32: 415–38.

Proctor, G. and Napier, M.B. (2004) *Encountering Feminism: Intersections Between Feminism and the Person Centred Approach*. Ross-on-Wye: PCCS Books.

Radford, J. (1990) Rape in Marriage: Make it a Crime! *Rights of Women Bulletin*, Spring: 12–14.

Radford, J. (1991) Rape in Marriage: Make it a Crime! *Rights of Women Bulletin*, Winter: 2–6.

Randall, V. (1998) Gender and Power: Women Engage in the State. In Randall, V. and Waylen, G. (Eds.) *Gender, Politics and the State*. London: Routledge.

Rapport (1999) *Violence against Women*. Swedish Government Offices, Stockholm.

Redstockings (1979) *Feminist Revolution*. New York: Random House.

Renzetti, C.M., Edleson, J.L. and Bergen, R.K. (Eds.) (2001) *Sourcebook on Violence Against Women*. Thousand Oaks, CA: Sage.

Rhodes, D. and McNeil, S. (1985) (Eds.) *Women Against Violence Against Women*. London: Onlywomen Press.

Roiphe, K. (1993) *The Morning After: Sex, Fear and Feminism on Campus*. Boston, MA: Little, Brown.

Russell, D. (1982) The Prevalence and Incidence of Forcible Rape and Attempted Rape of Females, *Victimology*, 7: 81–93.

Russell, D. (1984) *Sexual Exploitation: Rape, Child Sexual Abuse and Workplace Harassment*. California: Sage.

Ryan-Flood, R. (1998) *The Rape Crisis Services in Stockholm and Dublin: A Comparative Study*. Unpublished M.Phil. Thesis, Trinity College, Dublin.

Ryan-Larraghy, E. (1997) *A Case Study of the Dublin and Galway Rape Crisis Centres: The Therapist's Perspective*. Unpublished M.A. Thesis, Dublin City University.

Sampson, A. et al. (1988) Crime, Localities, and the Multi-Agency Approach. *British Journal of Criminology*, 28: 473–93.

Schechter, S. (1982) *Women and Male Violence: The Visions and Struggles of the Battered Women's Movement*. London: Pluto.

Scott, S. (2001) *The Politics and Experience of Ritual Abuse: Beyond Disbelief*. Buckingham: Open University Press.

Setch, E. (2003) Women's Liberation Anti-Violence Organisation. In Graham, H. et al. *The Feminist Seventies*. York: Raw Nerve Books. see http://www.feministseventies.net

Siddiqui, H. (1996) Domestic Violence in Asian Communities: The Experience of Southall Black Sisters. In Corrin, C. (Ed.) *Women in a Violent World: Feminist Analyses and Resistance Across 'Europe'*. Edinburgh: Edinburgh University Press.

Sinn Féin (2005) More Support for Rape Crisis Services Needed in Revised Estimates. http://sinnfein.ie/news/detail/9696

Skinner, T. (2000) Feminist Strategy and Tactics: Influencing State Provision of Counselling for Survivors. In Radford, J., Friedberg, M. and Harne, L. (Eds.) *Women, Violence and Strategies for Action*. Buckingham: Open University Press.

Smith, S.E. (2001) A Wolf in Sheep's Clothes? How Welfare Reform May Threaten Domestic Violence Services. *Affilia*, 16: 432–46.

Smyth, A. (1996) Seeing Red: Men's Violence Against Women in Ireland. In Corrin, C. (Ed.) *Women in a Violent World: Feminist Analyses and Resistance Across 'Europe'*. Edinburgh: EUP.

Spender, D. (1992) *Man Made Language*. London: Pandora.

Stanko, E. (1985) *Intimate Intrusions*. London: Routledge and Kegan Paul.

Stanko, E. (1990) *Everyday Violence*. London: Pandora Press.

Statistics Canada (1993) *The Violence Against Women Survey*. Ottawa: Statistics Canada.

Tara-Chand, A. (1999) Leeds Inter-Agency Project (Women and Violence): A Radical Approach? In Harwin, N. et al. (Eds.) *The Multi-Agency Approach To Domestic Violence: New Opportunities, Old Challenges*. London: Whiting and Birch.

Taylor, V. (1999) Gender and Social Movements: Gender Processes in Women's Self-Help Movements. *Gender and Society*, 13: 1, 8–33.

The Irish Revenue Commissioners (2007) *Charities Authorised at 23rd April 2007 Under the Scheme of Tax Relief for Donations to Eligible Charities and Other Approved Bodies Under the Terms of Section 848A Taxes Consolidation Act, 1997*. http://www.revenue.ie/pdf/sn45.pdf

Tuttle, L. (1986) *Encyclopaedia of Feminism*. Harlow: Longman.

Walby, S. and Allen, J. (2004) *Domestic Violence, Sexual Assault and Stalking: Findings from the British Crime Survey*. London: Home Office.

Walklate, S. (2001) *Gender, Crime and Criminal Justice*. Cullompton: Willan.

Ware, C. (1970) *Woman Power: The Movement for Women's Liberation*. New York: Tower Publications.

Wilcox, P. (2000) 'Me Mother's Bank and Me Nanan's, You Know, Support!': Women Who Left Domestic Violence in England and Issues of Informal Support. *Women's Studies International Forum*, 23: 1, 35–47.

Williams, B. (1999) *Working with Victims of Crime: Policies, Politics and Practice*. London: Jessica Kingsley.

Wilson, E. (1983) *What's to be Done about Violence Against Women?* London: Penguin.

WRC (2006) *The Crisis in Rape Crisis*. London: Women's Resource Centre.

Web Resources

Barrow and Geraldine Cadbury Trust –
http://www.bctrust.org.uk

Bush Telegraph – http://
www.bushtelegraph.uk.com

Charity Commission in England and Wales –
http://www.charity-commission.gov.uk

Choices – www.choicescounselling.co.uk

Department for Constitutional Affairs – http://
www.dca.gov.uk/criminal/auldcom/ar/
ar5.htm

Duke University – http://
scriptorium.lib.duke.edu/wlm/fem/
sarachild.html

Feminist Archive in the North –
http://www.feministarchivenorth.org.uk

Holla Back – http://hollabacknyc.blogspot.com

Home Office – http://press.homeoffice.gov.uk/
press-releases/support-victims-of-sexual-abuse

Irish Health website – http://
www.irishhealth.com/?level=4andid=8978

Irish Revenue Service – http://www.revenue.ie/
pdf/sn45.pdf

Justice for Women – http://www.jfw.org.uk/
index.htm

Make Poverty History – http://
www.makepovertyhistory.org

National Organisation of Women (NOW) –
http://www.now.org

New South Wales Rape Crisis –
http://www.nswrapecrisis.com.au

off our backs – http://www.offourbacks.org

Office of the Charity Regulator in Scotland –
http://www.oscr.org.uk

Rape Abuse and Incest National Network –
http://www.rainn.org

Rape Crisis – http://www.rapecrisis.org.uk

Rape Crisis and Sexual Abuse Centre –
http://www.rapecrisisni.com

Rape Crisis Network Europe –
http://www.rcne.com

Rape Crisis Network Ireland (2007a) *History.*
http://www.rcni.ie/abt . . . hist2.htm

Rape Crisis Network Ireland (2007b) *Strategic
Plans.* http://www.rcni.ie/abt . . . strat.htm

Rape Crisis Scotland (2007) *Statistics.* http://
www.rapecrisisscotland.org.uk/about_rape_
8.htm

Rape Crisis Scotland – http://
www.rapecrisisscotland.org.uk

Redstockings – http://www.afn.org/ ~ redstock/

Sinn Fein website – http://www.sinnfein.ie/
news/detail/16867

St Mary's Sexual Assault Referral Centre – http://
/www.cmht.nwest.nhs.uk/directorates/smc/
about.asp

Tokyo Rape Crisis – http://www.tokyo-rcc.org/
center-hp-english

Tyneside Rape Crisis – http://
www.tynesidercc.org.uk

Voluntary Activity Unit in Northern Ireland –
http://www.dsdni.gov.uk/index/voluntary_
and_community.htm

Washington DC Rape Crisis – http://
www.dcrcc.org

Women and Equality Unit – http://
www.womenandequalityunit.gov.uk

Women's Aid – http://www.womensaid.org

Women's Support Project – http://
www.womenssupportproject.co.uk

Zero Tolerance – http://
www.zerotolerance.org.uk

Glossary of Abbreviations

BAWAR	Bay Area Women Against Rape
BSARCH	Barnsley Sexual Abuse and Rape Crisis Helpline
CER	Campaign to End Rape
CR	Consciousness-raising
CSA	Child Sexual Abuse
DRCC	Dublin Rape Crisis Centre
GRCC	Galway Rape Crisis Centre
GP	General Practitioner
GUM	Genito-Urinary Medicine
ISVA	Independent Sexual Violence Advisor
JFW	Justice for Women
LRCC	London Rape Crisis Centre
NOW	National Organisation of Women
NYRW	New York Radical Women
RASA	Rape and Sexual Abuse Counselling Agency
RC	Rape Crisis
RCC	Rape Crisis Centre
RCF	Rape Crisis Federation
RCFRG	Rape Crisis Federating Reference Group
RCNI	Rape Crisis Network Ireland
SARC	Sexual Assault Referral Centre(s)
SATU	Sexual Assault Treatment Unit
SDS	Students for a Democratic Society
SERICC	South Essex Rape and Incest Crisis Centre
TAR	Truth About Rape
TWAG	Thurrock Women's Action Group
VVAPP	Victims of Violence and Abuse Prevention Programme
WAFE	Women's Aid Federation England
WAR	Women Against Rape
WAVAW	Women Against Violence Against Women
WLM	Women's Liberation Movement
WRCCS	Wirral Rape and Crisis Councelling Service
ZT	Zero Tolerance

Glossary

This section provides discussion of some of the terms and organisations referred to in the book.

Amnesty International UK: Stop Violence Against Women. On 5 March 2004 Amnesty International launched a global campaign to stop Violence Against Women. http://www.amnesty.org.uk/svaw/

Anti-oppressive practice. Anti-oppressive practice challenges the use and abuse of power not only in relation to individual behaviour which may be discriminatory but also in relation to broader social and organisational structures: for example, the criminal justice system, health and education, political and economic systems, media and other cultural groups. The aim of this should be to change practice from the root, rather than at the surface. It should generally describe a more radical approach than the more common 'equal opportunities' label.

Brighton Conference Violence, Abuse and Women's Citizenship: An International Conference. This was held on 10–15 November 1996 in Brighton and included workshops, speakers and sessions from women from around the world. The conference was co-ordinated by the Violence, Abuse and Gender Relations Research Unit at the University of Bradford. Included amongst the numerous topics addressed were: The National Centre for Battered and Raped Women in Sweden; The Campaign Against Rape in Nepal; A Feminist Perspective on Ritual Abuse (presented by women from Edinburgh and Dundee Rape Crisis centres) and 'Whatever Happened to Feminist Campaigns on Rape?' (facilitated by Liz Kelly, Jan Jordan and Kate Cook). This last workshop resulted in the formation of the Campaign to End Rape in the UK.

Bush Telegraph. This UK-based feminist online noticeboard started in October 2005 to generate support for the annual 16 days of activism against gender-based violence (see below for more, under International Day). The Bush Telegraph now acts as a place for UK feminist activists to advertise events etc. http://www.bushtelegraph.uk.com

Campaign to End Rape (CER). The Campaign to End Rape is a national coalition of radical feminist activists which formed in 1996 to campaign against rape and sexual violence, challenge women-blaming and hating myths that exist about rape and sexual violence, and challenge misogynist media reporting of sexual violence. http://www.cer.truthaboutrape.co.uk/. See further discussion within Chapter 6.

Collectives. Although women's groups today manifest themselves in a variety of styles and organisations, early Women's Liberation groups and the original Rape Crisis centres, took non-hierarchical, collective forms. Collectivity is a conscious attempt to challenge formal organisation, through an emphasis on participation by everyone, consensus decision-making and a shared common culture. Criticised as being utopian, many collectives within the UK Rape Crisis movement have ceded to a more traditional management structure. This is discussed in Chapters 1 and 2.

Consciousness-raising. Consciousness-raising (CR) and the fight for women's liberation go hand in hand. At http://scriptorium.lib.duke.edu/wlm/fem/sarachild.html Kathie Sarachild defines the radical roots of CR and the fact that 'it was seen as both a method for arriving at the truth and a means for action and organizing'. Women in CR groups focused on the situation of women from the perspective of individual women within the group, taking a theme, going round within the group, sharing our own experiences, and listening to the stories of others. This gave the opportunity to look at and understand women's position, not as a form of analysis of the individual woman but as a route to understanding the position of all women. All women within the group were encouraged to speak and their experiences were validated. We understood how difficult it was for women to initially speak the words describing their oppression, but it wasn't just about being able to speak the words, it was about being able to theorise out from the commonality of our experience. Not merely in order to speak and hear but in an attempt at understanding the route to oppression. For instance, where groups discussed women's own experiences of rape and sexual assault they would start the process of theorising 'why?' and this often enabled and encouraged a follow through to some form of political action, making the personal political. As this book details, Rape Crisis centres were born out of the early consciousness-raising groups formed by radical feminist activists during the late 60s and early 70s. From sharing their own experiences of rape and sexual violence, these feminist activists moved on to establish services aimed at all women. Importantly, many of the groundbreaking texts used as the foundation for second-wave radical feminist theory were born out of consciousness-raising. Susan Brownmiller's *Against Our Will* (1976), Robin Morgan's *Sisterhood is Powerful* (1970) and Liz Kelly's *Surviving Sexual Violence* (1988) are all works which benefited hugely from the writers' experiences within CR.

Eaves. Formed as Homeless Action in 1977, the core activity of the charity was to provide high quality supported housing to single homeless women. Today the organisation has over 150 supported bed spaces for women across nine London boroughs. They offer women support for up to two years to make the transition to independent living and provide domestic violence services, conduct violence against women research and are one of the few organisations to offer accommodation for women who have been trafficked or who are exiting prostitution. http://www.eaves4women.co.uk

Eve's Back. This was an independent feminist magazine for women in the Manchester area started by a small collective of women in 1994. The editorial statement of the original collective stated that aims included: 'keeping women in touch with each other; informing women of resources in and around Manchester; encouraging debate around issues of interest to women and . . . including articles of relevance to disabled women, black women, working-class women, lesbians, and woman of all ages' (from Issue 1). Due to lack of woman-power the magazine ceased production in 2004.

Fawcett (formerly the Fawcett Society). One of the longest established women's organisations in the UK. Fawcett is named for nineteenth century

suffragist Millicent Fawcett and is a liberal feminist organisation, with an interest in equality. Fawcett produces materials on a range of equality issues and responds to government consultations. An example of this is in Fawcett's response to the 'Safety and Justice' consultation on domestic violence. http://www.fawcettsociety.org.uk

Freedom Programme. Domestic violence project, developed from the Duluth model of power and control (http://www.duluth-model.org/). This is a free, 12-week, rolling programme which women can join at any time. It deals in detail with domestic and sexual violence. There is also a men's programme and venues exist across the UK. http://www.freedomprogramme.co.uk/site.htm

Greenham Common. In August 1981, 40 women marched from Cardiff to Greenham Common to protest at the decision to site US Cruise missiles there, and from this initial group the peace camp developed. Until 31 January 1982 the camp and some actions were mixed, women and men. Then women at the camp decided only women would live there, with men invited to visit and encouraged to offer support in other ways. Women participated in direct action at Greenham for many reasons. However, the majority would identify as feminists. Crucially, feminist consciousness-raising played a huge part in enabling women to fully participate in the various tasks necessary in the life at the camp: whether it was training others in non-violent direct action, supporting women in prison, public speaking, or legal briefings. However, the camp was incredibly mixed and diverse: the commitment to non-violence was the only real common principle. Over the following decade women took many and varied forms of direct action including: regular blockades of the gates at Greenham; 'keening' (i.e. traditional wailing), outside and inside parliament; organising up to 30,000 women to embrace the base; organising and taking part in a women-only 'die in' outside the stock exchange; blockading the economic heart of the city; at daybreak on New Year's Day 1983 entering the base and dancing on the silos; taking down the fence; and breaking into START talks in Geneva. www.guardian.co.uk/yourgreenham/ has videos, including those of women keening.

International Day for the Elimination of Violence Against Women. Officially designated by the UN in 1999, 25 November is used to mark successes in the battle against violence against women and to commemorate women who have died. The date was chosen because it is the anniversary of the death on 25 November 1960 of the three Mirabal sisters who were killed in the Dominican Republic for their political activism against the national regime. For many councils this date now begins the '16 Days of Action' (or activism) which ends on 10 December.

Justice for Women (JFW). Radical feminist campaign, formed in Leeds in 1990, in response to the case of Kiranjit Ahluwalia, found guilty of murder after killing her violent husband. This group continues to fight for justice for women who have killed violent men and currently has branches in London and Leeds. See: www.jfw.org.uk and Bindel, J., Cook, K. and Kelly, L. *Trials and Tribulations – Justice for Women: A Campaign for the 1990s,* in: Griffin, 1995.

National Council of Women (NCW). Formed in 1895 this is a British 'independent educational charity' whose vision is 'a world where it is no disadvantage to be born a girl'. The charity covers a wide spectrum of concerns: one of their special interest groups includes violence against women. http://www.ncwgb.org/

off our backs. Published since 1970, *off our backs* is the longest surviving feminist magazine produced in the US. It is run by a collective, and is a non-profit corporation. The mission statement is 'to provide news and information about women's lives and feminist activism; to educate the public about the status of women around the world; to serve as a forum for feminist ideas and theory; to be an information resource on feminist, women's, and lesbian culture; and to seek social justice and equality for women worldwide'. The back catalogue provides a great resource for learning more about feminism in the US. http://www.offourbacks.org

Professionalisation. In the 1970s and 1980s, feminists in the movement fought hard to expose the abuse of women and girls by men, and set up non-professional organisations to support each other. Once such large-scale abuse was the appearance of a whole industry of experts on sexual violence who medicalised women's responses to abuse, and created individualised treatment solutions. At the same time there was the fast growth of counselling and therapy, and

more recently the trauma industry; offering a whole range of trauma models to 'cure' distress following trauma. Sexual violence has become the vehicle for the production of a multitude of syndromes and disorders, all of which require 'treatment'. Such organisations also serve to dis-locate such violence from its social, political, powered, context. (Hester, Kelly and Radford, 1996: 11). A chapter by Monica Hill of Bradford Rape Crisis is also useful here (in: Proctor and Napier, 2004).

Radical Feminism. The word 'radical' has a Latin origin and means 'root'. Radical feminism therefore seeks to go to the root of female oppression and identifies patriarchy and associated hierarchical structures as the root cause. Radical feminism first emerged out of the Civil Rights movement in the US in the late 1960s and was adopted and developed by feminists in the UK in the 1970s. Radical feminism has been accused of being man-hating but such an accusation is based on a simplistic and erroneous conceptualisation of this social movement. Radical feminism argues that men as a group benefit from the oppression of women as a group. Radical feminism aims to eliminate patriarchy and other hierarchal systems which perpetuate the domination of one group over another, as the belief is that this will liberate everyone, women and men, from an unjust society. In the early years of its development, radical feminism used consciousness-raising sessions to better understand the nature and extent of the patriarchal domination of society and to develop a political ideology. (For other definitions and further discussion, see Chapter 1).

Rape Trauma Syndrome. This is a medicalised model for describing the responses of women to rape. It was first outlined by Ann Burgess and Lynda Holmstrom in 1974 with the intention of challenging the dominant idea that raped women are always hysterical. It is now recognised as a psychological disorder. It has sometimes been proposed that evidence of this syndrome could be used in court to support witness testimony of rape. However from a radical feminist perspective this is not a useful solution, since it involves medicalising women's responses to rape and can be used to judge that a woman has not been raped, simply because a medical expert views her responses as atypical.

Redstockings. The term Redstockings comes from the combination of 'bluestockings' (a patronising term coined to describe educated women in the eighteenth and nineteenth centuries) and 'red' for social revolution. Based in the US, the Redstockings is a radical feminist campaign group that formed in 1960s. Today, it continues to uphold the agenda of the Women's Liberation movement. http://www.afn.org/ ~ redstock/

Rights of Women (ROW). This is a London-based free-to-access organisation providing legal advice, training and a range of resources on using the law to address violence against women. http://www.rightsofwomen.org.uk

Second Wave Feminism. See Women's Liberation Movement.

Sexual Assault Referral Centres (SARC). Described as a one-stop location providing criminal justice and medical services for anyone who has experienced rape and/or sexual assault, this is a state-favoured non-feminist model for support. At present there are 15 SARCs across England and Wales. (For further discussion of this model see Chapters 2 and 5).

Spare Rib. *Spare Rib* a UK-based feminist magazine, was launched in June 1972 by a collective of six women, but many newsagents, including WH Smith, refused to stock it. According to an article in the National Housewives Register's Newsletter (no. 19, Autumn 1975: 10–11) it had a circulation of around 22,000 copies per month and aimed to challenge the traditional gender roles of women at the time. The *Spare Rib* editorial mission was cited thus: 'We are confronting the media image of Women's Liberation, of bra-burning and test tube babies, on its own ground. We are fighting the media with media of our own'. The magazine ceased in 1992. The Bristol University website shows some extracts: http://www.bristol.ac.uk/Depts/History/Sixties/Feminism/publications.htm.

Trouble and Strife. The first issue of this UK-based radical feminist magazine was published in late 1983. It was run by a collective and found support from *Spare Rib* (see above) who allowed them to use their office. The name was chosen as it is cockney rhyming slang for 'wife' and 'it acknowledges the reality of conflict in relations between women and men. As radical feminists, our politics come directly from this tension

between men's power and women's resistance' (first edition, inside front cover). Some university libraries and similar establishments hold back copies.

Truth About Rape (TAR). This feminist multimedia campaign was formed in 2002 to challenge myths about rape and to bring the truth and realities of rape back on to the public agenda. Membership is free and the campaign has a wide membership from across the globe. TAR is discussed in Chapter 6. http://www.truthaboutrape.co.uk

Thurrock Women's Action Group (TWAG) was formed in 1981 with an informal membership of 8/9 women. TWAG functioned from 1981 to 1985 as a consciousness-raising and anarchist/socialist feminist activism group tackling issues linked to toxic shock syndrome, equal pay, anti-nuclear war (Greenham) sexual harassment, lack of child care provision, wages for housework, gender division of housework, domestic violence, sexual violence etc. TWAG wrote regular feminist contributions for *Reverse Order*, a Thurrock political fanzine. Sheila Coates went on to set up what is now South Essex Rape and Incest Crisis Centre (SERICC) and Lee Eggleston went on to set up what is now Thurrock Women's Refuge (TWR).

Well Woman Centres. Primarily providing information on health matters, well woman centres have been established for over 20 years in the UK, provide services on relationship and emotional problems, and are sensitive to women who may not use more traditional health care channels.

WIRES. Women's Information Referral and Enquiry Service was set up in 1975 by the National Women's Liberation Conference, and has two main functions: (1) to provide an information service with comprehensive files of groups, contacts, campaigns etc.; (2) to issue a newsletter which aims to keep local groups in all areas in touch with each other's ideas.' This is taken from the collective statement in issue 169 of the WIRES newsletter. The Feminist Archive in the North website notes that this was a re-naming of an existing service, in 1975 (http://www.feministarchivenorth.org.uk/chronology/1975-1.htm).

Women Against Violence Against Women (WAVAW) was a network of autonomous groups set up at the Sexual Violence Against Women Conference in 1980 in Leeds. They were set up to campaign around all aspects of male violence against women. Very active campaigns included 'Free The Maw Sisters' in support of two women who killed their violent father and a longer campaign against sexual violence against women in films and videos and print media. In Leeds they succeeded ultimately in the removal of the 'Pin Up' from the evening paper, where it had often been placed next to stories of violence against women. WAVAW from the start determined to be a very public feminist voice, giving talks in schools, to Women's Institutes, to Trades Unions etc. They issued press releases and were available to speak on TV, radio and national newspapers on all relevant subjects from a sexual harassment storyline in Coronation Street to actual serial killers. Many groups lasted until 1985 (see: Rhodes and McNeill, 1985)

Women's Aid (WA). Women's Aid is the original feminist model for supporting women fleeing domestic violence. There are Women's Aid organisations throughout the UK and they perform a dual role in providing support services for abused women and in working for their safety by campaigning locally and nationally to raise awareness of the extent and impact of domestic violence in society. There are four nationally based Women's Aid organisations:

- Northern Ireland Women's Aid Federation http://www.niwaf.org/
- Scottish Women's Aid http://www.scottishwomensaid.co.uk/
- Welsh Women's Aid http://www.welshwomensaid.org
- Women's Aid Federation England http://www.womensaid.org.uk/index.htm

Women's Liberation Movement (WLM). A political movement of women begun in the late 1960s which grew rapidly worldwide during the 1970s. It comprised women's groups, campaigns, organisations, women's centres, newsletters, magazines, books and achieved a revolution in thinking. In the UK, in spite of constant ridicule in the media, the WLM established the idea that women should be equal not subordinate. Like all political movements the WLM experienced resistance and backlash but the vision of freedom remains. It is now sometimes called the 'Second Wave of Feminism' by younger women in the twenty-first century. The origins of this movement are discussed further in Chapter 1.

Women's National Commission (WNC). Established in 1969, the Women's National Commission (WNC) is an advisory Non-Departmental Public Body (NDPB), which means that although it is fully funded by government it claims independence to comment freely on government policy. The website includes a comprehensive list of women's organisations, many of which are WNC partners. The WNC has a specific section of its website dedicated to Violence Against Women. http://www.thewnc.org.uk/wnc work/violence against women.html

Women's Resource Centre (WRC). The WRC is a charity which was established to get gender onto the political agenda and support other women's organisations to be more effective and sustainable. Their work involves responding to government consultations, hosting conferences, delivering training and providing information and support to grassroots organisations. http://www.wrc.org.uk

Women's Studies. Delivered at local colleges and universities, Women's Studies courses have enabled students to reflect on their own experience in an analytical way and in its cultural and historical context, developing awareness of women's lives and their position in society, contemporarily and across history and geographical boundaries. Women's Studies draws on history, literature, politics, law, sociology, social policy, anthropology and psychology. It can be understood as the educational application of consciousness-raising. A fine example among many courses once offered was the Open University module entitled the 'Changing Experience of Women'. With a trend towards (liberalising) 'gender studies' and away from women-only provision, sadly these courses have now become rare.

YWCA. The YWCA was founded in 1855 for young women who were coming to London for the first time. Founded by Christian women, today the work is no longer faith-based and involves people of all faiths and none. Its aim is to raise the social and political profile of young women's issues and provide 'a voice for young women facing discrimination and disadvantage'. http://www.ywca-gb.org.uk

Appendix 1

Rape Crisis groups questionnaire

Name of Rape Crisis group:

What year was the group formed?

Has your group had any former names?

What was the original name?

When did your group's name change?

Do you know why the name was changed?

Size/structure of your group

How many women are in your Rape Crisis group currently?

On average, during its history, has your group been larger or smaller than this, or about the same?

If larger or smaller, what would you say was the average size of the group?

Is your group run as a collective?

If no, was it ever run as a collective?

And do you know when and why it changed?

If your group has a Management Committee, how many women are on that committee?

The work of your group

Does your group operate a helpline and if so, can you give the opening hours?

Roughly how many calls does your group take each week on the helpline?

Does your group provide face-to-face support to survivors and if so, how many sessions are run per week (roughly)?

Does your group run any other services for survivors, e.g. self-help groups, outreach groups, visits to women within institutions? If Yes, please give us some information about these services.

Finally, would you like to offer any further help in the process of producing a history of the Rape Crisis movement? If so, please complete the final section of this form, to enable us to get back in touch with you.

Yes, we/I would like to offer access to archive materials about our group, these are:

Yes, we/I would be willing to be interviewed for the book. The name of the person to contact is:

And contact phone number is:

Yes, we/I would like to offer further help, details as follows

The name of the person to contact is:

And contact phone number is:

Thank you for completing our questionnaire.

Respondents

Aylesbury Vale Rape Crisis
Barnsley Sexual Abuse and Rape Crisis Helpline (BSARCH)
Bradford Rape Crisis and Sexual Abuse Survivors Service
Colchester Rape Crisis Line
Coventry Rape and Sexual Abuse Centre
Doncaster Rape and Sexual Abuse Counselling Centre
Gloucester Rape Crisis Centre
Herts Area Rape Crisis and Sexual Abuse Centre
Manchester Rape Crisis – Rape and Sexual Abuse Counselling Service
Peterborough Rape Crisis Counselling Group
Plymouth Rape and Sexual Abuse Line
Rape and Sexual Abuse Counselling Agency (RASA, Wirral/Merserside)
Rape and Sexual Abuse Support Centre (RASASC, Croydon)
Rape and Sexual Abuse Support Centre (Guildford)
Rape and Sexual Abuse Support Centre (North West Wales)
Sheffield Rape and Sexual Abuse Counselling Service
Southampton Rape Crisis and Sexual Abuse Counselling Service
South Essex Rape and Incest Crisis Centre
The Rape and Sexual Abuse Counselling Centre (Durham)
Tyneside Rape Crisis Centre (TRCC)
Watford and SW Herts Rape Crisis
Women's Rape and Sexual Abuse Centre (Cornwall)
Women's Rape and Sexual Violence Service (North Staffs/South Cheshire)
Worcestershire Rape and Sexual Abuse Support Centre
Wycombe Rape Crisis
Up-to-date contact details for all groups can be found on the Rape Crisis website
    http://www.rapecrisis.org.uk

Appendix 2

Federating Flowchart

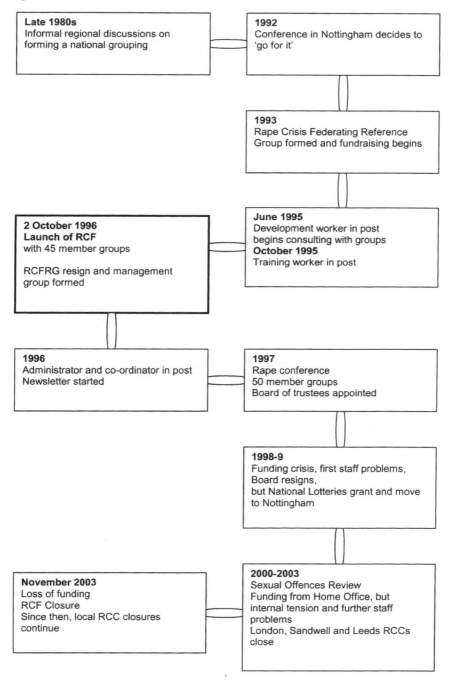

Late 1980s
Informal regional discussions on forming a national grouping

1992
Conference in Nottingham decides to 'go for it'

1993
Rape Crisis Federating Reference Group formed and fundraising begins

2 October 1996
Launch of RCF
with 45 member groups

RCFRG resign and management group formed

June 1995
Development worker in post begins consulting with groups
October 1995
Training worker in post

1996
Administrator and co-ordinator in post
Newsletter started

1997
Rape conference
50 member groups
Board of trustees appointed

1998-9
Funding crisis, first staff problems,
Board resigns,
but National Lotteries grant and move to Nottingham

November 2003
Loss of funding
RCF Closure
Since then, local RCC closures continue

2000-2003
Sexual Offences Review
Funding from Home Office, but internal tension and further staff problems
London, Sandwell and Leeds RCCs close

Appendix 3

Rape Crisis Network Ireland

Antrim
Carlow
Cork
Donegal
Dublin
Galway
Kerry
Kilkenny
Limerick
Louth
Mayo
Offaly
Sligo
Tipperary
Waterford
Westmeath
Wexford

Rape Crisis Scotland

Rape and Abuse Support – Aberdeen
Women's Rape and Sexual Abuse Centre – Dundee
Edinburgh Women's Rape and Sexual Abuse Centre
Rape Crisis Centre – Glasgow
The Rape Counselling and Resource Centre – Kilmarnock
Lanarkshire Rape Crisis Centre
Western Isles Rape Crisis Centre
Argyll and Bute Rape Crisis Centre
Perthshire Rape and Sexual Abuse Centre

Appendix 4

Sexual Assault Treatment Centres

The Rotunda Hospital in Dublin
The South Infirmary Hospital in Cork
Waterford Regional Hospital
Letterkenny General Hospital

Sexual Assault Referral Centres

Codnor, Derbyshire Millfield House
PO Box 142
Derby DE1 2HF
Tel: 01773 573840/1

Dartford, Kent Renton Clinic
Darent Valley Hospital
Dartford Kent
DA2 8DA
Tel: 01322 428 595

Durham The Meadowfield Suite
John Street (North)
Meadowfield
Durham DH7 8RS
Tel: 0191 301 8644

Gwent Laburnum House
Tredegar Street
Risca
Gwent
NP11 6BU
Tel: 01633 601943

Hampshire, Portsmouth The Treetops Centre
Northern Road
Cosham
Portsmouth
PO6 3EP
Tel: 02392210352

Leicester Juniper Lodge Sexual Assault Response
    Centre
Lodge One
Leicestershire General Hospital
Gwendolen Road
Leicester LE5 4PW
Tel and Fax: 0116 273 5461
24 hour helpline: 0116 273 3330
Email: juniperlodge@ukonline.co.uk

London Haven – Camberwell
King's College Hospital
Denmark Hill
London SE5 9RS
Tel: 020 7346 1599 (9 a.m.–5 p.m. Monday to
    Friday) or 020 7737 4000 at all other times.

Haven – Paddington
St Marys Hospital
Praed Street
London W2 1NY
Tel: 020 7886 1101 (9 a.m.–5 p.m. Monday to
    Friday) or 020 7886 6666 at all other times.

Haven – Whitechapel
The Royal London Hospital
9 Brady Street
London E1 5BD
Tel: 020 7247 4787 at any time.

Manchester St. Mary's Centre
St. Mary's Hospital
Hathersage Road
Manchester M13 0JH
Tel: 0161 276 6515
Website: www.stmaryscentre.org
Email: stmarys.sarc@cmmc.nhs.uk

Merthyr Tydfil, South Wales New Pathways
Willow House
57–58 Lower Thomas Street
Merthyr Tydfil CF47 0DA
Tel: 01685 379 310
Website: www.newpathways.co.uk
Email: enquiries@newpathways.co.uk

Northumbria The Reach Centres Ellis Fraser
    Centre in Sunderland
Tel: 0191 212 1551
Rhona Cross Centre in Newcastle
Tel: 0191 565 3725 Website:
    www.reachcentre.org.uk
Email: info@reachcentre.org.uk

Preston, Lancashire Lancashire SAFE Centre
Royal Preston Hospital
Sharoe Green Lane
Fulwood

Preston PR2 9HT
Tel: 01772 523344
Website: www.lancsteachinghospitals.nhs.uk/
    SAFE_Centre/index.shtml
Email: safe@lthtr.nhs.uk

Walsall, West Midlands The Rowan Centre
2 Ida Road
Walsall
West Midlands WS2 9SR
Tel: 01922 644 329 (8.30–5.30 Monday to Friday)
24 hour emergency line: 0800 73 111 62
Fax: 01922 622233
Website: www.crisispoint.org.uk
Email: crisis_point@btconnect.com

Swindon, Wiltshire The New Swindon Sanctuary
Sexual Assault Referral Centre
The Gables
Shrivenham Road
South Marston
Swindon
SN3 4RB
Open overnight 7 p.m.–7 a.m. Mon–Sat and
    throughout the weekend (after 1 p.m.
    Saturday).
Tel: 01793 709 512
Fax: 01793 709 513
Website: www.swindonpct.nhs.uk/our_services/
    sanct uary.htm
Email: info@swindonsanctuary.co.uk

All details correct at time of publishing. See the Home Office website for further details:
http://www.homeoffice.gov.uk/crime-victims/reducing-crime/sexual-offences/sexual-assa ult-
    referral-centres/referral-centre-locations/

Appendix 5

Victims Fund Grants 2007: breakdown by region of awards

East Midlands

Derbyshire Rape Crisis	£19,450
Nottingham Rape Crisis	£41,108
Sexual abuse and Incest Line (SAIL)	£17,767
Northamptonshire Rape and Incest Crisis	£20,000
Crisis point	£15,368
Walsall Street Teams (The Jigsaw Project)	£30,000

West Midlands

Sexual and Domestic Abuse and Rape Advise Centre (SARAC)	£15,250
Worcestershire Rape and Sexual Abuse Support Centre	£28,445
Coventry Rape Crisis	£35,424
The Rape and Sexual Abuse Violence Project (Birmingham)	£21,090

Yorkshire and Humberside

Bradford Rape Crisis and Sexual Abuse Survivors Service	£45,106
Doncaster Rape and Sexual Abuse Counselling Centre	£44,607
Grimsby and Scunthorpe Rape Crisis	£49,146
Sheffield Women's Counselling and Therapy Service	£18,672

North East

Women's Support Network	£28,038
Redcar and Cleveland Women's Aid	£41,724

North West

Rape and Sexual Abuse Support Centre Cheshire and Merseyside (previously Warrington Rape Crisis)	£35,370
Manchester Rape Crisis	£25,635

East

South Essex Rape and Crisis Centre (SERICC)	£49,291
HEAL (Helping Everyone Abused Live)	£38,038
Colchester Rape Crisis Line	£21,931

South East

RASAC – Rape and Sexual Abuse Counselling Service (Winchester)	£26,000
Survivors Network	£10,406
Southampton Rape Crisis and Sexual Abuse	£47,804
No Limits	£26,000

South West

WomanKind (Bristol Women's Therapy Centre)	£41,202
Survivors Swindon	£35,900
Plymouth Rape and Sexual Abuse Line	£12,450
Twelve's Company	£35,827
Womens Rape and Sexual Abuse Centre Cornwall (WRASAC)	£32,416

London

One-in-Four	£48,510
Lilith Project/Amina Project Eaves Housing for Women	£30,104
Step Forward	£32,190
Galup	£35,122

Wales

New Pathways	£23,660
Rape and Sexual Abuse Centre	£25,525

National

CIS'ters	£37,088
VOICE UK	£28,000
Respond	£50,000
Survivors UK	£30,000

Index

Russell House Publishing

We publish a wide range of professional, reference and educational books including:

Strong Mothers
**A resource for mothers and carers of children
who have been sexually assulted**
By Anne Peake and Marion Fletcher   1997 ISBN 978-1-898924-04-3

Mothers of Sexually Abused Children
**A framework for assessment, understanding
and support**
By Martin C. Calder with Anne Peake and Kate Rose   2001 ISBN 978-1-898924-77-7

Helping Mothers Move Forward
**A workbook to help provide assessment
and support to the safe carers of children
who have been sexually abused**
By Lynda Regan   2006 ISBN 978-1-903855-87-4

Safeguarding Adults
By Jackie Martin   2007 ISBN 978-1-903855-98-0

Safeguarding Vulnerable Adults
By Denis Hart   2008 ISBN 978-1-905540-37-9

Power and Empowerment

By Neil Thompson   2007 ISBN 978-1-903855-99-7

Gender in Social Work: Promoting Equality

Edited by Christine Gruber and Helga Stefanov   2002 ISBN 978-1-903855-15-7

For more details on specific books, please visit our website:

www.russellhouse.co.uk

Or we can send you our catalogue if you contact us at:

Russell House Publishing,
4 St Georges House,
Uplyme Road Business Park,
Lyme Regis, DT7 3LS,
England

Tel: (UK) 01297 443948
Fax: (UK) 01297 442722

Email: help@russellhouse.co.uk